Separatist Christianity

Separatist Christianity

Spirit and Matter in the Early Church Fathers

David A. Lopez

The Johns Hopkins University Press
Baltimore and London

The Johns Hopkins University Press
2715 North Charles Street
Baltimore, Maryland 21218-4363
www.press.jhu.edu

Library of Congress Cataloging-in-Publication Data

Lopez, David A., 1971–
   Separatist Christianity : spirit and matter in the early church fathers /
David A. Lopez.
      p. cm.
Includes bibliographical references and index.
   ISBN 0-8018-7939-6 (alk. paper)
   1. Church and the world—History of doctrines—Early church, ca.
30–600. 2. Separation from sin—Christianity—History of doctrines—
Early church, ca. 30–600. I. Title.
   BR195.C53L67 2004
   270.1—dc22

                                          2003023416

A catalog record for this book is available from the British Library.

For my wife,
without whose daily encouragement
I could never have finished

Contents

	Acknowledgments	*ix*
1	The Origins of Separatist Christianity	1
2	The Ideal of Separation after AD 135	14
3	Separatist Christianity and the Roman Empire	38
4	Martyrdom and Salvation	57
5	The Martyr and the Community	73
6	Apocalyptic Expectations	89
7	The Apologetic Evidence	109
8	Constantine, Eusebius, and the Triumph of Christianity	134
	Conclusions	149
	Notes	*155*
	Select Bibliography	*179*
	Index	*187*

Acknowledgments

This study ultimately arose from an undergraduate paper I wrote in 1992. Through all of its various permutations, many people have helped to shape it and me. I am deeply indebted to so many of you, and most especially to those without whose support I could not have persevered to this point.

I thank all those at Yale University who graciously made it possible for me to complete two years of my work *in absentia* while at the Medieval Institute of the University of Notre Dame. I must single out for especial gratitude Jaroslav Pelikan; Deborah G. Thomas, associate dean of the Graduate School; and Lee Patterson, director of graduate studies in the Department of Medieval Studies. I thank also all those at Notre Dame and at the Medieval Institute who welcomed me and encouraged me during my stay there. I am especially grateful to James Powell, associate dean of the Graduate School, who made miles of red tape disappear in moments; John Van Engen, director of the Medieval Institute; Marsha Kopacz, secretary of the Institute; and all the graduate students (too numerous to mention by name) who befriended me.

I am indebted particularly deeply to Paul Freedman, whose generous contributions of time and advice have prevented me from making numerous and grievous errors in this work; and to Keith Sweet, Johnny Gravois, Jacob Hundt, and Ben Dueholm, whose ravenous intellects both daunted and inspired me in my first year of teaching.

Most especially, I thank Jonathan Boulton, mentor and friend, for his judicious application of both carrot and stick, for so many hours of thoughtful conversation offered so freely, and for the abiding concern shown throughout the years for my professional welfare.

Lastly, I thank Henry Tom and Michael Lonegro, my editors at the Johns Hopkins University Press, for their support and, most especially, their patience.

All of these people have contributed in many ways to the work I have been able to complete. Any errors which persist are entirely my own.

The Origins of
Separatist Christianity

In the first four centuries of Christian development, Christian writers used the dichotomy between the spiritual and the corporeal in varying ways. As Christianity's relations with both Judaism and the Roman world changed, the distinction between spirit and matter also shifted. This division dictated what ideas, actions, and things could have salvific significance to Christians, and therefore reflected a crucial component of the relation to non-Christians at a given time.

The relations of Christians with Jews and the Romans changed dramatically during two crucial transitional periods. The first transition, between the opening of the First Jewish Revolt in AD 66 and the razing of Jerusalem in 135, made permanent the division between Judaism and Christianity. In 66, the followers of Jesus seem still to have thought of themselves essentially as Jews, one among many first-century varieties of Judaism. By 135, however, Christians and Jews were identifiably different, even to outsiders. This difference also meant that Romans identified Christianity as an illicit religion.

The second transition comprised that long, awkward truce between Christianity and the Roman Empire during the last four decades of the third century. Between the persecutions of the emperors Valerian (258–259) and Diocletian (303–311), the number of Christians increased significantly, straining established behavioral norms and controls, especially at the margins of Christian communities. After Constantine's seizure of power in 312, these changes offered new bases of cooperation between the state and Christian leaders, which over the course of the fourth century led to a fairly thorough Christianization of Roman imperial institutions.

Between these two transitional moments, Christianity offered a distinctive resistance to the problem of interpenetration with uncommitted Christians and non-Christians in daily life. Such resistance, of course, has never been considered unique to the second and third centuries. Before the Jewish Revolts, recruitment among Gentiles on the margins of Hellenized Jewish communities challenged the Jewish identity of Christ's followers; after Constantine, communities of Jews, pagans, and heterodox Christians challenged the imperial ideology of unity. Nevertheless, during the period between 135 and 312, Christian authors resisted these challenges in a different way than they had before or would since. They developed a unique interpretation of the traditional division between spiritual and corporeal things, in order to support Christian separation from non-Christians to an extraordinary extent.

The Contrasting Theme of the Spiritual and the Corporeal

Origen, that most prolific and influential of patristic exegetes, offers in his *Fifth Homily on Judges* a striking interpretation of the story of Jahel and Sisera from the fourth chapter of that book. Sisera, a Canaanite lord, has been allowed by God to oppress the Israelites for two decades as a punishment for their sins; finally, the prophetess Deborah summons Barac to lead the Israelites against him. There is a great battle, in which Sisera's host is overcome by the power of God and completely destroyed, and Sisera himself flees the field. Coming to the tents of Jahel, an Israelite woman married to a Canaanite, Sisera begs her to hide him from Barac's pursuit. She covers him with a blanket, promising that no one will find him; then she drives a tent peg through his head, and gives his body to Barac.[1]

Origen's allegorical interpretation of this story claims that Sisera represents "the carnal and vicious world" (*carnalium vitiorum*) in which the early Christian communities lived, while the woman Jahel represents the

"Ecclesia." Just as Sisera was the oppressor of the Israelites, the world is the oppressor of contemporary Christians, who, like Jahel, Origen says, must "kill Sisera" (*extinguere Sisaram*) in order to live fully as Christians.[2] What did Origen mean by this?

In Origen's homilies, as in all early Christian writing, a predominant theme is the contrast between "spiritual" and "corporeal" things. Understanding the nature of this distinction in the minds of Christian authors is crucial to our understanding of these texts. On the most basic level, "spiritual" (Latin *spiritualis*, Greek *pneumatikós*) refers to the immortal and incorporeal substance of which God, angels, and human souls are constituted; and "corporeal" (Latin *saecularis*, Greek *kosmikós*) refers to the perishable, material substance of which human bodies and all other created things are composed. By extension, these categories can be applied to behaviors and phenomena associated with one or the other substance. It is this extended level of interpretation that is most significant for understanding the intended meanings of a given source.

The earliest Christian interpretation of this theme can be derived from the letters of Paul. The Pauline letters are fundamentally ambiguous in stating the proper relation of Christians to the world, both physical and political, in which they lived. For Paul, human society and its institutions were established by God for some providential purpose. Among these institutions, the Roman Empire particularly was created by God as an institution whose goal was justice;[3] and yet simultaneously, because of idolatry, that same empire and the society it embodied were foolish in God's sight, and would surely perish both literally and figuratively.[4] Thus, Paul implied, cooperation with the Empire could be proper in some circumstances, but not in others. What this usually meant for both Christians and Jews in the first century was that demands from imperial officials for idolatrous actions needed to be rejected. This ambiguity is significant; it was characteristic of first-century Christianity in its Jewish context, and would again be visible in a new way following the conversion of Constantine.

For this later period, the clearest and most influential definition of this ambiguity was provided by Augustine in the early fifth century. Augustine, Bishop of Hippo in North Africa from 394 to 430, wrote extensively about his faith during that whole period, leaving hundreds of letters and sermons, and dozens of major treatises. In two of his most prominent works, *On Christian Doctrine* and *On the City of God*,[5] he defined how the dichotomy should be applied in the context of a Christian empire. By "spiritual," Augustine really meant "salvific"; hence he implied meanings like "moral" and "ecclesiastical." By "corporeal," he meant "non-salvific" (but not necessarily *anti*-salvific); hence he implied meanings like "immoral," "amoral," or "imperial." This double connotation is rooted in two fundamental distinctions, which Augustine makes in the same works.

The first distinction is between what Augustine calls "use" and "enjoyment" (*uti, frui*), thereby connoting licit versus illicit exploitation of corporeal things. This distinction makes it possible for him to claim that corporeal objects and behaviors may contribute to spiritual ends. In Augustine's view, a Christian may *use* a corporeal object (such as money or a spouse) to achieve not only an intermediate, corporeal end (buying food or being loved), but also an eventual, spiritual end (salvation through living for God or through learning to love, the better to love God). What a Christian may not do, however, is *enjoy* using these corporeal objects for their own sakes. When the object becomes only an end in itself, rather than also a means to a more significant if more distant spiritual end, use of the object becomes illicit. Thus the *intention* of the user is a crucial factor in determining proper from improper use; only ends that are ultimately spiritual, even if immediately material, can justify use of corporeal things.

The second distinction made by Augustine is between religion and politics. Augustine defined a separation of secular from ecclesiastical powers; in the fifth century, this was a fairly radical idea. He argued that the "City of God," the Heaven where God and angels live, also exists in the physical world, in order to serve ultimately spiritual ends. Within this city, God rules justly and harmoniously through the Logos. This city, however, overlaps with the earthly "City of Man," which, as a corporeal phenomenon, serves purely corporeal ends. God makes use of the earthly city (which Augustine identifies as the Roman Empire) to further the goals of the heavenly city, just as men may make use of corporeal objects to further their own spiritual goals. In recent centuries, for example, God had established the Roman Empire to facilitate the spread of Christianity and the establishment of episcopal authority. Yet despite this providential cooperation, the Church and the Empire remained distinct entities, with separate purposes and separate means of achieving them.

In these ways, Augustine clarified and codified ambiguities in Christianity's relation to the physical and political world, ambiguities that dated back to Paul in the mid-first century. For the small, isolated minority

Christian communities of the first century, Paul's core criterion for establishing norms of Christian behavior while living among non-Christians — namely, Christlikeness with respect to sin, and especially idolatry — could be sufficient.[6] For the large, heterogeneous majority Christian communities of the fourth and fifth centuries, however, this core criterion was too vague to be useful. Augustine showed how fifth-century Christians, in a society now nominally Christian from top to bottom, should interpret Paul's ambiguous relation to imperial authority. He argued that avoiding sin now meant avoiding enjoyment of the material world in quotidian activities. Augustine's distinctions between use and enjoyment and between state and religion thus rendered Paul's ambiguities clear to a wider group of Christians than comprised Paul's original audience.

Like Paul and Augustine, Origen too describes Christianity as interpenetrated with secular society. All these authors agree that there is no immediately visible distinction among devoted Christians, weak Christians, and non-Christians. Origen admitted that even Christian leaders sometimes fail to live up to the ideals of Christianity; their authority within the community, which ideally ought to correspond to their spiritual progress toward God, could thus conceal mere lip service to those ideals.[7] Likewise, Paul and Augustine distinguished between carnal and spiritual men primarily on the basis of an orientation of the will.[8] True Christians subordinated their will to God's will; weak and non-Christians, in contrast, preferred to follow their own will in their actions. This orientation of the will, however, is not always visible; not all sinners will be judged (and hence picked out from the rest of humanity) before the last day,[9] and even Adam in the garden willed improperly before the tangible evidence of his sin, that is, his eating of the forbidden fruit.[10] Moreover, since no man is perfect while living in this world, even the will of good Christians may sometimes err and become divided in its objects.[11]

Moreover, Augustine's use of the spiritual/corporeal theme has provided Christians from the fifth to the twenty-first century with distinctions between use and enjoyment, and between state and religion. These have made it possible for Christian leaders to cooperate with secular authorities, working toward goals beneficial to both church and state; and they have made it possible too for ordinary Christians to participate in various activities with no immediate spiritual end. Although new in their precise formulation by Augustine, these distinctions are clearly rooted in Paul's ambiguous use of this theme; the world and participation in it could be seen as either good or evil, according to how it was used and to what end it was being put. Furthermore, these distinctions seem also to invoke a similar mingling of Christians with non-Christians in daily living both before and after Constantine. It seems, then, superficially reasonable to believe that the Augustinian distinctions are implicit in the Pauline ambiguity, and that most if not all Christian writers between Paul and Augustine also imply these distinctions in their discussions of Christians' roles in the physical and political worlds.

However, the attitude revealed in second- and third-century sources toward corporeal things generally, and toward Roman society and government in particular, was notably dissimilar to that of either Paul or Augustine. The differences are aptly epitomized in Origen's allegorical reading of the story of Jahel and Sisera. Unlike either Paul or Augustine, Origen implies that Christians of his day—that is, between the crushing of the Second Jewish Revolt in 135 and the conversion of Constantine in 312—ideally made *no* distinction either between use and enjoyment of corporeal things, or between state and religion; and that they were therefore predisposed to view the whole of the Roman Empire, and any cooperation with or participation in it, as "corporeal"—that is, as opposed to God's will and their own salvation. This is what Origen meant by "killing Sisera": rejecting the "carnal and vicious world" of the Roman Empire in favor of the "Ecclesia."

There is a further difference among the approaches to worldly engagement described by Paul, Origen, and Augustine. For Paul, as described above, the imminence of Christ's return and judging of humanity defined the problem of living among non-Christians. Although the proper orientation of the will in true Christians was not necessarily visible to men, it was clearly visible to God; God's perception made obvious the division of humanity into saved and damned. For Augustine, God's perception of the human will is again the key element in resolving the problem. Only time could make a completely accurate distinction among devoted Christians, weak Christians, and non-Christians; only after death was the orientation of an individual's will made fully plain, by the reward offered to it: namely, punishment or entrance into Heaven. For Origen, however, God's perception is not the only point of view from which salvation or damnation may be clearly seen. Continual persecution made it evident even here in this world; one did not need to share God's perception to be able to separate the righteous from the impious. Persecution revealed the extent of one's commitment to God: only those whose will was properly oriented to "spiritual" things and away from "corporeal" things could receive the fortitude to endure martyrdom. This was the point at which all ambiguity must be dropped; the true Christians died and were saved; the weak and the idolatrous failed the test and were condemned. Thus, in the second and third centuries, interpenetration of Christians and non-Christians in daily life did not raise the problem of assurance of salvation, as it did for both Paul and Augustine. Christians in this period did not imply the twin distinctions ultimately codified by Augustine; rather, they attached their own significance to this theme, which affected in distinctive ways their attitudes toward the world, the Empire, civic participation, social status, money, death, salvation, and Christ's return.

This is not to say that no Christians at all between 135 and 312 ever compromised this "ideal of separation" (as I will call it), especially under the pressure of Roman demands for participation in civic society. Rather, it means that the sources that are extant for study were preserved as authoritative documents precisely because they promoted the separatist ideal. In their official capacities as Christian leaders and bishops, the authors of the surviving sources consistently taught that Christians must not compromise between these conflicting demands. However, it was surely the case, in the second and third centuries no less than in the twenty-first, that individual Christians both could and did think and act in ways that differed from the promoted ideal. But the existence of Christians who did not support the ideal in every facet of their lives does not alter the significance of the ideal itself. The extreme consistency with which separation was promoted for nearly two centuries indicates its general success. This in turn implies that the majority of Christians of the period accepted the ideal at some level and conformed to it to some degree; the martyrs whose deaths were remembered and written about were the most exemplary, but by no means the only, such Christians.

Pauline Christianity and the Jewish Revolts

How did it come about that Christians between 135 and 312 had this divergent use of spiritual and corporeal categories? I believe that the failure of the Zealot movement between 66 and 135, and most especially the destruction of the Temple in 70, limited the ways in which both Christians and Jews perceived their relation to the world.

Messianic and apocalyptic traditions were deliberately exploited by the Jewish revolutionaries to gain support.[12] When their movement failed so dramatically, with the mass suicide at Massada in AD 73, and the total expulsion of the Jews (and Jewish Christians) from Jerusalem in 135, these messianic and apocalyptic overtones backfired. Among Jews, the loss of the Temple and their homeland actually strengthened pro-Roman accommodation, and led to the predominance of rabbinical Judaism at the expense of other first-century sects.[13]

Among Christians, these events curtailed the pro-Roman side of the Pauline tradition, but they also strengthened the emphasis on spiritual at the expense of corporeal ideas. Because Zealots had made messianic claims about their hoped-for kingdom, it was vital that Christians differentiate *their* messianic claims about a hoped-for kingdom. This they accomplished by relegating Zealot claims to the corporeal realm (this also explained the Zealots' failure),[14] while elevating their own claims to the spiritual realm.[15]

But such thorough emphasis on spiritual expectations had consequences: also under the influence of persecution, the boundaries between "spiritual" and "corporeal" were redrawn. Corporeal came to mean a conflation of the material world with both idolatry and the Roman Empire — thus obscuring Paul's fundamental ambiguity. In these terms, the Empire itself could no longer be represented as potentially positive; because inherently pagan, it was universally bad. While it could often be ignored in practice, the pagan Empire could never be condoned in theory. This is very different from both Paul's ambiguity and Augustine's distinction between church and state.

Distinctiveness of the Period 135–312

Events between 66 and 135 altered the worldviews of both Christians and Jews. Under growing external pressures, the Pauline ambiguities of the mid-first century became increasingly less ambiguous during these decades; the pro-state and pro-world possibilities were more and more excluded, until by the 130s they had no place in Christianity's worldview. This separatist Christianity rejected both world and state as corporeal, the antithesis of spiritual; no compromise could be accepted with either, despite the reality of interpenetration of Christian living into the Roman world.

This separatist ideal endured—partly under the force of persecution and partly because of the small size of Christian communities—until late in the third century. Between 259, the end of Valerian's persecution, and 303, the beginning of Diocletian's, the Roman government largely ignored Christians as such, and Christian communities were growing steadily larger. Traditional episcopal controls over the daily lives of separated Christians weakened. This gradual erosion of the ideal of separation led to the possibility of Constantine's support for Christianity, not as a replacement for paganism but rather as another, more successful attempt to reestablish internal harmony within the Empire after the final failure of Diocletian's persecution in 311. Constantine's supporter Eusebius reintegrated the Empire into Christian ideals, offering in his *Ecclesiastical History* Paul's original ambiguities as a "traditional" basis of support for a new, pro-imperial Christianity.

There are three distinctive features of Christianity in the separatist period. First, there is the splitting off of Christianity from its Jewish roots. This took place in two main stages.[16] For the first four decades of its existence, from the death of Christ to the destruction of the Temple in 70, the dominant form of Christianity had been that of the followers of James in Jerusalem. The followers of Paul, who wanted to dispense with literal obedience to Old Testament law, seem to have remained peripheral. With the destruction of the Temple, however, it became impossible for the followers of James to maintain a foot in each camp; for both Jews and Christians, attention had to be refocused away from Jerusalem. This allowed the Pauline Christians to become dominant in the second stage.[17]

This new dominance of Pauline Christians, however, led to a bitter dispute with Pharisaic Judaism over the proper interpretation of the Old Testament. Was it to be literal, as the Jews claimed, or figurative, as the Pauline Christians claimed?[18] After the destruction of the Temple in 70, the polemic between Christians and Jews to possess the salvific history of the Old Testament created great animosity on both sides, and made it henceforth impossible to reconcile the two traditions.

Moreover, the need to define themselves in opposition to each other pushed Jews and Christians further apart in their view of the Roman Empire. Throughout the first century, Pharisaic Judaism, which would become normative rabbinical Judaism, favored accommodation in order to secure the peace in which to practice their religion unmolested.[19] Jewish Zealots favored armed resistance, in order to create an independent

Jewish state.[20] The political sympathies of the Christians had often tended toward the Zealots as allies against the Pharisees,[21] and increasingly hardened after 70 due to the embittered struggle for identity with Pharisaic Judaism.

When the Second Jewish Revolt was crushed in 135, however, the tendency within Christianity toward Zealotry was also suppressed. Thenceforth, until the conversion of Constantine, the majority of Christians believed not only that the Old Testament must be understood figuratively, but also that the promises of the New Testament for a "kingdom of God" must likewise be understood figuratively (that is, "spiritually," as we shall see later), not as political expectations for this world. Thus by 135 only two groups out of the numerous first-century Jewish sects survived: the Pharisees, who were world-engaging and pro-imperial, and who interpreted the Old Testament literally; and the Pauline Christians, who were separatist and anti-imperial, and who interpreted the Old Testament figuratively.

The second distinctive characteristic of the period was persecution by the Romans.[22] Although Christians were certainly executed by Nero after the burning of Rome in 64, it seems likely that he did not persecute Christians as a dissident religious group, but rather as a convenient scapegoat group. The fact that they were Christians and held particular views on particular issues had little to do with their being singled out by Nero; more important was the fact that they were few, new, and unprotected. Likewise, in the 90s under Domitian, who made it compulsory to swear by the imperial *genius* at all public ceremonies, some Christians were probably executed for refusing to do so. But again, their being Christian had less to do with the crisis than their refusing to swear; Jews too, as well as some Romans, refused to swear by the imperial *genius*, and were treated no differently than were Christians.

Thus, through most of the Apostolic period, there was no persecution of Christians as such. From the reign of the emperor Trajan (98–117), however, Christians began to be singled out *as Christians*, and accused as Christians of various moral and political crimes. Trajan's famous letter to the governor Pliny the Younger (written about 112) reveals that Christians were by this time a recognizable dissident group. From at least 112, then, until 312, Christian communities in various cities were persecuted by violent mobs, by zealous local or regional officials, and even—under Decius in 251, Valerian in 259, and Diocletian in 303—by official imperial pronouncement. After 312, however, orthodox Christians in the Roman Empire were never again persecuted in this way.

The third distinctive feature of the separatist period was its production of literature of the type labeled "apologetic," or defensive. The earliest known apologist was Quadratus, who wrote an *apología,* or "defense" (not extant) about 130. Similar tracts were written by Aristides about 140, Justin about 155, and many others, down to Arnobius about 300. Prior to Quadratus, material with apologetic purpose was not relevant to Christianity; after 312, comparable material was produced and continued to be called apologetic, but actually served quite a different purpose[23] (and ought to be reclassified). Thus Christian apologetic was both characteristic of and particular to the separatist period.

A Note on Primary Sources

The primary sources available for our period are both numerous and varied. To assist the reader and to avoid frequent repetition in the chapters that follow, I offer here a summary of the most important and most frequently cited works and authors, and an indication of the genres the sources fall into.

Hermas, the earliest author of our period, recorded certain dreams or visions he had, probably about 130 or so. Little else is known of him. His work entitled *The Shepherd* enjoyed a wide audience throughout the period, and has sometimes been considered part of the New Testament Apocrypha. It includes themes common to both apocalyptic and exegetical writings.

Aristides of Athens was well educated and probably came to Christianity through Platonic philosophy. Little is known of his life. His *Apology* (ca. 140) is the earliest extant apologetic work.

Justin Martyr was another well-educated Christian who converted from Platonic philosophy. He lived and taught in Rome in the 140s and was martyred about 156. A number of his works are extant (some in fragmentary condition); the most important for our purposes are his *First* and *Second Apologies* (ca. the early 150s).

In the 170s, four Greek apologists wrote, almost simultaneously, four works with almost identical themes and content: Tatian (*Apology*) and Athenagoras (*Presbeia* or *Legatio*) were leaders in their Christian communities, but seem not to have been clerics of any sort, while Melito (*Apology,* extant in Greek and Syriac fragments) and Theophilus (*To Autolycus*) were both bishops.

About 195, another bishop, Commodianus, wrote a lengthy verse treatise called *Instructions,* notable more for its disciplinary content than its rhetorical skill.

About 210, the Roman Minucius Felix wrote an apology in the form of a dialogue, which he called the *Octavian.* Minucius is most significant for what his text reveals about the relatively strong presence of Christianity in Rome itself at the beginning of the third century. His text is also significant for its presentation of a coherent pagan view of Christianity.

In Carthage in the last decade of the second century and first decade of the third, Tertullian wrote a very large number of treatises on all aspects of Christianity. He was a native of Carthage, seemingly of a Christian family. He studied law and rhetoric, probably in Rome, and served some time as a lawyer, perhaps also in Rome. He eventually became an extremely influential Christian writer, though he does not seem to have been ordained. Tertullian's influence on later generations of Latin, and especially North African, Christians cannot be overstated. The most important of his works for our purposes are his exegetical *On Prayer* and *On Baptism;* his disciplinary *Antivenom against the Gnostics* and *On Spectacles;* his martyrial *To the Martyrs, On the Crown,* and *On Flight from Persecution;* and his apologetic *To Scapula, To the Nations,* and *Apologetic.*

At the same time that Tertullian dominated Latin Christianity, the Alexandrian school was dominating Greek Christianity. Clement was its first leader whose works we have; in his time Clement was at least as influential as Tertullian, but he would be overshadowed in the next generation by Origen. Clement's most important works are the *Instructor* and the *Stromata,* both of which include exegetical and disciplinary themes. Clement also left a shorter apologetic *Exhortation to the Nations.*

In the second quarter of the third century, Christianity was completely dominated by the most famous product of the Alexandrian school, Origen. What we know of his life comes to us from Eusebius's *Ecclesiastical History;* he was certainly the most brilliant and creative thinker of the separatist period. Despite the increasing disfavor his works and reputation fell into from the fourth century on, many are extant, though often not in the original version. His most productive period was the 230s and 240s; he was imprisoned and tortured during the Decianic persecution of

250–251, and died about 256. His most important works for our purposes are the prolific Old Testament *Homilies* preserved in Latin by Rufinus; the exegetical *On Prayer;* the apologetic *Against Celsus;* and the martyrial *Exhortation to Martyrdom.*

Origen's contemporary and Tertullian's successor as intellectual leader of the Carthaginian Church in the 240s was the bishop Cyprian. Little is known of his early life, but he clearly received a good education, and was highly influential as bishop. He championed the desire of the Christians who had lapsed during Decian's persecution to be readmitted to the Church, against the much more conservative Novatian, bishop of Rome. His most important works for our purposes are his exegetical *On Prayer;* his disciplinary *On the Lapsed, On Mortality,* and many of his extant letters; his martyrial *To Fortunatus;* and his apologetic tract *To Demetrian.*

From the last half of the third century, considerably less material is extant. Only two authors from this period, one Greek and one Latin, are significant. Methodius, the Greek, wrote his *Banquet of the Ten Virgins* in the last decade of the third century, while Arnobius, a Latin North African, wrote his apologetic *Disputation against the Nations* about 300. Arnobius was apparently still a catechumen at the time he wrote, and so his text is highly significant for revealing what a contemporary Christian considered most important to learn first about that religion.

There are, finally, a large number of anonymous works from throughout the period, primarily the *Acts* or *Passions* of martyrs. The earliest such is probably the *Martyrdom of Polycarp,* concerning the bishop of Smyrna who was martyred about 156; this text was circulating not long after the event. The latest such *Acts* are contemporaneous with the persecution of Diocletian (303–311), from the very end of our period. These martyrial texts have most recently been collected and edited by Herbert Musurillo, whose work remains the most accessible edition of the whole martyrial corpus.

CHAPTER TWO

The Ideal of Separation
after AD 135

Christian leaders after 135 tried to promote a fundamental division between worldly pagans and spiritual Christians. Ideally, this division was
insurmountable, except by conversion to Christianity and the consequent
replacement of the set of Roman ideals (*Romanitas*) with the set of Christian ideals (*Christianitas*, as it would eventually be called). The crux of
this division was one's attitude toward the world (Latin *saeculum*, Greek
kósmos) and its demands of involvement; the line was drawn between
those (theoretically, all non-Christians) who remained "mired"[1] in the
world and those (ideally, all Christians) who renounced (Latin *renuntiare*,
Greek *apotássō*) the world. This renunciation demanded both a complete
rejection of political involvement in the Roman state—an involvement
that could not be separated from state-supporting pagan ritual,[2] which
Christians considered idolatrous[3]—and, to the greatest extent possible, a
rejection of the physical means of living a material existence.

This renouncing of the world defined Christians' relationship to matter, to civic society, and to the Empire. Oppositional development from 66
on had gradually pruned away any positive connection between the Logos

and these aspects of the corporeal world. Renunciation was necessary because none of these things could participate in the Logos. To the extent that Christians remained attached to non-Christian values, then, they too were impeded from participating in the Logos, and thus from achieving Christianity's promise of salvation.

Martyrial Literature

As might be expected from this sort of idea, the theme of renunciation is most strongly presented in sources directly concerned with martyrdom itself. This is because separatist Christians saw martyrdom as the ultimate way to renounce the world.[4] Tertullian, for example, writing in 203 to a group of Christians in prison and awaiting judgment, claims: "Thence [i.e., in prison] you were set apart from this world; how much more from its worldliness and its affairs? But do not let [the fact] that you were set apart from the world disturb you. For if we think this world is more the prison, then we understand that you have gone out of a prison, and not into a prison. For the Christian outside the prison has renounced the world, but inside the prison, he has renounced also a prison. It matters nothing where you are in the world, you who are outside of the world."[5] This passage very strongly expresses the opposition between Christian renunciation and pagan involvement. At this moment of crisis for the Christian community, the defining characteristic of the Christian for Tertullian is "renunciation of the world." The world and its daily demands constitute "a prison," which can best be escaped by entering a literal prison (from which the most likely release is death). The Christian, by definition not part of the world, feels no more constrained in a prison cell than in any other geographic location, because the affairs of the world have nothing to do with him. His imminent death is not a matter of concern, because his relationships with the divine and with the world change in no way when he enters the prison.

Similarly, in his tract *On the Crown*, Tertullian claims that military service—a common demand of the world for a broad class of people within the Roman Empire—should not be accepted by Christians.[6] This text again derives from a martyrial context; Tertullian was writing in the aftermath of the following event, which took place about 211.[7] An unnamed Roman centurion, called forward to receive a military decoration at a

formal assembly, declines his award on the grounds that he is a Christian.
In a subsequent judicial examination, he bluntly refuses to offer sacrifice
to the traditional gods, and is therefore put to death. Tertullian lauds this
man as a martyr:

> I think first it is necessary to inquire whether military service is at all
> appropriate for Christians. Are we to believe it permissible to add a
> mortal oath to the divine, and to obey another lord after Christ? Will it
> be permitted to take up the sword, when the Lord has pronounced that
> the one who lives by the sword will perish by the sword?[8] And will the
> son of peace fight in battle, to whom it is not proper to bring legal
> action?[9] And will he apply chains and prison and tortures and sen-
> tences, [who is] not the avenger of his own injuries?[10] For military
> service does not offer impunity from sins nor immunity from martyr-
> dom. The Christian never is anything other.[11]

Again, in the context of praise for a martyred Christian soldier, Tertullian
unequivocally claims that military service to the Roman state is incompatible with the service of God. Quite aside from the unavoidable problem of
the necessity of violent actions, the baptismal "divine oath" of the Christian supersedes any mere mortal oath, and obedience to God's commands
precludes obedience to any other lord. In Tertullian's view, one cannot be
a soldier without sinning against God, because one cannot be both a
soldier and a martyr. Thus the only acceptable solution to this dilemma for
a soldier who, like the centurion in question, becomes Christian while
serving, is to renounce his soldierly duties and to accept martyrdom.

A century after Tertullian, the incompatibility between the obligations
of a soldier and a Christian could still be insisted upon by Christians as
grounds to refuse military service. Under the emperor Diocletian in 284, a
young Christian named Maximilian, called to serve in the army, refused.
When Dion, the proconsul, said, "Serve, lest you perish," Maximilian
responded, "I will not serve. Cut off my head, I will not serve the world;
but I serve my God."[12] In the 280s, Maximilian's extreme response to the
military summons appears to be an isolated event,[13] since in the tolerance
of the late third century, few Christians found it necessary to insist quite
so strenuously on ideal renunciation.[14] Those who did, however, could
draw on an established and accepted tradition to support their interpretation; indeed, for the recorder of Maximilian's martyrdom, this tradition

was normative. The demands of the world and the demands of God, this passage claims, are mutually exclusive; it is better for a Christian to accept death than to compromise the divine commandments. Renouncing the world is the only way, suggests the text, to understand the actions of Maximilian; the audience of this text was expected to accept this ideal regardless of any quotidian compromises they might ordinarily make.

In addition to military service, other demands for worldly participation by the Roman Empire were supposed to be rejected by Christians. Encounters with the imperial cult were particularly likely to precipitate confrontations.[15] Especially in the context of a more general crisis, the demand that an emperor be treated as a god was used by Christian leaders to underscore the impossibility of any reconciliation with the Empire.[16] Polycarp of Smyrna, for example, bluntly refused even to answer when asked why he would not conform to this practice: "And the *eirenarch* [i.e., captain] Herod and his father Nicetes came to meet him [Polycarp], and placing him in the carriage and sitting beside [him], they pleaded with him, saying, 'What is the harm in saying, "Caesar is lord," and in sacrificing and [doing] what follows after, and thereby in preserving your life?' At first he did not answer them, but when they persisted, he said, 'I do not intend to do what you desire for me [to do].' "[17] The *Martyrdom of Polycarp* was composed during a very significant moment of crisis for the Christian communities of western Asia Minor, probably in the late 150s.[18] In the passage cited here, Polycarp, the Christian bishop of Smyrna, has just been arrested by the authorities and is being brought into Smyrna for trial. Herod and Nicetes attempt to defuse a tense situation, made more volatile by a sudden increase in Smyrna of popular resentment toward Christians;[19] they hope to persuade Polycarp to perform a public declaration of loyalty to the Empire,[20] thus appeasing the popular resentment of Christian non-participation. In the Christian presentation of this event, however, the goal of Herod and Nicetes is not to prevent mob violence, but to prevent the desired and predestined[21] martyrdom of the bishop. In the text, not only do pagans like Herod and Nicetes entirely fail to understand the nature of the irreconcilable divide that separates Christians from pagans, but Polycarp himself cannot possibly imagine any other attitude toward the Empire and the world. His refusal to answer the question posed to him, then, indicates the ideal rejection by Christians of Roman demands for participation. Polycarp's silence recalls to the text's audience the extent of the gulf that separated Christian from Roman, and the necessary failure of any attempt to bridge that gulf. What is in fact wrong with saying "Caesar is Lord" is that such a statement undermines the ideal of renunciation by involving Christians in political affairs, which they should ideally avoid altogether.

A century later than Polycarp, under the violent and Empire-wide persecution of Valerian,[22] the author of the *Martyrdom of Marian and James* evinced the same opposition to the Empire, in even more intractable language: "O the great and excellent favor of God for his own! O the true and paternal compassion of Jesus Christ our lord, who grants such great benefits to his beloved ones and reveals [himself] before bestowing the gifts of his clemency! The day after the vision dawned, and now the judgment of the magistrate complied with the promises of God, such that the judgment to punish with death sent forth Marian and James and the other clerics from the distractions of the world, and restored them at last to the patriarchs with glory."[23] In the context of Valerian's persecution, it is not surprising that such extreme language was used to praise the Christian martyrs. Martyrdom is here described as a "favor," a "benefit," and a "gift of clemency" from God. The martyrs' deaths free them from "worldly distractions" and rejoin them to the heavenly community "with glory."[24] The position of the servants of the Empire in this martyrdom is also unambiguous. God uses the Empire and its authority to fulfill the promises he has made to Christians.[25] The instrumentality of the magistrate in fulfilling God's plan for the world does not, however, lessen his culpability for having ordered the deaths of Christians.[26] Divine favor for Christians, who renounce the world and desire martyrdom, is strongly contrasted to the unwitting compliance of pagans, who serve the world and thus oppose God and Christians.

These five passages demonstrate how the ideal of renunciation could be deployed in martyrial texts. The unbridgeable division between Christian separation and pagan involvement is consistently stressed, without ever evoking any potentially pro-imperial themes to balance this division. Christian audiences of martyrial texts were thus repeatedly exposed to an unpaired anti-Roman sentiment, which conflated as "corporeal" three significant objects: the prison of the physical world and its many distracting attributes; the political world of the Empire and its many demands for civic participation; and the idolatrous ritual activities of Roman paganism that that participation inevitably implied, especially for soldiers and officials, whose careers directly supported the Empire.

Apologetic Literature

The theme of renunciation from the world also appears strongly in the apologetic literature of separatist Christianity.[27] Although apologetic literature appears to contain a distinction between state and religion very similar to what Augustine defined in the early fifth century, it should be read as conflating, rather than distinguishing between, pagan ritual and Roman imperial government. In one early apologetic text, Justin Martyr describes a renunciation from the world that seems to correspond with that already derived from martyrial sources:

> And you, having heard that we await a kingdom, rashly suppose that we speak of a human [kingdom], but we are speaking of one concerning God, as appears also from the fact that Christians examined by you confess that they are [Christian], knowing that death is the penalty laid down for the one confessing. For if we expected a human kingdom, we would deny [Christ] so that we might not be destroyed, and we would seek to escape [your] notice, so that we might achieve what we seek. But since we hold our expectations not on the present, we have not concerned ourselves with those who kill [us], because beyond doubt everyone is bound to die.[28]

Here Justin clearly describes the contrast between the "spiritual" expectations of Christians and the "corporeal" concerns of non-Christians. Indeed, while the pagan is so bound by these concerns that he cannot imagine any other interpretation of the "kingdom" promised to Christians, the Christian nevertheless is so unconcerned with the world that death itself holds no fear. Justin is also careful to speak of Christians as unanimous in the desire for separation; whether or not such a unity of opinion actually existed among Christians in Rome about 150, the appearance of unity was certainly being promoted by Christian leaders.

The same ideal of renunciation is also present in the apologetic literature of Tertullian. Like Justin, Tertullian in his *Apologetic* accuses the Roman authorities of ignorance of Christian "truth"; they wrongly assume that Christians are involved in the world. Christian "truth," however, remains disengaged from the world, concerned only with otherworldly affairs:

> If it is not permitted to you, judges of the Roman state, sitting in judge-ment in that open and elevated almost-peak[29] of the city, to look down openly and to examine personally what is certain in the trial of the Chris-tians; if, in this unique sort [of trial], your *auctoritas* either fears or is ashamed to inquire in public with the diligence of justice; if, finally, as has recently happened, the disturbance of this way of life, carried out[30] too severely by local judgments, obstructs the path of defense, then let it be permitted to the truth to reach your ears by the hidden path of silent letters. She [i.e., the truth] disdains her trial, because she does not won-der at her condition. She knows that she is a wanderer in the world, that it is easy to find enemies among strangers, and moreover that she has her origin, homeland, hope, recompense, and dignity in the heavens.[31]

Tertullian's accusations of the leaders of the Empire are biting. These officials are described as "jumped up" judges who refuse to perform their official duty[32] to examine for themselves the nature of accusations against Christians. They fear mob violence if carrying out their duty creates the appearance that they even tolerate Christians. The trials over which these judges preside are no trials at all, but mere cursory condemnations. As a result of the failures of these magistrates, Christians suffer unjust disturbances.

It is not, however, the disturbance itself to which Tertullian objects. Tertullian expects the pagan "stranger" not to understand the Christian "truth," and to be inimical to it and its adherents. Christian "truth" is clearly dissociated from worldly affairs, and centered on spiritual goals. The martyrdoms of Christians which result from the ignorance of the worldly are not to be avoided, Tertullian claims;[33] the perpetrators, how-ever, are still to be punished.[34] Tertullian's biting depiction of the leaders of the Empire underscores their inability to perform their most central function—the keeping of order and the punishment of disorder and vio-lence within the Empire—and thereby emphasizes the contrast between the worldly pagan and the disengaged Christian.

Clement of Alexandria, writing in the early third century, does not insist as strongly as his contemporary Tertullian upon the ignorance and culpability of the Roman authorities; yet the ideal of renunciation from the world is no less clear in his *Exhortation to the Nations:* "It is possible for you, if you desire, to purchase the high-priced salvation with your own treasure, with love and living faith, which is a worthy payment. God accepts this worship gladly; for 'We have hoped in the living God, who is the savior of all mankind, especially of the faithful.'[35] But the others, overgrown by the world like rocks on a shore by seaweed, neglect immortality."[36] Clement presents the gaining of Christian salvation as the result of personal choice. If one chooses to love and obey God, one will be saved. This to Clement means renunciation from the world: the opposite of love and obedience to God, Clement here claims, is continued involvement in the world. The affairs of the world overwhelm such people; salvation cannot be chosen by them because of their worldliness.

Very early in the fourth century, Arnobius of Sicca[37] offered a reprise of the same confrontational opposition as Justin and Tertullian in his *Disputation against the Nations*:

> You ask: since therefore you serve almighty God, and trust him to have concern for your salvation and well-being, why does he suffer you to endure so many persecutions, and to undergo every kind of penalty and torture? And we inquire in rebuttal: why, since you cherish so many and so innumerable gods, aren't you immune to as many dangers and storms, by which every day the fatalities and multiplicities of fortune move you? Why, I ask, do your gods cease to avert from you so many kinds of disease and sickness, shipwrecks, destructions, fires, plagues, barrenness, loss of securities and confiscation of goods, discords, wars, enmities, captures of cities, and enslavements endured by the free-born? But God aids us but little in these misfortunes. The reason is clear and manifest. For nothing is promised to us in this life, nor for accommodations in the husk of this bit of flesh; no help is offered or aid decreed: but indeed, we have been taught to reckon and esteem lightly every menace of fortune, whatsoever they be.[38]

Arnobius poses a question in the voice of a hypothetical pagan: why doesn't the Christian God prevent misfortune for his adherents? The question underscores the pagan character's central ignorance. The Christian God, Arnobius tells the reader, is not concerned with worldly affairs; the benefits of Christian belief are not material, but spiritual. For the pagan, however, this renunciation is incomprehensible. Protection from physical misfortune is precisely (and solely) what Arnobius's pagan desires from religion; a multiplicity of gods merely increases the opportunities for divine benefaction. Clearly, however, Arnobius's pagan does not realize even this desire, for mundane misfortunes still befall him. In contrast to Arnobius's Christian voice, the pagan character is thus doubly wrong, in his beliefs and in his desires.

Nothing in these passages (or in many similar passages throughout the apologetic corpus) necessarily implies a distinction between state and religion such as Augustine defined. Rather, these texts seem to contrast the spiritual kingdom of heaven with the corporeal kingdom of the Romans, and to conflate with the concerns of the Empire both all forms of matter and all kinds of pagan ritual, in precisely the same manner as martyrial texts conflated these three ideas. Thus, in apologetic texts, just as in martyrial texts, renunciation of the world is a central criterion for distinguishing pagan (sinful, corporeal) from Christian (salvific, spiritual).

Moreover, the consistency with which this idea was presented between Justin about 150 and Arnobius in 302/3 is highly significant. It is very likely that Arnobius was still a catechumen at the time he composed his *Disputation*.[39] The fourth-century author Jerome tells us that Arnobius wrote the text to demonstrate the strength of his Christian convictions for his new community.[40] This forces us to realize the importance of renunciation in Arnobius's text: renunciation appears as the foremost criterion for identity as a Christian, even to an early fourth-century convert with little lived experience of the faith, and only catechetical training! This shows that the ideal of separation has not lost much of its centrality by the closing years of our period.

Disciplinary Literature

The theme of renouncing the world is also prominent in literature intended to regulate Christian behavior. Such literature is of particular importance in this argument, for its context is necessarily nonmartyrial. The behavior expected of Christians during moments of crisis may not have been representative of Christianity's broader claims and goals. The behavior expected of Christians in normative situations, however, is precisely what this disciplinary corpus defines. Again, it is possible to read the theme of renunciation in disciplinary literature as conflating rather than separating matter, empire, and paganism.

Tertullian, for example, in his tract *On Spectacles*, exhorts Christians not to attend any events in the circus or theater. Such displays only involve their audiences more deeply in worldly affairs: "You are addicted to pleasure, Christian, if you also[41] desire enjoyment in the world; yes indeed, [you are] a complete fool, if you esteem this[42] to be enjoyment."[43] Tertullian asserts not only that the desire to enjoy one's current life is foolish for the Christian, but also that no true enjoyment can be had in this world. Such a foolish "addiction" is certainly sinful in Tertullian's view, and thus incompatible with Christian living.

If Tertullian's "enjoyment" corresponds to Augustine's distinction between enjoyment and use, then Tertullian here contrasts enjoyment of the world, and specifically of its theaters and circuses, with mere use of the world for spiritual ends. Thus one could argue that Tertullian objected to Christian participation in public spectacles both because the shows were inherently imbued with elements of pagan ritual and because the shows deliberately excited enjoyment of mundane affairs, as a way of fostering community sentiment, but not because the shows themselves (apart from their pagan content or anti-spiritual effects) were antithetical to Christian morals.[44]

But is this the only possible interpretation? Tertullian's "enjoyment" here may not correspond with Augustine's codification. If not, then by "enjoyment" Tertullian means any participation in worldly events. Enjoyment subsumes use, as Tertullian makes plain: "What is more enjoyable than to have God the Father and our Lord at peace with us, than revelation of the truth, than confession of our errors, than pardon for the innumerable sins of our past life? What greater pleasure is there than distaste for pleasure itself, contempt for all that the world can give, true liberty, a pure conscience, a contented life, and freedom from all fear of death?"[45] The Christian "desiring enjoyment in the world" is wrong-thinking, not because enjoyment of material things (as opposed to their use) is wrong, but because having anything to do with material things is antithetical to divine commands for Christian renunciation. Worldly pleasure is *by definition* opposed to the will of God, regardless of the purpose or utility of that pleasure. Only "contempt for all that the world can give" makes possible the sinless living promised by baptism. The pagan content of the shows and the world-embracing response engendered in the audience, therefore, cannot be separated from the event itself. Christians should not attend spectacles, not merely because of the negative effects these spectacles can have, but more fundamentally because shows themselves are inherently "foolish" and unspiritual. The term *enjoyment* in Tertullian's writings thus conflates matter, empire, and paganism into one category.

Clement of Alexandria states explicitly that renunciation of these three together is a quotidian obligation for separatist Christians, and not merely one that arises in crisis situations: "It must now be described summarily, in what way someone must live throughout the whole of a life that is called Christian. For whenever anyone, compelled by the Word away from external things and even from the burden itself of the body to the mind, will have learned thoroughly the contemplation of the conditions which befall man precisely according to nature, he will know to be anxious not for external things, but rather for the things particular to man, and [he will know] to cleanse out the eye of his soul, and also to consecrate his flesh."[46] Clement's Christianity has little room for "external things," for involvement in the world and the concerns of the body. Quite the contrary; Clement insists on renunciation from the world as the only manner of proper care for the soul. Those who, by spiritual grace, learn that the "natural conditions" of the body have little effect on the soul,[47] will learn also to have proper concern for the soul, and consequentially, proper concern for the body, "consecrating" it by removing to the greatest extent possible any "external things."

Clement's demand for renunciation does not imply that physical necessities must be neglected, but rather that anything beyond what is strictly necessary should be avoided. This applies firstly to nourishment: "[Some live to eat,] but the Pedagogue commands us to eat so that we may live; for neither is nourishment our labor, nor pleasure our goal; but [food is] for the sake of continuance in this material world, [continued life] which the Word instructs towards immortality; on account of which also, [excessive] nourishment is condemned."[48] Clement explicitly condemns anything eaten for pleasure or in excess of the body's basic requirements. The Christian must eat only "to live"; Clement's ambiguity here is deliberate. The body needs a certain minimum nourishment to function, to live in the world until the expected ending;[49] this amount is not condemned. The soul, however, needs only the Word to live "towards immortality," and is hindered by any bodily excess. "Eating to live" therefore implies the support of both the body's physical (and temporary) life, and the soul's spiritual (and unending) life. But these two goals may be simultaneously accomplished only by avoiding every extraneous thing. This support of the life of the body, then, must not be taken as a vindication of material existence; Clement is clear that continued life in this world is merely a means to an end, an opportunity to improve the life of the soul. Life in the world is a necessary precursor to eternal life, but enjoying life in the world hinders salvation.

Because physical living is to be restricted to bare necessities, the avoidance of extraneous things applies also to wine: "Therefore I admire those who have taken up an austere life, and who desire water, the medicine of temperance; and who flee wine to the greatest extent possible, as if it were a threat of fire."[50] Clement praises those who prefer water to wine, and compares the "fiery" effects of wine on the body to the fiery torments of a soul which succumbs to temptation.[51] Wine itself may not be an evil, but it brings on a heated excitation in the body, which can reduce one's ability to resist temptation. Water, by contrast, is the "medicine of temperance," of renunciation and avoidance of pleasure, and is therefore preferable.

The avoidance of extraneous things applies, lastly, to material goods: "Follow God, stripped of false pretension, stripped of mortal escort; possessing what is yours, what is good, what alone cannot be taken away: faith in God, confession in the one who has suffered, beneficence towards man, the most precious of possessions. I, moreover, approve of Plato, who rightly establishes as a law, that one must not surround oneself with treasures of silver or gold, nor with useless equipment which does not concern an enforced necessity or is [not] moderate; so that the same thing may be suitable for many [uses], and [so that] a multitude of possessions may be pruned away."[52] Clement here draws an explicit contrast between Christian faith, the "most precious possession" of the soul, and material goods, the "mortal escort" which surrounds the body and hinders the progress of the soul. Faith, Clement asserts, is the only "good" possession, the only one that cannot be taken away from the Christian. Material goods, by contrast, are to be shunned to the greatest extent possible. Clement does not insist that the Christian own nothing; he does insist that the Christian own no more than is necessary. Every object possessed by a Christian should be devoid of ornament, and should have a specific and necessary use, or more preferably, several uses. Practicality is the sole criterion for judging the value of any object.

These works of Clement, and this last passage in particular, have often been cited to argue that Clement intended to permit the use of corporeal objects for ultimately spiritual goals, in the same way that Augustine would two centuries later.[53] Indeed, at a first reading, Clement does seem to be authorizing use of material things along the same lines as Augustine. There is, however, a fundamental difference. Augustine's use/enjoyment contrast permits the use of most material objects, and of secular institutions and processes, in direct support of nonmaterial, that is, spiritual, goals. That is not what Clement is saying in these passages. Rather, he is attempting to define the extent to which accommodation must be made to the fact of material existence. Within this extent, use of material things is permitted for the sake of the body, but not of the soul. These licit material things may not impede the soul, since the body is also given by God for a purpose; but these things certainly do not contribute positively to the salvific welfare of the soul. Beyond this very basic level, moreover, there is still no implication that material things can contribute in any way to spiritual goals; and indeed, beyond this level, the use of material things explicitly impedes spiritual goals. The interpretation of the spiritual/ corporeal dichotomy as understood by Clement is thus fundamentally different from Augustine's understanding.

A generation after Clement, Cyprian describes more explicitly the dangers of all material possessions, licit or not, for Christians: "But how can they follow Christ, who are held back by the chain of inheritance? Or how do they seek heaven and ascend to high and sublime things, who are weighed down by earthly desires? They believe themselves to possess, who are rather possessed, slaves of their own property, not lords over their own wealth but rather slaves of wealth."[54] Cyprian in this passage argues that salvation and material possessions are mutually exclusive. Lack of renunciation prevents Christians from achieving the proper goal of following Christ. The proper orientation on spiritual things is hindered by any unnecessary attention paid to material things; those who pay such attention are "enslaved" to the world and its demands, incapable of following Christ or being in any way Christian. Such people, for Cyprian, fail to "follow Christ."

It is significant that this passage occurs in Cyprian's tract on the proper status of Christians who lapsed during the Decianic persecution. In this tract, Cyprian argues that God allowed the Decianic persecution because of the sins of the Christian communities—sins such as avarice and internal dissent.[55] The persecution is a warning to Christians to return to traditional "harmony" and "simplicity."[56] Yet if Cyprian meant to imply an Augustinian-like use/enjoyment distinction, then he undermines his main point: namely, the necessity of renouncing both use *and* enjoyment of material goods in order to avoid idolatry. The inutility of wealth for the salvation of the whole Christian community, including those who lapsed during the persecution, is a necessary corollary to renouncing the world.

Clement's contemporary, Commodianus, evinced much the same attitude toward renunciation in his verse *Instructions*. Renunciation defines the essence of Christian behavior, in opposition to pagan worldliness:

> If certain learned ones, while they await your gifts or fear your persons, relax individual things for you, I do not grieve, but I am compelled to speak the truth. With the crowd of evil people you go to useless spectacles, where Satan is at work in the commotions in the circus. You persuade [yourself] that whatever pleases you is permissible. Child of the Most High amongst the sons of Zabulus,[57] do you now desire to look again on the former things which you have renounced? Do you dwell again among them? What does the One profit [you]? Do not desire to love the world, nor its ostentation; such is the voice of God, and proper it seems to you. If you seek to live as a native [of the world, while still] a man of faith, the pleasures of the world remove you from the grace of Christ.[58]

Like Tertullian, Commodianus inveighs against "useless spectacles," and for much the same reasons. Enjoyment of the world is incompatible with Christian renunciation; the events of the circus draw the disengaged Christian back into material, and indeed idolatrous, concerns which should not involve him. These events are deliberately conceived by Satan to tempt mankind;[59] pagans have fallen to this temptation, but the Christian must remain aloof from such concerns.

In these disciplinary sources, renunciation again conflates rather than distinguishes among matter, empire, and pagan practices. This is the same meaning seen in the martyrial and apologetic literature.

Exegetical Literature

The final genre to be considered here is exegetical literature: literature, that is, intended to interpret the Scriptures. This exegetical material provides scholars with the most direct evidence of contemporary interpretations of canonical texts. Exegetical texts were intended to have instructional value independent of context.[60] They rely on traditional themes and images to reinforce standards of Christian behavior in their audience.

Once again, the theme of renunciation seems to conflate the same three objects as "corporeal."

Origen asserts that a "spiritual" interpretation of biblical texts is necessary: "If indeed we, following the opinion of Paul that 'the law is spiritual,'[61] believe and hear spiritually what [the Bible] contains, an enormous profit for the soul will appear in those things which are written."[62] Following this spiritual interpretation, the benefits expected from Christianity are also spiritual: "If the law is not spiritual, but carnal, it is not to be doubted that, observed carnally, [the law] offers equally carnal blessings to those who observe it. But if, as it seemed to the Apostle Paul, 'the law is spiritual,' then without doubt it must be observed spiritually, and the remuneration of blessings hoped for from it is spiritual. And so it follows from all this that a spiritual law gives spiritual blessings, and it even follows no less from this that the curses and punishments of a spiritual law are not corporeal."[63] Origen further describes this crucial distinction between "spiritual" and "carnal": "When indeed they [i.e., the Old Testament Israelites] began to neglect the divine commandments, a stronger and more powerful enemy hand was raised up against them. And against that first people, when they had sinned, corporeal enemies rose up; but against us, who are called Israel according to the spirit, without doubt a spiritual enemy rises up, and when we neglect the commandments of God, when we despise the precepts of Christ, the hand of demons is raised more powerfully; and we are given over to [these] enemies when we are separated from grace."[64] These texts again establish the theme of renunciation, just as it emerged from martyrial, apologetic, and disciplinary texts. The Christian is ideally concerned only with spiritual, otherworldly things, and not with mundane affairs. The chief enemy of the Christian is also spiritual, and presents obstacles to the progress of the soul toward God. These obstacles, however, are themselves primarily corporeal temptations—including, for example, the circus spectacles described above, denounced by Tertullian and Commodianus. These obstacles are intended by their demonic inventors to cause Christians to neglect the divine precepts demanding renunciation, and to become involved in secular affairs to the peril of their souls.

In his tract *On Prayer*, Tertullian describes the same spiritual Christian goal as Origen: "It [the prayer "Our Father"] begins with a testimony to God, and with the reward of faith, when we say, '[Our] Father who art in Heaven.' For we pray to God, and we commend faith, whose reward is this address."[65] For Tertullian, the "reward of faith" is twofold. First, it is to enter Heaven, to live after death in the presence of God; second, it is to know God as Father. Both these rewards are the common goal of Christians, and both are closely linked; one cannot enter Heaven without knowing God as Father, nor know God as Father without ultimately entering Heaven.

Clement of Alexandria describes explicitly in his *Instructor* what knowing God as Father implies for Christians:

> We, then, who are children,[66] no longer roll ourselves along on the ground like serpents, nor walk slowly on the ground as formerly, crawling in the manner of serpents with the whole body after foolish desires; but, stretching ourselves upwards by our will, having renounced the world and sins, touching the ground on tip-toe in order to pretend to be in the world, we pursue holy wisdom, which seems folly to those who have been goaded into villainy. Suitably, then, [we are called] children, who have known God alone as father. And so, to those who have made progress in the Word, he announced this utterance,[67] bidding [them] to care nothing for the affairs of this [world], and exhorting [them] to cleave to the Father alone, in imitation of children.[68]

Clement, like Tertullian, asserts that only those who "know God as Father," who have renounced the world and its sinfully corporeal demands, are truly Christian. The childlike Christian trusts fully in God and cares nothing for what is not godly. The more fully Christian one is, the less one cares for mundane affairs, and the more one turns toward God and "pursues holy wisdom." The Christian, having thus renounced the world and hopeful for the "reward of Heaven," is explicitly contrasted to the non-Christian, who "crawls in the manner of serpents after foolish desires" and who has been "goaded into villainy." These foolish desires are material concerns; villainy is involvement in unspiritual affairs.

A generation after Tertullian and Clement, Origen, in his *Treatise on Prayer*, maintained a similar distinction between the spiritual and the corporeal: "Just so, if we have spiritual gifts and are illuminated by God for the complete possession of true goods, we will not split hairs over the paltry affairs of what concerns a shadow. For all material and corporeal things, of whatsoever kind they happen [to be], are reckoned a feeble and useless shadow, in no wise able to be compared with the saving and holy gifts of the God of all. And how will the mind which views the kingdom of the ruling Christ not despise as not at all worthy of thought every worldly kingdom?"[69] Origen again, like Clement and Tertullian, distinguishes between the true and good possession, which is faith and knowledge of God, and material possessions. These latter are reckoned "feeble and useless," of little importance in comparison to faith and other divine gifts. The Christian, who necessarily realizes this, will consequently desire not to be involved with "what concerns a shadow." Origen, indeed, asserts that a Christian, once he understands the true relationship between the material and the divine, cannot possibly do otherwise than "despise" the affairs of this world.

Moreover, in the same work, Origen quite strongly asserts the incompatibility, described equally by Clement, of spiritual with secular pursuits:

> Just as there is not a partnership between righteousness and lawlessness,[70] just so the kingdom of sin is incapable of coexisting with the kingdom of God. If, then, we desire to be ruled by God, let sin rule in no way in our mortal body,[71] nor let us obey its commands when it summons our soul to the works of the flesh and to what is alien to God, but rather, putting to death the useless things belonging to the earth,[72] let us cultivate the fruits of the Spirit,[73] so that the Lord may, as it were, walk about in us as in a spiritual garden,[74] ruling alone over us with his Christ, until every rule and authority and power is destroyed from us.[75]

Here again, Origen identifies sin with mundane distraction from proper spiritual goals. The "kingdom of sin" tempts the soul with "works of the flesh" which are "alien to God." The Christian, who is ruled by the "kingdom of God," must avoid this temptation; he must "put to death the useless things" of this world and "cultivate the fruits of the Spirit." Renunciation of the world is explicitly defined as the opposite of sin, and as the equivalent of rule by God. The Christian, unless he opposes every divine gift offered, must necessarily renounce the world. Those who do not, but who remain involved with worldly affairs, cannot be Christians; "sinful" worldliness is incompatible with Christian renunciation.

Origen admits that the ideal of renunciation is difficult to uphold; but the challenge of living up to such an ideal[76] is part of what separates Christian from pagan:

> This order is chiefly shown from the fruits of labors, but also no less from excellence of understanding. For often it happens that those who

care for an earthly and worthless understanding and who occupy themselves with earthly things, occupy the elevated rank of priest or the
throne of a learned [bishop], and he who is spiritual and free by turning
away from earthly things, so that he may "examine all things and be
judged by none,"[77] holds the rank of a lower minister or even is rele-
gated among the multitudinous [lay] people. But this is to despise the
statutes of both law and gospel, and to care for nothing at all according
to order.

But if anyone among us is solicitous of food or drink, and directs all
his cares to worldly affairs—even indeed if he allot to God one or two
hours from the whole day, or come to pray in the church or hear the
word of God in passing—and indeed measures his chief care against
concern for the world and his stomach, this one does not obey the
commandment which says that "man must advance according to his
order,"[78] or the one that says that "all things must be done according to
order."[79] For order, instituted by Christ, is "to seek first the kingdom of
God and his justice,"[80] and to believe that those things which are in the
second place "will be added to us"[81] by God. Therefore, "let man advance according to his order."[82]

Origen expects to observe a correlation between level of renunciation and
social standing within the Christian community. Such a correlation represents the "order instituted by Christ." That this order is not always
achieved, and that even the leaders of the community are susceptible to
involvement in worldly affairs, is the result of human fallibility, of "not
obeying the commandments" of God. Christian renunciation demands an
otherworldly orientation, and a trust in God rather than in oneself to
provide mundane necessities. There may be among Christians those who
feign this orientation and this trust, who only pay lip service to God and
rely on themselves to provide for physical needs; but they are not Christian "according to the order" of God. They fail to live up to the ideals and
standards demanded by Christianity. They are bad Christians.

Origen's expected correlation between renunciation and moral stature
is also evident in the late-third-century *Banquet of the Ten Virgins* by Methodius: "For those who are the better and who already have drawn in the
truth more clearly, withdrawn from the offences of the flesh through perfect purification and faith, become a church and an assistant of Christ."[83]
Methodius shows that the significance of renunciation has not changed in

the course of the third century. The Christian still must strive to "with-draw" from attention to physical being, and to orient himself instead to the otherworldly and the divine. Those who come closer to this ideal are "the better," who perceive "the truth more clearly." In this way, Methodius's virgins stand closer to the goal of salvation: "Virginity is something exceedingly great and admirable and esteemed; and, if one must speak openly and according to the holy Scriptures, [it is] the most fertile source of immortality, and its flower and its first-fruit. For just as the ichors and the putrid humors of meats, and all things which cause it ruin, are melted out by salt, thus in the same manner also all the irrational desires of a virgin are drawn out of the body by [divine] teaching."[84] Methodius states explicitly that virginity leads to salvation. Virginity here has a broader sense than its literal meaning—not merely sexual abstinence but more broadly a commitment to divine teaching, to living a fully Christian life.[85] Only such an austere life is "great, admirable, and esteemed." For true Christians, the "irrational desires" brought on by material temptations are "melted out" by "divine teaching," in the same way that salt preserves meat from rotting.

Moreover, Methodius understands this "virginal" life to be one of renunciation: "And so now, O virgins, daughters of undefiled prudence, our zeal [is] for life free from envy and [for] the kingdom of heaven. You also be zealously of one mind with those prior to you toward this same glory of purity, having little concern for this life."[86] Methodius's virgins are spiritually oriented, "having little concern for this life," in precisely the same way as their predecessors were throughout the separatist period. In the closing years of the third century, the same ideals for Christian behavior are invoked as in the middle years of the second century.

Renunciation and the Logos

Renunciation in the separatist period, as we have seen, conflated together under the "corporeal" category three things: matter, the Roman Empire, and paganism. All of these had a common characteristic that allowed this mutual identification: separation from the divine. No aspect of this broad corporeal category could participate in the Logos, in the saving wisdom of God's providence, except through the transformation of baptism.

The development of this ideal during and after the period of Zealot activity (66 to 135) resulted in a complete dissociation of each of these three things from their ambiguous Pauline context. In the separatist era, neither matter nor the Roman Empire nor paganism were seen ambiguously: all were certainly opposed to Christian wisdom and discipline, and Christian participation in any of these threatened one's salvation. Only by rejecting all of these unspiritual affairs could the fullness of the promised salvation be attained. Irenaeus of Lyons, when summarizing the differences between orthodox and Gnostic teaching at the conclusion of his *Against Heresies*, claims the importance of such a rejection for conversion:

> God does, however, exercise a providence over all things, and therefore he also gives counsel; and when giving counsel, he is present with those who attend to moral discipline. It follows that the things which are watched over and governed should be acquainted with their ruler; which things are not irrational and vain, but have understanding derived from the providence of God. For this reason, certain of the Gentiles, who were less addicted to allurements and voluptuousness and were not led away to such a degree of superstition regarding idols, being moved by his providence were convinced that they should call the maker of this universe the Father.[87]

Irenaeus here notes the providential activity of God in promoting conversion to Christianity. Only those whose "addiction" to worldly, political, and pagan affairs was not complete to begin with are susceptible to "being moved" by God's providence. Having been introduced to the "moral discipline" of renunciation, they are progressively "convinced that they should call the Creator 'Father.'" We have already noted the significance of calling God "Father," in the earlier discussion of exegetical literature. Conversion for Irenaeus is thus a rational process of increasingly complete separation from corporeal affairs; in other words, an acceptance of the ideal of renunciation.

Moreover, the corporeal affairs of the physical, political, and pagan world are *not* ruled over by God. Irenaeus defines the "things watched over and governed" by God's providence as "not irrational and vain." According to the ideal of renunciation, corporeal affairs are rejected precisely because they are irrational and vain; they contribute nothing to the goal of salvation, but rather hinder that goal for Christians. In Paul's ambiguous relation between creation and God, corporeal affairs do not directly or necessarily hinder salvation. Creation (including the Empire, but excluding idolatrous paganism) is good because made by

God for good purposes. In separatist Christianity, however, matter and the Empire are conflated with idolatrous paganism, not because they were not made by God for good purposes (a fact that separatist Christians readily accepted), but rather because they have fallen away from those purposes along with Lucifer. God maintains direct control only over "spiritual" things; corporeal affairs (matter, empire, and paganism) are under demonic control, as the second-century apologist Athenagoras makes clear:

> To the good that is in God, the spirit which is about matter, who was created by God just as the other angels were created by him and entrusted with the control of matter and forms of matter, is opposed. For this is the office of the angels: to exercise providence for God over the things created and ordered by him. Some continued in those things for which God had made them, but some outraged both the constitution of their nature and the government entrusted to them: namely, this ruler of matter and its various forms.[88]

Lucifer's original duties included ruling the material world on God's behalf. When he rebelled against divine authority, he was not removed from this office, but rather caused matter to fall away from participation in the divine; the world has become solely a corporeal place, having nothing in it of the spiritual Logos, until Christ's incarnation.

This demonization of matter is much different, however, from "heretical" attempts to posit a dual godhood. Satan is never God's equal, but rather even in a state of rebellion continues to serve God's providential purpose.[89] Moreover, the demonization of matter is temporary. Although in the present age matter is a hindrance to salvation, after the Parousia matter will be restored to its intended place in God's perfect creation; matter will be reinfused with the Logos. Tertullian makes this clear in his refutation of Marcion's dualistic theology, in which the demonization of matter is eternal: "If that is a plenary grace and a substantial mercy which brings salvation to the soul alone, this is the better life which we now enjoy whole and entire; while to rise again in part only will be a chastisement, not a liberation. The proof of the perfect goodness [of the unique God] is that man, after his rescue, will be delivered from the domicile and power of the malignant deity into the protection of the most good and merciful God."[90] According to Marcion, salvation pertains to the soul only, not to the body. Tertullian rejects this kind of thinking, not because matter itself is a good — Tertullian respects matter no more than Marcion does *in the present age* — but because Marcion's salvation denies Tertullian's fuller description of God's providence and mercy. God made humans with both a body and a soul, even before the fall of Adam; salvation, the "liberation" of complete human nature from the corruption engendered by the fall, must thus include both elements. Salvation for the soul alone, rather than for both soul and body, is incomplete salvation for humans, since it fails to "liberate" the body also into a state of incorruption.

In this debate between Gnostic dualism and orthodoxy, the inheritance of Pauline theology, even as it was read in the separatist period, still supported explicit statements of the goodness of creation and explicit promises of bodily resurrection. Separatist theologians like Tertullian, Athenagoras, and Irenaeus never sought to deny these Pauline tenets, only to read them in light of the apparent meaning of the events between 66 and 135. Indeed, this makes the importance of second- and third-century refutations of Gnostic-type heresies much more understandable to modern scholars. As this chapter has argued, separatist self-identity was rooted in an opposition between spiritual and corporeal affairs, in which "corporeal" conflated matter, empire, and paganism all together, but in which also the promise of perfecting the corporeal remained fundamental. If this was true, then the alternatives proposed by Marcion, Valentinus, and other Gnostic-type thinkers threatened to undermine not merely the *political* boundaries of Christian communities[91] but Christ's very purpose in coming into the world. By challenging such aspects of separatist Christianity as the perfection of matter through the Parousia, these alternatives — which also tended to reject engagement with the physical and political worlds, but for very different reasons — challenged the very nature of separatist Christianity.

Hippolytus of Rome, in his *Refutation of All Heresies*, describes the significance of this challenge in Christological terms. Even in separatist Christianity, which sought political and physical renunciation, the Incarnation of Christ in a fully human body (denied by Gnostic dualism like that of Marcion) was absolutely crucial to the successful salvation of both soul and body:

> This Logos we know to have received a body from a virgin, to have remade the old [i.e., fallen and corrupted] man by a new creation, to have passed through every period of this life, in order that he himself

might serve as a law for every age, and that, by being present among us, he might exhibit his own [incorrupt] manhood as an aim for all men. This [Logos] we know to have been made out of the compound of our humanity. For if he were not of the same nature as ourselves, in vain does he ordain that we imitate the Teacher. In order, however, that he might not be supposed to be different from us, he even underwent toil, and was willing to endure hunger, and did not refuse to feel thirst, and fell into the stillness of death. He did not protest against his own Passion, but became obedient unto death, and manifested his resurrection. In all these acts, he offered up as first-fruits his own manhood, in order that you, when you are in tribulation, may not be disheartened, but, confessing yourself to be a man of like nature with the Redeemer, may expect also to receive what the Father has granted to his Son.[92]

Hippolytus insists on the crucial fact that Christ, the Logos incarnate, did indeed have a fully human body, not merely the appearance of one. Only because the Logos was fully human could all matter, and especially human bodies, hope for an eventual perfection and reconciliation with God. The proper means of perfection in the current state of material corruption is to live as Christ lived: toiling, hungry, thirsty, and prepared for death—in other words, the ideal of renunciation. Ultimately there will be no need for renunciation, because with the Parousia all creation will once again participate perfectly in the Logos, and there will be no further separation of spiritual from corporeal.[93]

By challenging the Incarnation, Gnostic alternatives threatened to appropriate the revelatory truth of the Logos from orthodox Christianity. If the Christianity of Irenaeus, Hippolytus, or Tertullian was no longer unique and distinctive, it could have no unique purpose; salvation, in other words, could not in fact be both universal and through Christ alone. Christian teaching would not be "the Truth," and the sacrifices converts made to adhere to the ideal of renunciation would be meaningless. Gnostic sects like those of Marcion and Valentinus did not merely compete with orthodox Christianity to attract and retain converts; Gnostic dualism, by denying the eventual salvation of the corporeal, offered a different definition of the Logos and man's relation to it; this alternative threatened the very existence of Christian "Truth." It was for this reason that Irenaeus, Tertullian, Hippolytus, Origen, Clement, and many other Christian authors expended so much time and energy on refutations of Gnosticism.

Conclusion

In all four genres of separatist literature, the theme of renunciation not only surfaces consistently but also appears without its Pauline pro-imperial and pro-worldly complements. The material world, the demonic snares of pagan ritual, and the worldly authority of the Empire are all three repeatedly conflated under the "corporeal" category by separatist Christian authors; all these things are explicitly opposed to what is "spiritual" and Christian. The audiences of these texts were over and over exposed to an ideal asserting that accommodation between Christians and the material and political worlds in which they lived was not acceptable; it was not possible to remain both a Christian and in the world.

Moreover, because of the perceived threat of Gnostic-type sects, this opposition of spiritual to corporeal is tied closely to Christian definitions of the Logos and man's relationship to the Logos. Thus, not only was the message of renunciation one which Christians were continuously exposed to, more significantly it was one whose emphasis was inseparably linked to the very nature of being a follower of Christ.

The remaining chapters of this work will examine some consequences of this ideal of renunciation, describing how renunciation intersected other ideas central to the development of Christianity in the second and third centuries: relations between Christians and Romans, martyrdom, apocalypticism, apologetic, and the bases of Constantine's conversion.

CHAPTER THREE

Separatist Christianity and the Roman Empire

If the conflation of matter, empire, and paganism underlay the separatist ideal of renouncing the physical and political worlds, this ideal still had to incorporate biblical statements about the divine origins of worldly authority and the necessity for Christians to obey these authorities. Separatist Christians interpreted New Testament statements about the providential activity of worldly authority in light of the failed Zealot revolts before 135. The pro-imperial aspects of Pauline ambiguity were read according to the ideal of separation. Human institutions like the Roman Empire had indeed been created by God for providential purposes, but had since fallen from those purposes through the idolatry of material pursuits. Because Rome was inherently pagan, its authority was inherently corrupt, even demonic. God made providential use even of this demonic authority to test and punish Christians, but ultimately earthly Rome would be fully replaced by the Heavenly Jerusalem; in the meantime, Christians were not under Roman authority, but under Christ's.

The three biblical passages considered here exhibit typical pro-imperial sentiment in the New Testament. These passages claim that the Roman state was instituted by God as the highest form of government until the

Parousia, and that for this reason Christians should be obedient to the state, to the extent that this obedience does not involve transgressing explicit divine sanction, particularly against idolatry. Before the outbreak of the First Jewish Revolt in 66, Christians could still hope that the Empire would be a positive providential device, and that obedience to it would provide to Christians (as to Jews) earthly benefits such as protection from persecution and peace in which to seek converts. But the failure of the Zealot movement between 66 and 135 meant that Christians could no longer see the Roman Empire as contributing positively to God's salvific plan, but only as a source of persecution for God's true followers.

Pro-imperial Sentiment in the Synoptic Gospels

Although written shortly after the destruction of the Temple of Jerusalem in 70, the Gospel of Matthew shows little effect of the failed revolt in describing proper Christian attitudes toward the Empire.[1] Matthew describes how certain pro-imperial Jews, suspecting Jesus of Zealot sympathies, tried to trick him into transgressing either Jewish or Roman law:

> Then the Pharisees went out and laid plans to trap him in his words. They sent their disciples to him along with the Herodians. "Teacher," they said, "we know you are a man of integrity and that you teach the way of God in accordance with the truth. You aren't swayed by men, because you pay no attention to who they are. Tell us then, what is your opinion? Is it right to pay taxes to Caesar or not?" But Jesus, knowing their evil intent, said, "You hypocrites, why are you trying to trap me? Show me the coin used for paying the tax." They brought him a denarius, and he asked them, "Whose portrait is this? And whose inscription?" "Caesar's," they replied. Then he said to them, "Give to Caesar what is Caesar's, and to God what is God's."[2]

In this passage a group of Pharisaic Jews attempts to impale Jesus on the horns of a political dilemma. It is significant that in the first century the Pharisees were the predominant sect of Palestinian Judaism.[3] Religiously, they observed an extensive legal code drawn from both the Pentateuch and oral tradition; politically, they collaborated with the pro-Roman Herodian government, in order to obtain the freedom to practice their religion unmolested. The question they pose to Jesus is extremely well chosen to trap him: should Jews pay Roman taxes; or, in other words, should Jews accommodate themselves to the Roman occupation of Judea? This question is presented primed for a yes-or-no answer, either of which responses could be catastrophic for Jesus. If he says yes, then the Zealots[4]—the anticollaborationist opponents of the Pharisees, who could be found among Jesus's followers—would either abandon him or turn on him; if he says no, he would be subject to the harsh Roman penalties for rebellion.

Jesus's answer is equally well chosen, for it sidesteps neatly the two horns of the dilemma. He refuses to say either yes or no; instead, he demands a coin, and on it points to the imperial likeness and inscription. If the coin so obviously belongs to the emperor, then clearly it is not wrong to return it to him; but, he adds, be sure to observe equally the divine law. Neither the Pharisees nor the Zealots can find fault with this answer, and so Jesus escapes the intended trap.

This passage could be interpreted to support a distinction between church and state, such as Augustine made.[5] But did separatist Christians interpret it in this way? I argue that they did not. Because the ideal of separation consistently conflated the Empire and paganism together, such a distinction was not made during the separatist period.

Irenaeus clearly evokes the ideal of renunciation and its conflation of the Empire with paganism in interpreting this passage:

> The Lord himself directed us to "render unto Caesar the things which are Caesar's, and to God the things which are God's," naming Caesar as Caesar, but confessing God as God. In like manner also, that which says, "You cannot serve two masters,"[6] he does himself interpret, saying, "You cannot serve God and mammon,"[7] acknowledging God as God, but mentioning mammon, a thing also having an existence. He does not call mammon Lord when he says, "You cannot serve two masters," but he teaches his disciples who serve God, not to be subject to mammon nor to be ruled by it. For he says, "He who commits sin is the slave of sin."[8] Since he calls those "the slaves of sin" who serve sin, but does not call sin itself God, then also he calls those who serve mammon "the slaves of mammon," not calling mammon God. For mammon is, according to the Jewish language, which the Samaritans also use, a covetous man, and one who wishes to have more than he ought. But according to the Hebrew, it signifies one whose gullet is insatiable. Therefore, according to both these things which are indicated, we cannot serve God and mammon.[9]

Irenaeus interprets the "things which are Caesar's" as opposed to the "things which are God's," in the same way in which one "cannot serve two masters." Christians, the followers of Christ, are commanded to reject sin. Anyone who does not reject sin is a "slave of sin," which Irenaeus equates with a "slave of mammon." Mammon, which Irenaeus defines as covetousness, that is, as the opposite of renunciation, is identical with sin *because* it is corporeal. Thus, just as the corporeal pursuits of sinful men are opposed to the spiritual pursuits of followers of Christ, just so the "things which are Caesar's" are opposed to the "things which are God's." The Christian must "give to Caesar the things which are Caesar's," because "you cannot serve both God" and the Empire. Failing to "give to Caesar" is a failure of renunciation.

The idealized equation made by Irenaeus of Caesar, sin, and mammon works only because separatist Christians defined the category of corporeal things so broadly. If Irenaeus intended a distinction between state and religion, then his identification of sin-as-mammon with Caesar makes little sense; it would be possible to serve both God and Caesar, as Augustine would show, because Caesar too serves God. Irenaeus, however, was working from within the separatist tradition; he already conflated the Roman Empire with sin, with worldliness and idolatry. Thus it was logical for him to extend the claim "mammon equals sin" to include Caesar as well.

Tertullian makes exactly the same identification between mammon and Caesar in his tract *On the Crown,* which denied that Christians could rightly serve as Roman soldiers:

> But first I say a word about the crown itself. The laurel is sacred to Apollo or Bacchus: to the former as the god of archery, to the latter as the god of triumphs. In like manner Claudius teaches, when he tells us that soldiers are wont to be wreathed in myrtle, for myrtle belongs to Venus. When again military service is crowned with olive, the idolatry has respect to Minerva, who is equally the goddess of arms, but who got a crown of [olive] because of the peace she made with Neptune. In these respects, the superstition of the military garland will be everywhere defiled and all-defiling. And it is further defiled, I think, also in the grounds of it. Consider the annual public pronouncement of vows: what does that seem on its face to be? It takes place first in the part of the camp where the general's tent is, and then in the temples. Observe also

the words, "We vow that you, O Jupiter, will have an ox with gold-decorated horns." What does this utterance mean? Without a doubt the denial of Christ. Even if the Christian says nothing with his mouth in these places, he still makes his response by having the crown on his head. The laurel is likewise ordered at the distribution of the largess. So you see idolatry is not without its gain, selling as it does Christ for pieces of gold, as Judas did for pieces of silver. Will it be, "You cannot serve God and mammon" to devote your energies to mammon, and to depart from God? Will it be, "Render to Caesar the things which are Caesar's, and to God the things which are God's," not only not to render the human being to God, but even to take the denarius from Caesar? But even then you are still the soldier and servant of another; and if of two masters, then of God and of Caesar. But assuredly not then of Caesar, when you owe yourself to God.[10]

Tertullian, like Irenaeus, ties the distinction between God and Caesar in Matthew's passage to the command not to serve any master besides God. Military service is one example of imperial demands for engagement which cannot be harmonized with being a follower of God. The necessary idolatry of the legions' pagan rituals prevents Christian participation. But, Tertullian continues, even if the army were not imbued with pagan ritual, the idolatry inherent in corporeal things still makes serving for pay an unacceptable activity for Christians. The Christian "owes himself" *only* "to God"; and this obligation (ideally) demands a *total* commitment to spiritual goals and away from corporeal goals. Mammon here, as for Irenaeus, is not merely paganism; mammon is also "taking the denarius from Caesar," idolatry in the conflated sense. The Empire and all its servants are pursuing corporeal goals; Tertullian insists that Christians must pursue only spiritual goals, and hence cannot "serve Caesar."

Justin Martyr seems to be saying something rather different from Tertullian and Irenaeus in his commentary on this passage of Matthew in the *First Apology:*

And everywhere we, more readily than all men, endeavor to pay to those appointed by you the taxes both ordinary and extraordinary, as we have been taught by Christ; for at that time some came to him and asked him if one ought to pay tribute to Caesar, and he answered, "Tell me, whose image does the coin bear?" And they said, "Caesar's." And again he answered them, "Render therefore to Caesar the things which are Caesar's, and to God the things which are God's." Whence to God alone we render worship, but in other things we gladly serve you, acknowledging you as kings and rulers of men, and praying that with your kingly power you be found to possess also sound judgement. But if you pay no regard to our prayers and frank explanations, we shall suffer no loss, since we believe (or rather, indeed, are convinced) that every man will suffer punishment in eternal fire according to the merit of his deed, and will render account according to the power he has received from God, as Christ intimated when he said,[11] "To whom God has given more, of him more shall be required."[12]

Justin makes two crucial claims in this apologetic passage: that Christians willingly serve the Empire, and that Christians pray for the emperor. However, these claims can only be literally true if Christians like Justin could and did distinguish both between use and enjoyment and between state and religion. Only an Augustinian-like use/enjoyment distinction would have allowed Justin to conceive of worldly pursuits having ultimately spiritual ends; likewise, only an Augustinian-like state/religion distinction would have allowed Justin to support a pagan empire while simultaneously rejecting paganism.

I do not believe such distinctions were intended in this passage. A separatist interpretation of the spiritual/corporeal theme has already been demonstrated in Justin's *First Apology*. If, then, Justin intended a broad conflation of the corporeal category throughout his apology, how should the two claims he makes about Christian activity be read?

Justin claims that Christians pay their taxes "more readily than all men." According to the ideal of renunciation, there is only one plausible reading for this key phrase. Christians pay taxes "more readily" because they understand better than any others the proper relationship between spirit and matter: namely, renunciation. Material goods, and especially money, are not "good" for disengaged Christians. Paying taxes, then, is merely an opportunity to reduce the community's material accumulation; because of the ideal of renunciation, this is a necessary corollary of "rendering worship to God alone." For the same reason, the claim that "in other things we gladly serve you" is suspicious.[13] Christians did pay taxes and obey some Roman laws, though for their own reasons; but it has already been shown that, on the grounds of renunciation, Christians rejected other normative demands of the Empire: military or administrative service and public acts of political and religious loyalty. Justin's claim that Christians willingly serve the state is thus true only in a limited way, and not for the reasons he seems at first to provide.

Similarly, Justin's claim that Christians pray for the emperor should also not be taken at face value. Christians pray that the emperor maintain both "kingly power" and "sound judgment." "Sound judgment" for Justin means action and belief in accord with the precepts of Christianity, as this passage shows:

> Of old these evil demons, effecting apparitions of themselves, both de-filed men and corrupted boys, and showed such fearful sights to men that those who did not use their reason to judge these actions were struck with terror; and, carried away by fear, they called them gods. And when Socrates endeavored through true reason and examination to bring these things to light and to deliver man from demons, then the demons themselves, by means of men who rejoiced in iniquity, con-trived his death. Not only among the Greeks did reason (Logos) prevail to condemn these things through Socrates, but also among the barbar-ians they were condemned by Reason (Logos) Himself, who took shape, and became man, and was called Jesus Christ.[14]

"Sound judgement," then, is both the opposite of idolatry and identical with the Logos. Demons rely on fear and corporeal pleasures to threaten and entice men away from the truth; but those who, like Socrates or Justin himself, use "sound judgment" know that spiritual truth (Logos, Christ) cannot be attained through corporeal actions. Reason is opposed to the body. This is the ideal of renunciation; "sound judgment" is antithet-ical to the idolatry of both pagan ritual and corporeal pursuits.

Christians, Justin thus claims, pray that imperial officials, by employ-ing their God-given "sound judgment," may become convinced of the *rational* truth of Christian teaching—but if they were thus to convert, they would immediately and necessarily abandon their public careers, which, we have already seen, are incompatible with renunciation of the world. Moreover, Justin (in a rather unconciliatory move) concludes this pas-sage by threatening imperial officials with damnation if they fail to heed reason and continue to persecute Christians. By using their God-given authority for such an unjust end, they clearly damn themselves; but more significantly, by committing themselves to Roman ideals and by pursuing corporeal ends (like the collection of taxes), they reject reason. True reason (Logos) demands renunciation; corrupt reason justifies just the kind of corporeal goals embraced by the Empire, whose officials reject both renunciation and the Logos. Thus, even if Roman officials do not persecute Christians, Justin is saying, they are still accountable to God for having failed to renounce their worldly positions. Christians, however, regardless of whether or not Roman officials persecute them, and regardless of whether or not Roman officials convert, "suffer no loss," because they live properly, according to the ideal of renunciation.

During the separatist period, then, passages from the synoptic Gospels, like the passage from Matthew considered here, which in the first century were taken to imply support for worldly authority, were reinterpreted after 135 to avoid such an implication. The conflation of matter, empire, and paganism forced a rejection of accommodation. Accordingly, separatist Christians read in this passage a strategy for avoiding worldly engagement when pressed by governmental demands for taxes in money or kind. Because Christianity existed within the Roman state, such demands would regularly be placed on the Christian community. Jesus seemed to be saying to separatist Christians that such demands should be met *only* because of the ideal of renunciation. Those who serve the Roman state are damned by their actions; they cannot understand or benefit from Christian renunciation; they remain concerned with money and goods. Christians, on the other hand, who *do* understand renunciation, are not concerned with money or goods, and the paying of taxes is merely one more opportunity to reduce the salvation-impeding wealth of the community. "Giving to Caesar" the things that are his—money and goods, which prevent salvation—is a necessary corollary of "giving to God" what God demands—renunciation of the world, faith, and prayer.

Pro-imperial Sentiment in Non-Pauline Epistles

Precisely the same conclusions can be drawn from a second New Testament passage, this one from the *First Letter of Peter:*

> Submit yourselves for the Lord's sake to every authority instituted among men: whether to the king, as the supreme authority, or to governors, who are sent by him to punish those who do wrong and to commend those who do right. For it is God's will that by doing good you should silence the ignorant talk of foolish men. Live as free men, but do

not use your freedom as a cover-up for evil; live as servants[15] of God. Show proper respect to everyone: Love the brotherhood of believers, fear God, honor the king.

Slaves, submit yourselves to your masters with all respect, not only to those who are good and considerate, but also to those who are harsh. For it is commendable if a man bears up under the pain of unjust suffering because he is conscious of God. But how is it to your credit if you receive a beating for doing wrong and endure it? But if you suffer for doing good and endure it, this is commendable before God. To this you were called, because Christ suffered for you, leaving you an example, that you should follow in his steps.[16]

This passage is typical of pro-imperial sentiment in canonical, non-Pauline epistles. In the first verses Roman authority is portrayed as the source of justice, reward for right action, and the punishment for evil. Christians should obey that authority, then, as long as it is right, that is, nonidolatrous. Likewise, social institutions such as slavery are also upheld. Masters of slaves, like Roman officials, owe "consideration" to their slaves; but if they are not considerate, so much more will God reward the slaves who endure as Christ endured.

This passage, like the previous one, could be interpreted as distinguishing between state and religion.[17] But again, the ideal of separation forced separatist thinkers to interpret it differently. Polycarp of Smyrna offers such a reinterpretation in his *Epistle to the Philippians:*

Follow the example of the Lord, being firm and unchangeable in the faith, loving the brotherhood, and being attached to one another, joined together in the truth, exhibiting the meekness of the Lord in your intercourse with one another, and despising no one. When you can do good, defer it not, because alms deliver from death.[18] Be all of you subject to one another, having your conduct blameless among the Gentiles, that you may both receive praise for your good works, and the Lord may not be blasphemed through you. Woe to him by whom the name of the Lord is blasphemed! Teach, therefore, sobriety to all, and manifest it also in your own conduct.[19]

Polycarp here reinterprets the passage from 1 Peter rather unsubtly. He advises his audience to be "subject to one another," rather than to Roman authorities. This reinforces the separation of Christians from Roman society, turning the community inward toward itself. Consequently, the proper relation with Roman officials is not submission, but rather "blamelessness." By this, Polycarp means conformity to the highest moral standards and avoidance of idolatry. If Christians maintain "sobriety" in both internal and external dealings, then neither God nor pagans will be displeased. This "blameless sobriety" thus seems to imply renunciation as a primary means of "following the example of the Lord." Renunciation is both good for the Christian community and may attract converts through Christians' superior moral reputation;[20] more fundamentally, failing to live up to the ideal of renunciation is itself a form of idolatry, of "blaspheming" against God.

The second-century apologist Tatian offers a similar reinterpretation of this passage in his *Address against the Greeks:*

> For what reason, men of Greece, do you wish to bring the civil powers into collision with us, as in a pugilistic encounter? If I am not disposed to comply with the usages of some of them, why am I to be abhorred as a vile miscreant? If the sovereign orders the payment of tribute, I am ready to pay it. If my master commands me to serve as a bondsman, I acknowledge the servitude. Man is to be honored as fellow-man; God alone is to be feared. Only when I am commanded to deny him will I not obey. God is a spirit, not pervading matter but the maker of matter and the forms that are in matter. But the Spirit that pervades matter is inferior to the more divine spirit, and is not to be honored equally with the perfect God.[21]

Tatian here does not explicitly reinterpret the command for obedience as meaning obedience to other Christians rather than to Roman authorities, but implicitly he strongly undermines the legitimacy of Rome, first by understating the significance of Roman demands for participation, and second by comparing Roman rule with demonic rule. Tatian presents Christian rejection of participation in military or administrative service, and in public acts of loyalty, as "an indisposition to comply" with mere "usages," compliance with which, the reader supposes, is incidental enough to be voluntary. Tatian then admits that Christians pay taxes and do not seek to alter their legal status, as if these were the most crucial tests of one's commitment to the ideals of Rome. Moreover, he concludes by identifying the object of pagan ritual with "the spirit that pervades matter": that is, as we have already noted, Satan. By defining idolatry in this

way, Tatian evokes renunciation's conflation of paganism with both matter and empire; in other words, Tatian is claiming, *all* of the Empire,
not merely its pagan rituals, is incompatible with "fearing God alone,"
which requires renunciation and rejects participation. Thus, for Tatian as
for Polycarp, the obedience of Christians to Roman authority happens
not because of any legitimate claim these demonic authorities have over
Christians but only by accidental congruence between Christian and Roman precepts. Roman officials are to be respected "as fellow-men": not as
Roman officials, but as creatures of God and as potential converts.

Thus the same reinterpretation that was applied to passages from the
synoptic Gospels was also employed to read pro-imperial non-Gospel
passages in a way other than as pro-imperial. The idolatry of the state that
Christians must avoid is not merely pagan ritual; it is corporeal pursuit in
all guises. The ideal of renunciation again conflates matter, the Empire,
and paganism together as idolatry.

Pro-imperial Sentiment in Pauline Epistles

The final passage considered here is the well-known Romans 13:1–12.
This passage, like the previous two, seems clearly to uphold the authority
of the Roman government and the necessity for Christians to obey that
authority.[22] This passage is typical of such pro-imperial passages in the
Pauline corpus:

> Everyone must submit himself to the governing authorities, for there is
> no authority except that which God has established. The authorities
> that exist have been established by God. Consequently, he who rebels
> against the authority is rebelling against what God has instituted, and
> those who do so will bring judgment on themselves. For rulers hold no
> terror for those who do right, but for those who do wrong. Do you want
> to be free from the fear of the one in authority? Then do what is right
> and he will commend you. For he is God's servant to do you good. But if
> you do wrong, be afraid, for he does not bear the sword for nothing. He
> is God's servant, an agent of wrath to bring punishment on the wrong-
> doer. Therefore, it is necessary to submit to the authorities, not only
> because of possible punishment, but also because of conscience.
>
> This is also why you pay taxes, for the authorities are God's servants,
> who give their full time to governing. Give everyone what you owe him:

If you owe taxes, pay taxes; if revenue, then revenue; if respect, then respect; if honor, then honor.

Let no debt remain outstanding, except the continuing debt to love one another, for he who loves his fellowman has fulfilled the law. The commandments, "Do not commit adultery," "Do not murder," "Do not steal," "Do not covet," and whatever other commandment there may be, are summed up in this one rule: "Love your neighbor as yourself." Love does no harm to its neighbor. Therefore love is the fulfillment of law.

And do this, understanding the present time. The hour has come for you to wake up from your slumber, because our salvation is nearer now than when we first believed. The night is nearly over; the day is almost here. So let us put aside the deeds of darkness and put on the armor of light.[23]

The opening verses of this passage state very clearly a positive relationship between worldly, Roman authority and divine authority. God has established the Roman government to serve the divine purpose in the world, "bearing the sword" of justice and punishment of evil. Those who "do right" need have no fear of reprisal, while those who "do wrong" will be subject to divine punishment, through the agency of Roman law. Christians should therefore "do right," obeying all the commandments of God, especially to "love your neighbor as yourself," since love is "the fulfillment of law," both divine and divinely inspired. The imminence of the Parousia makes these commands all the more urgent, but does not undermine in any fundamental way the providential nature of Roman authority in this first-century context.

However, separatist Christianity saw the imminence of the Parousia and the urgency of obedience differently than did Apostolic Christianity.[24] Rather than enjoining obedience to the state, such imminence and urgency for separatist Christians enjoined obedience to the ideal of renunciation. In separatist reinterpretations of this Pauline passage, the Empire is again idolatrous in the broad rather than the narrow sense. Origen, in his apologetic tract *Against Celsus*, points out the accidental nature of Christian obedience to Roman law created by renunciation: "While we do nothing which is contrary to the law and word of God, we are not so mad as to stir up against ourselves the wrath of kings and princes, which will bring upon us sufferings and torture, and even death. For we read, 'Let everyone be subject to the higher powers. For there is no power except from God; the powers that be are ordained by God.' "[25] Christians, Origen claims, "do nothing contrary" to what God has commanded: they don't lie, or commit adultery, or kill, but try to live simply and harmoniously; they also support the ideal of renunciation. They live this way because God has ordained it; if this Christian life diverges from Roman social norms, Origen continues, it is not "madness" or flagrant fomenting of dissent, but a necessary consequence of living according to divine commands. By the same token, however, Christians obey Roman laws and norms (to the extent that they do), also because God has commanded this lifestyle. The "subjection" of Christians to Romans happens only to the extent that Roman customs coincide with divine commands.

The coincidence of Roman and Christian norms is not purely accidental. God's providential salvation was active in establishing Roman norms, to encourage pagans ignorant of the truth to behave properly, under threat of human punishments for wrong acts, as Irenaeus argues:

> Paul the apostle also says on this subject, "Be subject to all the higher powers; for there is no power but from God, and all powers which are, have been ordained by God." And again, in reference to them he says, "For the ruler bears not the sword in vain; for he is the minister of God, the avenger for wrath to him who does evil." He spoke these words, not in regard to angelic powers, but of actual human rulers, as he says, "For this reason pay tribute also; for they are God's ministers, doing service for this reason." This also the Lord himself confirmed, when he did not do what the devil tempted him to do, but rather gave directions that tribute should be paid [to Caesar]. For since man, by departing from God, reached such a pitch of fury as to look upon even his brother as his enemy, and engaged without fear in every kind of murder and avarice, God imposed upon mankind the fear of man, since they did not acknowledge the fear of God, in order that, being subject to the authority of men, and kept under restraint by human laws, they might attain to some degree of justice and forbear to sin through dread of the sword suspended in full view. Earthly rule, therefore, has been ordained by God for the benefit of nations, and not by the devil, who does not love to see nations conducting themselves in a quiet manner. Some of these rulers are given for the correction and benefit of their subjects, and for the preservation of justice; others, for fear and punishment and rebuke; others for deception, disgrace, and pride; while the just judgment of

God passes equally upon all. The devil, however, as he is the apostate angel, can only, as he did in the beginning, deceive and lead astray the mind of man into disobeying the commandments of God, into forgetting the true God, and into the adoration of himself as God.[26]

God's providence has permitted the elaboration of human laws and institutions "for the benefit of nations." Pagans had need of standards of conduct, which human laws establish and enforce. Threat of punishment at law compels pagans to conform to (minimal) divine standards of behavior. If Christian and Roman customs overlap, then, it is because both ultimately come from the same source, and share a similarity of purpose.

Satan, however, has influenced how these human laws are enforced in practice. The inherence of pagan ritual in Roman politics only proves that divinely ordained institutions have been corrupted (to one extent or another) through human error. God may have molded the Empire with the intention of leading people toward the truth; but the devil filled the mold with idolatry and corruption, hoping to lead people away from the truth. At some times and in some places, the devil largely failed to entice people into idolatry; these governments are those described by Irenaeus as "for the correction and benefit" of subjects. At other times, the devil was more successful; these governments are thus "for fear and punishment." When the devil is most successful, governments essentially fail in their providential purpose, serving only "deception, disgrace, and pride." But, Irenaeus points out, "the just judgment of God passes equally upon all"; regardless of how successfully Satan may lead men into idolatrous ritual, those who serve worldly governments are *necessarily* judged by God as failing in renunciation. Even governments that are just by human standards still seem unjust when seen against the absolute standard of Christian truth; commitment even to a just government still "disobeys the commandments of God," replacing God's command to be disengaged with the idolatrous ideal of serving what is not God.

Tertullian finds an example of how this idolatrous corruption has tainted Roman authority from its beginnings in the story of the Sabine rape:

> Then Romulus dedicated the Equiria to Mars, though they also claim the Consualia for Romulus, because he dedicated them to Consus the god, as they have it, of counsel; the counsel, namely, by which he then contrived the rape of the Sabine virgins, [so that they became] wives for

his soldiers. An excellent counsel, truly; and even now among those Romans [held] just and proper, but not, I might say, under God. For it creates a blemish on the origin, unless you esteem to be good, what receives its beginning from evil, from shamelessness, from violence, from hatred, from a fratricidal founder, from a son of Mars.[27]

Tertullian here places the contemporary Roman government into the third of Irenaeus's categories, that of deception and disgrace. He decries the hypocrisy of holding a solemn feast in honor of a legendary divine event which, by Christian standards, involved clearly immoral action. The pagan festival in question, the *Consualia,* was dedicated to the god Consus, whose advice to Rome's founder Romulus—who was faced with a shortage of marriageable women in Rome—resulted in the kidnapping of the Sabine women and the perpetuation of the Roman race. This immoral action "creates a blemish on the origin," therefore rendering all subsequent action by the Roman government suspect. Tertullian states clearly that such advice and such action is not considered "just and proper" by God, either at the time or "even now"; the fact that such unjust counsel is celebrated and perpetuated through a public festival proves the malicious deception practiced regularly by Romans.

In practice, then, the Roman Empire is not helpful for leading people toward salvation, because it has been corporeally corrupted; and Christians, who know the full truth of the matter, are in fact *not* subject to Roman authority, but only to the higher authority of God himself, as Tertullian implied in the previous passage, and as Origen explicitly claims here:

If someone found himself among the Scythians (who have unlawful customs), and had no opportunity of returning, and were forced to live among them, he would do this rightly on account of the law of truth, which for the Scythians is lawlessness: he would make a convention with those of like mind, against what is for them lawful. In the same way, judging according to truth, the laws of the nations concerning images and godless polytheism are the laws of the Scythians; and [this law] is more irreverent than any [law] of the Scythians. And so it is not unreasonable to make a convention on behalf of truth, against what is lawful. For, just as, if certain ones make a secret convention on behalf of the removal of a tyrant who has seized control of a city, they do so rightly; just so the Christians, when they are tyrannized by falsehood and by the one they call the devil, make conventions contrary to what is for the devil lawful, against the devil and for the sake of the salvation of those whom they may be able to persuade to free themselves from the law of a tyrant and, as it were, of Scythians.[28]

The corruption of idolatry, injected into the providential purpose of states by an envious devil, renders mere human law "unlawful" for Christians, armed as they are with the truth of revelation. The rejection by Christians of all social norms and laws that fail to conform to revealed truth is, Origen claims, right and proper; moreover, the failure to do so is itself idolatry, the "tyranny" of the corporeal. Only when Roman customs coincide with Christian norms can Christians obey them, but explicitly *not* because the Roman customs are authoritative; they are only accidentally correct.

Thus, in Pauline passages as in other parts of the New Testament, separatist Christian ideals rejected the authority of the Empire on the grounds of idolatry; but by idolatry, these writers meant not just pagan ritual, but all unlawful pursuits, as defined by the ideal of renunciation.

Demonization of the State in Martyrial Literature

With explicit biblical texts such as the three cited here in front of them, separatist Christians could not deny the divine origins of Roman authority. As we have just seen, however, they had no real need to make such a denial; what they could and did deny was the legitimacy of that authority over Christian (as distinct from pagan) communities. Because the Roman Empire was a corporeal institution that denied the spiritual law of God, it forfeited its right to obedience from Christians. Its authority, in effect, became demonic in the same transformation that made demons out of angels: namely, the rejection of the spiritual (Logos) in favor of what is neither God or godly.

At many times and in many places the separatist opposition to the Roman Empire remained latent; in many ordinary matters, Christian morality and Roman morality were not so far apart, and both Christians and Romans were usually content not to precipitate crises. When such crises did occur, however, Christians were already prepared with a sanctioned set of attitudes and actions with which to resist the demands of what was perceived as an illegitimate state. Thus the martyrial sources naturally convey a much stronger version of anti-Roman attitudes than other genres of Christian literature; but this attitude is not opposed to any pro-Roman sentiment elsewhere. Even the apologetic literature, we have seen, contains a rejection of Roman authority on the grounds of (conflated) idolatry; because separatist Christianity did *not* distinguish between state and religion, the rejection of idolatrous Rome necessarily included a rejection of all facets of the Empire.

The martyrial sources' more extreme rejection of Roman authority can be found, for example, in the late-second-century *Passion of the Scillitan Martyrs*, in which "Speratus said, 'I do not recognize the authority of this world; but I serve that God which no man with these eyes has seen or may see. I have committed no theft, but if I purchase anything I give the tax, because I recognize my lord, the commander of kings and of all nations.' "[29] Speratus is the leader of a group of twelve Christians being examined by the provincial proconsul, Saturninus. The proconsul asks these Christians to swear their loyalty to the Empire by the *genius* of the emperor Commodus. Speratus refuses to swear this oath, and refuses even to recognize that the Empire holds any legitimate authority over Christians; this lack of legitimate authority would of course nullify any oath. Instead, he recognizes only the authority of God. Insisting on his innocence of any crime,[30] Speratus asserts his obedience to formal Roman law on the basis of his tax payments, themselves due to his "recognition" of "my lord."

The final sentence of this passage is ambiguous. Speratus has just denied the authority of the emperor; does he then retract that denial in acknowledging the emperor as "my lord, the commander of kings and of all nations?" He might have meant this;[31] but I argue that Speratus is here referring not to the Roman emperor but to God, the divine emperor.[32] Speratus admits paying Roman taxes; but, in keeping with the separatist reinterpretation of the pro-imperial New Testament sentiment, he does so not out of obedience to Rome, but rather from obedience to Christ. It is Christ, and Christ alone, whom Speratus recognizes as "my lord."

Moreover, far from being the lord of Christians like Speratus, the emperor can be portrayed as a willing servant of the devil, as in the early-fourth-century *Passion of the Thessalonikan Martyrs*, wherein "Dulcitius the prefect said, 'What do you say, Irenê? Why didn't you obey the command of our lords the kings and Caesars?' Irenê said, 'Out of fear of God.' And he added, 'What do you say, Agapê? Will you perform all these things which we perform and dedicate to our lords the kings and Caesars?' Agapê said, 'It is not possible for Satan; he cannot move my reason; our reason is invincible.' "[33] The three Christian women, Irenê, Agapê, and Chionê, being examined by the prefect Dulcitius, have been ordered to obey the imperial command to sacrifice to the traditional tutelary deities for the good of the Empire. The three women refuse to do so, "out of fear of God." Moreover, Agapê asserts that the command to sacrifice is itself demonic; if the emperor Diocletian and his tetrarchic peers desire from her an action to which "Satan cannot move her reason," then clearly they themselves are tools of the devil, jealous of Christian salvation and bent on corruption.

Thus, the explicit rejection of Roman authority in martyrial sources appears as merely a stronger version of anti-Roman sentiment in other genres, including apologetic. What is objectionable to Christians in all kinds of literature is the corporeal nature of Roman norms; Rome is idolatrous, not merely in the sense of pagan but in the conflated sense of anti-spiritual. The ideal of renunciation prevents any accommodation with the Empire.

Conclusion

This chapter has shown how pro-imperial sentiment in the New Testament was reinterpreted according to the ideal of renunciation during the separatist period. Separatist Christians did not support the state as a divinely ordained institution worthy of respect, as these biblical passages present it. Rather, they acknowledged the divine origins of institutions of human authority, but then claimed that these institutions were corrupted by demonic forces into purely corporeal (idolatrous) affairs, sharing nothing "divine" or "spiritual" in practice. Because separatist Christians were themselves (ideally) only spiritual, they could have nothing to do with institutions wholly corporeal. Roman authority, corrupted as it was by an envious devil, had no claim on Christian loyalties.

This anti-Roman attitude, based on the ideal of renunciation, is prevalent in all genres of separatist Christian literature. Although it appears to be weaker in apologetic and stronger in martyrial sources, there is no fundamental difference in attitude between these two genres. The ideal of renunciation's conflation of matter, empire, and paganism all together as corporeal is active in both apologetic and martyrial texts, and both, despite their differing purposes, come to similar conclusions about the relationship between Christians and Romans.

Thus, for separatist Christians in the second and third centuries, the state was not a positive providential force. Providence, however, still made use of the state for positive ends: testing Christians' commitment to renunciation, making martyrs to prove Christian truth, and encouraging conversion in some non-Christians. The next two chapters will examine the significance of this martyr-creating role of the state.

CHAPTER FOUR

Martyrdom and Salvation

At most times in most places, Christians' opposition to what they saw as a corporeally ordered and motivated empire was relatively passive. Roman leaders largely ignored the small numbers of Christians in the cities as long as Christians appeared to obey Roman law, while Christians, for their part, mostly refrained from precipitating confrontations as long as no attempt was made to force idolatrous actions on them. At other times, however, the opposition between Christianity and Romanitas surfaced violently. These moments of crisis had varied causes, but similar results. The *Acta* of the Christian martyrs and other martyrial texts indicate the response to crisis which the leaders of the Christian communities consistently promoted: martyrdom (Greek *martyría*, literally "witness") was put forth as the only appropriate Christian response in immediate circumstances of violent confrontation between Christians and Romans. As we shall see, among more rigorist Christians such as Tertullian, death was preferable even to the *appearance* of accommodation with the illegitimate, idolatrous authority of the Roman state; this most profound act of rejecting accommodation was believed to be a necessary step for one's salvation. Among less rigorist Christians, such as Clement of Alexandria, martyrdom was promoted somewhat less strongly, and was believed to be necessary for salvation only in situations in which it became the sole defense against idolatry. Despite these differences, no Christian writer of the separatist period, however nonrigorist, considered compromise with the demands of the Empire or of the world an acceptable alternative to martyrdom.

There were two broad bases for this promotion of martyrdom, both of which tied it closely to Christian ideas of history and providence: a "three-fold" conception derived largely from the Old Testament, and a Christo-logical conception derived from the New.

The "Threefold" Theory

Separatist Christians understood martyrdom in the Old Testament[1] to be presented simultaneously in three distinct yet closely related forms: as a test (Latin *probatio*, Greek *dokímion*) of the martyr's love of and faith in God; as a punishment (Latin *censura* or *castigatio*, Greek *timôría*) for any sins that might have been committed since the martyr's baptism, purifying the martyr to enter Heaven; and as a reward (Latin *gloria*, Greek *dóxa* or *chárisma*) for the martyr's steadfast faith, granting direct contact with the divine godhead even before death, and immediate entrance into Heaven after death.[2] These three core ideas appear throughout separatist litera-ture,[3] both independently and together.

Martyrdom as a Test of Faith

The first aspect of the Old Testament understanding of martyrdom is that of testing. Opportunities for martyrdom occur as divinely willed tests of Christians' faith; this testing is necessary when and where it occurs, for it proves that Christians are worthy of following God. Origen describes martyrdom as test in his homilies on the Book of Judges: "For our testing does not extend only to blows, but it goes as far as the pouring out of blood."[4] Origen here is commenting on the story of Gideon's defeat of the Madianites (Jg 7:1–25), whom God had previously allowed to conquer Israel on account of Israel's sins.[5] Gideon leads three hundred warriors, whom God has "tried" or "chosen" (*ekkatharô*),[6] into battle against the Madianites; with God helping them, they overcome their enemies. Origen interprets these three hundred warriors as prefiguring Christians: "These three hundred therefore were alone, who prefigured the form of this sacrament [i.e., baptism], these chosen ones, these tested ones, these ones consecrated to victory."[7] Just as these proven warriors faced the same threats and "blows" that all soldiers face, so too Christians, in their proving, must be prepared to accept not only beatings—torture, confiscation of property, enslavement—but even "the pouring out of blood"; in other words, martyrdom. Being chosen by God leads to such a testing; passing through the test "consecrates" the martyr "to victory."

The very same idea of martyrdom as test which appears in this exegetical passage surfaces equally strongly in Origen's martyrial work as well: "And so we must deem that the present temptation has occurred as a proving and an auditing of love towards God; as it is written in Deuteronomy,[8] 'For the Lord tempts you, in order to know if you love the Lord your God with all your heart and with all your soul.' "[9] As in the passage above, here the depth of the Christian's faith in God is tested through a direct and violent confrontation of Roman and Christian values. God desires to know whether the devotion of the Christian is strong enough to withstand any adverse conditions. Just as the three hundred warriors of Gideon were chosen by their reaction in a testing situation, Christians too expect to have such an opportunity. By accepting martyrdom in the "testing situation" of violent confrontation, the Christian demonstrates the extreme commitment desired by God, and proves his worthiness to be among the most select group of God's followers.

This testing of faith occurs only by the will of God; however, as in the commentary on Judges above, God's agents in this testing are his enemies. The officials of the Roman Empire who carry out judicial examinations of Christians stand in the same relationship to Christians as the Madianites to Israel. Tertullian makes this precise relationship clear in his tract *On Flight during Persecution:*

> If, because injustice is not from God, but from the devil, while persecution consists of injustice, it therefore seems that persecution comes from the devil, by whom injustice occurs, of which persecution consists, then we must know, since there is neither persecution without the injustice of the devil, nor testing of the faith without persecution, that injustice, which is necessary on account of the testing of faith, does not maintain a defense of persecution, but rather an agency; that the will of God concerning the testing of faith, which is the reason for persecution, comes first, but the injustice of the devil follows as an instrument of persecution, which is the reason for testing.[10]

In this rather convoluted passage, Tertullian makes a number of points: that God wills persecution of Christians as a test of faith; that persecution entails injustice; that the devil rather than God causes this injustice, but only with the permission of God; and that the devil is thus responsible for this injustice. The theme of martyrdom as test surfaces here in the context of its greatest significance. Tertullian's purpose in the tract *On Flight* is to demonstrate that persecution is never to be avoided by Christians. The crucial assumption on which this passage, and indeed the entire argument, turns is that the testing of faith by persecution, which is the opportunity for martyrdom, is *necessary*. Without the necessity of a test of faith, the avoidance of persecution would be justified; Tertullian asserts in contrast that a test of faith must absolutely be necessary, for if it were not, God's just providence would not allow unjust persecution to arise in the first place.

Tertullian's disciplinary writing also presents a test of faith as necessary to salvation. In his *Antivenom against the Gnostics*, Tertullian draws a striking comparison between Roman civic games, which prove the contestants' skills and abilities, and Christian martyrdoms, which do the same for a different audience:

> Thus the trial of the arenas is accounted by this age a most worthy [manner] to contest skills, to exhibit the excellence of bodies and of voices, when the prize is the witness, when the spectacle is the judge, when pleasure [of winning] is the sentence. However insignificant the contest, the wounds are not insignificant; fists batter, heels ram, boxing gloves tear to pieces, whips tear apart. Yet no one will revile the games' presider because he subjects men to violence; suits of damages [belong] outside the arena. But to the extent that they traffic in bruises and blood and welts, he holds out [prizes]: namely crowns, and glory, and endowment, political privileges, civic stipends, images, statues, and eternal fame such as this world is capable of, a resurrection of memory. The contestant himself does not complain that he hurts, but rather desires it; the crown erases the wound, the palm wipes off the blood; he is excited more by victory than by injury. Do you consider this one injured, whom you see joyful? Not even the vanquished himself will reproach the *agonothete* [i.e., the presider of the games] his case. Will it be unseemly for God to bring forth in public his skills and his teachings, in this arena of the world, in the sight of men and angels and the powers of the

universe; to test the constancy and endurance of flesh and of soul; to give to this one the palm, to this one honor, to that one the city [i.e., the Heavenly Jerusalem], to that one his stipend; or even to reject certain ones, and to send the punished ones away with ignominy?[11]

For Tertullian, Roman games offer an opportunity to prove one's worth in a public manner, and to gain some reward from the civic body as a recognition of that worth. This opportunity is not without hazard: the games are often violent and result in injury; yet there is no thought on the part of the contestants to reproach their adversaries or their judges for their injuries. The risk is part of the game and must be accepted in agreeing to compete. If, then, Tertullian argues, pagans are willing to accept such risk of injury for the sake of mere worldly glories and honors, so much the more must Christians accept the risk of injury for the sake of eternal, heavenly reward. The testing of faith in a public forum, where all can witness the steadfastness of the "contestants," is the demonstration of worthiness which God requires. It is necessary for Christians to compete in this way; by doing so, they gain the reward they seek, while by failing in the test they prove themselves unworthy of that reward.[12]

Cyprian likewise presents the necessity of a test of faith in martyrdom, in his tractate *To Fortunata,* and does so by assembling scriptural passages to support this idea:

> [It says] in Deuteronomy: "The Lord your God tests you," in order to know if you love the Lord your God "with all your heart, and with all your soul," and with all your strength.[13] And again, according to Solomon: "The furnace proves the potter's vessel, and just men, the trial of tribulation."[14] Paul also speaks and attests the same things, saying:[15] "We glory in the hope of the splendor of God; but not only that, we glory also in afflictions, knowing that affliction causes endurance, and endurance testing, and testing hope: but hope does not bring into disorder, since the love of God is infused in our hearts by the Holy Spirit who is given to us."[16]

Cyprian's attitude toward the "trial of tribulation" in this passage is no different from Origen's or Tertullian's; persecution by the state is necessary in order to prove the devotion demanded by God from his followers. Affliction provides an opportunity to endure suffering, which is intimately connected to one's hope of salvation. Suffering is the test of faith that must necessarily be passed to attain the *gloria,* the reward of salvation, which is the goal of Christians.

Indeed, the idea that persecution and martyrdom are necessary because willed by God could easily become a criterion for exclusivity among different groups of Christians. For example, in the late-second-century polemic over the followers of Montanus, an early anti-Montanist writer, Apollonius, fragments of whose writings were preserved by Eusebius, attacked Montanus's followers exactly on this point: "Themison also, who wore a trustworthy robe of covetousness, who declined to bear the sign of the confessor, but who by a large sum of money put away from him the chains of martyrdom, yet had the hardihood to boast that he was a martyr. He, in imitation of the apostle, composed a general epistle, in which he attempted to instruct in the elements of the faith those who had believed to better purpose than himself. He defended the doctrines of the new-fangled teaching, and moreover uttered blasphemy against the Lord and the apostles and the holy Church."[17] The "trustworthiness" of Themison's faith is obvious from his actions. When given the opportunity, he fails to confess Christ at all; he bribes his way out of a test of faith. He thus proves himself weak in faith, unworthy to follow Christ; and his "attempt to instruct" (perhaps to justify his actions?) is therefore mere pretense of knowledge rather than true Christian teaching.

This idea could also support inclusion, however. None of the martyrial passages already quoted explicitly precludes other, nonmartyrial, means of salvation for Christians; while they do imply more or less strongly the exclusive efficacy of martyrdom, this implication is not borne out in other kinds of sources. Not all Christian leaders are quite as rigorist as Tertullian in equating flight from persecution with apostasy.[18] During the persecution of Decius, for example, Dionysius, Bishop of Alexandria, first hid in his home and then attempted to flee the city, before being arrested;[19] while Cyprian, Bishop of Carthage, managed to spend the entire period hidden from the authorities.[20] These actions, however, were not entirely well regarded by their rigorist contemporaries,[21] and the letters of both bishops, and in particular those of Cyprian from this period, are at pains to justify the avoidance of a test of faith. It is significant that the rationale chosen for this justification did not allude in any way to using the bishop's political position to alleviate the persecution for local Christians; instead, it portrayed both bishops as concerned to promote the martyrial constancy of their communities through continuous and multiple exhortations, rather than through a single exemplary act.[22]

Both the martyrial and the disciplinary sources quoted above uphold the testing of faith as a good both in itself and for its consequences. The salvific potential of martyrdom is of central importance in both contexts. The conclusion that the audience of both kinds of sources is supposed to reach is identical: the successful passing of a test of faith leads to salvation. In the martyrial texts cited in this chapter, the implication that martyrdom is the only means of salvation is stronger than in the nonmartyrial texts — regardless of whether the author was rigorist or nonrigorist. This is a natural side effect of the exhortatory nature of martyrial writing, and applies equally to both traditions. But it is only in nonmartyrial literature that the distinction between rigorist and nonrigorist Christians is at all observable.

Martyrdom as Punishment for Sin

The second way in which separatist Christians understood the Old Testament depiction of martyrdom was as a punishment and purgation for sin. It is important to note that separatist Christianity had not yet developed a sacramental means of dealing with postbaptismal sin,[23] comparable to later penitential traditions. While institutional means were developed for dealing with minor transgressions by individuals, no such means were available to help the community cope with the major transgressions (and in large numbers) of apostasy and idolatry. The only recognized means of purging these sins was baptism; yet baptism could only be had once.[24] Martyrdom, however, the "second baptism," could serve as well: "Let us also remember that we have sinned; and that there is no remission of sins other than accepting Baptism; and that it is impossible according to the Evangelical laws to be baptized again with water and the Spirit for the remission of sins; and that we have been given the baptism of martyrdom."[25] Origen in this passage draws a clear parallel between baptism and martyrdom. Baptism, the sacral initiation into the Christian community, is the sole means of remission for previous sins. Baptism is only available once, however; subsequent sins must be purged in some other way. Origen notes that martyrdom is also a baptism, of blood rather than of water; as such, it is equally effective in remitting postbaptismal sins.[26]

The martyrial remission of sins is not solely through the implied pres-

ence of the Holy Spirit in the martyr, as in baptism. The suffering itself of a martyrdom is a punishment for having transgressed the divine
mandates:

> Rutilius the most holy martyr, since he had fled persecution so many
> times from one place into another, and the peril (as he thought) had suf-
> ficiently diminished, after the complete safety which he had looked for-
> ward to for himself, was apprehended unexpectedly, and [was] brought
> before the judge, was overcome with tortures, I believe as a punishment
> for his flight, [and] was then given to the flames; he gave back his
> passion, which he had avoided, to the mercy of God. What else does
> God wish to show us by this example, than that one must not flee, since
> no flight can succeed if God does not wish it?[27]

In this anecdotal passage, Tertullian describes how Rutilius avoids persecution by fleeing the cities until the crisis has passed. Upon his return, however, he is arrested and tortured, and so dies. Tertullian notes
that Rutilius's arrest and torture were inspired by God in order to punish
him for avoiding the original persecution. By suffering, Rutilius expunges
that transgression, and thus, despite having initially apostatized through
his avoidance of martyrdom, is still worthy of memory as a "most holy
martyr."

Similarly, Cyprian attributes the persecution of Decius to lax behavior
by Christians in the years preceding 251:

> Yet, most beloved brothers, the reason of truth must be had, and the
> shadowy obscurity of hostile persecution should not have so blinded
> mind and feeling, that there remain nothing of light and illumination
> whence the divine precepts may be perceived. If the cause of misfor-
> tune is recognized, then redress for the injury will be found. The Lord
> wished to test his household; and since a long peace had corrupted
> the teaching handed down to us from heaven, a heavenly judgment
> aroused faith lying down and almost, as I might say, sleeping; and
> though we deserved more for our sins, the most clement Lord is so mod-
> erate in all things that everything which has occurred seemed rather an
> examination than a persecution.[28]

Decius's persecution is here described as a test of faith, a notion already ex-
plored. Cyprian notes, moreover, that God required a test in this instance
because "a long peace had corrupted the teaching handed down to us from

heaven"; in other words, Christians were not living in accordance with the central ideals of renunciation and communal harmony. God's judgment falls upon them; their behavior is corrected by the persecution, and their previous laxity is simultaneously punished. Despite the severity of Decius's persecution, Cyprian believes that God was lenient to his followers, punishing them less than they deserved. The persecution is thus less an affliction than an "examination," a test that is both probative and corrective.

Most Christians in the third century continued to hold the opinion that only martyrdom could remove the stain of major postbaptismal transgressions, especially apostasy. This traditional view was strongly championed in the aftermath of Decius's persecution by Novatian, Bishop of Rome.[29] Cyprian of Carthage, however, recognizing the unprecedented effectiveness of the Decianic persecution, took the novel and opposing view that the stain of having apostatized under duress could be removed by other means less drastic than martyrdom.[30] Cyprian's less strict viewpoint offered several long-term, institutional advantages for increasing episcopal control over both apostates and confessors, and these no doubt contributed significantly to its eventual success. During the remainder of the third century, the question of the efficacy of these alternative means of remitting sin still remained undecided, but as reaction to Diocletian's persecution from 303 to 311 showed, the effectiveness of martyrdom for salvation was never in doubt.

Martyrdom as Heavenly Reward

The third way in which separatist Christians understood the Old Testament depiction of martyrdom was as a reward for firm adherence to the faith. Martyrs, because they had suffered and thus been purged of sin, and also because they had passed the test of their faith and thus had proven themselves worthy of Christ's name, were believed to be admitted immediately into the divine presence.[31] As a sign of the divine approbation thus implied, the splendor of the divine presence was visible to witnesses even before death occurred.

Cyprian makes use of this heavenly hope to encourage Christians to accept martyrdom during Decius's persecution:

> And now let nothing be considered in your hearts and minds, except the divine precepts and heavenly mandates, by which the Holy Spirit has always animated us for the endurance of suffering. Let no one contem-

plate death, but immortality; not the temporary penalty, but eternal glory, since it is written: "Precious in the sight of God is the death of his righteous ones."[32] And again: "An afflicted soul is a sacrifice to God; a contrite and humble heart God does not despise."[33] And again, where the divine scripture speaks of the tortures which consecrate and sanctify by the same test of suffering the martyrs of God:[34] "And if tortures are suffered in the presence of men, their hope for immortality is fulfilled. And if they are afflicted in a few things, they are well disposed in many, since God has tested them and found them worthy. As gold in a furnace he has tested them and has received them as a burnt-offering sacrifice. And in time they will have consideration. They will judge nations and rule peoples, and their Lord will reign forever."[35]

Cyprian in this passage links the test of faith—that is, persecution and torture—with its outcome, salvation. The "test of suffering" endured by the martyrs both "consecrates and sanctifies" them. By observing "the divine precepts" to accept martyrdom, the martyrs gain the reward hoped for by Christians. Cyprian reinforces this hope for heavenly reward with carefully chosen Old Testament citations, making his association of test and reward entirely traditional.

The reward Cyprian holds out to potential martyrs is not an intangible one. The *Acta* of Christian martyrs contain many examples of prefigurative visions of Christ suffering with and in the martyr.[36] These visions were both proof of the salvific nature of martyrdom and a promise that the martyrs too would enter Heaven with Christ: "But this suffering, this helplessness, this time of inevitability belongs to God, most beloved brothers. For he who wished to test us, showed himself so that we might have an exhortation[37] in this testing."[38] In this martyrial passage, a group of Christians is in prison in Carthage during Valerian's persecution; before their martyrdoms in February 259, they write down their experiences and visions for the remainder of the community. The passage goes on to describe the vision of Christ seen by Victor, one of their number. What is significant here is the meaning attributed to the vision. Christ's appearance "exhorts" and "consoles" (*adlocutio*) the prisoners; Christ promises them more suffering to come, but the reward of Heaven thereafter.

Separatist Christians, whether rigorist or nonrigorist, thus perceived martyrdom in three related, Old Testament-based ways: as test, as punishment, and as reward. Martyrdom was the second baptism that purged postbaptismal sins from the martyr, ensuring salvation even while reject-ing accommodation in an extreme manner. Avoiding martyrdom was a risky endeavor in the eyes of other Christians, difficult to justify and easy to perceive as idolatry.

Imitation of Christ

Complementing this "threefold" Old Testament interpretation of mar-tyrdom, separatist Christians also developed a Christological interpreta-tion of martyrdom. Just as Christ suffered and died, so too must his followers suffer and die with him. Christ is present in these sufferings, defeating death for the martyrs so that they may enter Heaven. To reject martyrdom, then, is ultimately to deny Christ.[39]

The sources indicate a high level of conviction among separatist Chris-tian writers that imitating Christ to the greatest possible extent—in all manner of daily activities, but most especially in accepting martyrdom—represented the highest ideal of Christian living. This ideal was not always possible to choose, for persecution was not omnipresent; nor in practice was it always chosen when persecution arose. As an ideal, however, it represented the most committed way in which a Christian could follow Christ, and therefore its importance in understanding Christianity in the separatist period cannot be overstated.

Tertullian, in his *Antivenom against the Gnostics*, describes to what extent Christians must be willing to imitate Christ:

> "But he who will endure until the end, he will be saved."[40] What must be endured, if not persecution, if not betrayal, if not death? For enduring to the end is nothing other than suffering the end. And therefore, "the disciple is not above the teacher." Immediately there follows, "nor the servant above his master;"[41] since, when the teacher and master himself has steadfastly endured persecution and betrayal and death, so much more should servants and disciples suffer the same, lest they seem to be exempt from injustice, as if they were better.[42]

Tertullian here insists that martyrdom, "suffering the end" which Christ suffered, must be required of Christians since it was required of Christ. Those who reject this extent of imitating Christ are in effect claiming "to be exempt from injustice" and persecution, "as if they were better" than their acknowledged master and teacher.

Cyprian makes a similar claim in his tractate *To Fortunata:*

> And Peter in his Epistle sets down and says:[43] "Dearly beloved, do not
> wonder at flame befalling you, which happens for your trial; and do not
> fall away, as if some new thing were happening to you. But as often as
> you share the sufferings of Christ, rejoice in all things, so that, rejoicing,
> you may also exult in the revelation made of his splendor. If it [i.e., the
> flame] is hastened for you in the name of Christ, you are blessed, since
> the name of the God of majesty and strength rests in you: which [i.e., the
> name] indeed among them is blasphemed, but among us is honored."[44]

Cyprian asserts that those who "share the sufferings of Christ," namely
persecution and martyrdom, will "rejoice" in Christ's "splendor," the divine presence visible in the martyr both as proof of approbation and as
reward. Cyprian also explicitly connects this imitation of Christ with the
themes of test and reward already discussed, and reinforces this concep-
tual link with extensive biblical citation.

A more extensive assertion of the same idea is found in another of
Cyprian's letters:

> The Lord in himself constitutes an example to all, teaching that none
> may arrive in his kingdom except those who follow him throughout his
> way, saying: "Whoever loves his soul in this world will lose it. And
> whoever hates his soul in this world will preserve it in eternal life."[45]
> And again: "Do not fear those who kill the body, for they cannot kill the
> soul. But fear greatly him who can kill both body and soul into hell."[46]
> Paul also admonishes us that we who desire to come to the promises of
> the Lord must imitate the Lord in all things. He says, "We are the sons
> of God; but if sons and heirs of God, then coheirs with Christ, if indeed
> we suffer with him so that we may be glorified with him."[47] And he adds
> a comparison of present time and future splendor, saying, "The suffer-
> ings of this time are not worthy of comparison with the splendor to
> come, which will be revealed in us."[48] It behooves us to endure all
> afflictions and persecutions, thinking on the glory of this splendor, since
> also the afflictions of the righteous are many, yet those who believe in
> God will be delivered from them all.[49]

Here Cyprian is explicit that the Christian's path to salvation is uniquely
the imitation of Christ in all things: first, in the renunciation of the world,
which is the foundation of separatist identity; and second, in the martyr-

dom that Christ suffered for others. The follower of Christ is glorified and approved of by God to the extent that he suffers as a martyr and "coheir" with Christ. Therefore, Cyprian argues, persecution must be accepted by Christians; for it is only through suffering that the righteous can prove themselves and gain their reward.

This imitation of Christ as martyr was consciously promoted by the authors of martyrial literature. In the *Passion of Polycarp*, for example, the author claims that the bishop's martyrdom saved not only himself but also those witnesses whom it exhorted to become martyrs: "For just as the Lord [did], he awaited and was given up, so that we also might become his [i.e., Christ's[50]] imitators, 'looking out not only for ourselves, but also for our neighbors';[51] for it is true and secure love to desire not only oneself to be saved, but also all the brothers."[52] Polycarp, this passage claims, accepted his martyrdom, not only for the sake of his own soul, but also for "all the brothers" of his community at Smyrna whom he could inspire with his example. He hoped that, by watching him die, they would "imitate him" imitating Christ. This "true and secure love" was in fact the culmination of his career as bishop of Smyrna.

Origen later promoted the same message in his *Exhortation to Martyrdom*: "'Jesus once endured the cross, despising shame, and because of this he is seated at the right hand of God.'[53] And those who imitate him, despising his shame, will sit and rule in the heavens with him who 'desires[54] to bring not peace on earth, but the sword.'"[55] Origen here makes two explicit claims about the salvific nature of martyrdom. First, Christ's position in Heaven "at the right hand of God" results from his own death on the cross, the first Christian martyrdom; and second, a similar position can be had by those who endure martyrdom in imitation of Christ. Martyrdom is "the sword" that Christ "desired to bring" to his followers; they can expect no better fulfilment of their Christianity than to die for Christ.

This conscious promotion of the ideal of martyrdom as the unique path of Christian salvation is characteristic of martyrial literature. Its immediate relevance to an abnormal, crisis situation should not, however, prevent scholars from noting the wider importance of martyrdom for Christians in other situations. During the separatist period, Christians in noncrisis situations were encouraged to live up to the ideal of renunciation, centered not on the world and its affairs but on God. This ideal limited Christians' Christ-imitating possibilities for a face-to-face encounter with God in this world to three:[56] baptism, which could only be had once; Eucharist;[57] and martyrdom. Baptism was the symbolic initiation into the new Christian renunciation of worldliness; it marked the transition from one state to another. Baptism therefore was a central symbol and requirement of Christianity. It is thus all the more striking that martyrdom is described as a "second baptism":

> For we have a second washing, one with the former, namely, of blood; about which the Lord said, "I have to be washed by baptism,"[58] when he had already been washed. For he had come by means of "water and blood,"[59] as John wrote, so that he might be washed by water, glorified by blood, in order to make us in the same manner called by water,[60] chosen by blood. He sent out these two baptisms from the wound pierced in his side, so that whoever would believe in his blood, would be washed with water; whoever would wash with water, would also drink the blood. This is the baptism which replaces the washing [with water] not received, and restores the lost [washing with water].[61]

In this passage, Tertullian identifies martyrdom as a "baptism of blood," like that which Christ underwent on the cross. He thus links both baptisms, that of water and that of blood, with imitating Christ. Christ in his life received first one, then the other, baptism; by imitating Christ in baptism and in martyrdom, Christians conform to the most central conception of their common identity in the separatist period.

Tertullian here makes explicit the salvific demand for martyrdom typical of rigorist, martyrial texts; Christians must endure martyrdom, as Christ both commanded and exemplified, in order to be saved. Yet this text is not martyrial, it is exegetical. The unusually rigorist attitude found in this exegetical source merely reinforces the importance of martyrdom in separatist Christianity's ideal of renunciation.

Origen likewise expresses considerable rigor in his attitude toward martyrdom, even in exegetical texts:

> For our testing does not only extend to blows, but it goes as far as the pouring out of blood, since also Christ, whom we follow, poured out his blood for our redemption, so that we might go forth from here bathed in our blood. For the baptism of blood is the only [baptism] which renders us more pure than that of water renders [us]. And I do not presume this, but the Scriptures announce [this], when the Lord says to his disciples, "I am to be baptized with a baptism which you do not know. And how I

am driven that it be accomplished!"[62] Therefore you see that the pouring out of blood he named his baptism.[63]

Origen here also identifies Christ's death as a "baptism of blood," on the basis of precisely the same scriptural passages as Tertullian. For such separatist Christian leaders, martyrdom, the test of faith willed by God, is an even more efficacious baptism than that of water. It purifies the martyr of all postbaptismal sin, and even stands in lieu of baptism of water for unbaptised martyrs.

Moreover, martyrdom as the imitation of Christ entailed an even larger reward than salvation. Because the martyr affirms his willingness to follow Christ absolutely through his martyrdom, Christ is present in and with the martyr, even before the martyr's death. This joining with Christ before death is called a "splendor" or "glory" (Latin *gloria*, Greek *δόξα* or *chárisma*) in separatist sources. Cyprian describes Christ's presence with the martyr in spiritual terms in one of his letters:

> Blood was flowing which could have extinguished the fire of persecution, which could have quieted the flames and fires of hell with glorious bloodshed. O what a spectacle that was to the Lord, how sublime, how great, how acceptable to the eyes of God through the sacrament [i.e., martyrdom] and devotion of his soldiers, as it is written in the psalms when the Holy Spirit speaks and admonishes us equally, "Precious in the sight of God is the death of his righteous ones."[64] Precious is this death which bought immortality with the price of its blood, which receives the crown of God through the consummation of strength.
>
> How happy there was Christ, how willingly the protector of faith fought and conquered in such servants of his, giving to believers as much as he who chooses believes himself to receive. He was present at his own battle; he lifts up, strengthens, animates the combatants and defenders of his name. And he who once conquered death for us, conquers [death] always in us.[65]

Cyprian in this letter extols the martyrs of the Decianic persecution in Carthage. He passes briefly over themes already discussed in this chapter: martyrdom as public testing willed by God; martyrdom as baptismal sacrament; martyrdom as immediate salvation. He then describes how Christ is present in the martyrs. Christ, the "protector of faith," is "happy" that his "servants" choose martyrdom; Christ "fights and conquers death" in the martyrs, just as he fought and conquered death in his own martyrdom on the cross. By imitating Christ even in death, the martyrs are joined with Christ even before leaving this world and entering Heaven.

In the *Martyrs of Lyons*, furthermore, Christ's presence in the martyr Sanctus undergoing multiple tortures is not merely spiritual; Christ is visibly present with Sanctus through the miraculous healing of his inflicted wounds, a physical proof of the martyr's spiritual salvation:

> But his body was a witness to the tortures, being one whole wound and bruise, shriveled up by fire and degraded beyond human shape; in which Christ, suffering, was bringing to perfection great expectations, rendering ineffective the one opposing him [i.e., the devil] and teaching in the pattern of his followers that there is no fear where there is the Father's love, no pain where there is Christ's glory. For the wicked one [i.e., Satan] after some days again tortured the martyr, thinking that, since his body was inflamed, if they applied the same tortures they would gain the victory over him. But contrary to every expectation of man, his body unbent itself and became straight during the subsequent tortures, and resumed its former appearance and the use of its limbs, so that the second torture became through the grace of Christ a cure not an affliction.[66]

"Christ's glory (*δόξα*)" here refers both to the "expectation" of martyrdom as the fulfillment of following Christ, and to the "splendor" and "grace" of Christ present and revealed in the martyr. Christ, by suffering with the tortured martyr, "brings to perfection great expectations," namely, salvation for the hopeful Christian. The visible presence of Christ in healing the martyr's body gives testimony to all those who witness the torture, both Christian and pagan, that the Christian promises are true and achievable. The presence of Christ in the tortured Sanctus becomes a "cure," both physically, in that he gains release from his pain, and spiritually, in that he then immediately dies and enters Heaven with Christ.

Separatist Christians thus conceived of martyrdom as the most profound following of Christ available to them. Not only did martyrdom fulfill absolutely all the divine commands that Christians sought to live by, it also won for the martyr the presence of Christ, reenacting his own death through the martyr and thus conquering death again for the martyr. Thus the martyr was immediately and fully saved, entering Heaven to enjoy the eternal vision of God.

CHAPTER FIVE

The Martyr and the Community

The various meanings that separatist Christians attached to the concept of martyrdom promoted martyrdom in moments of toleration as much as in moments of persecution. The ideal of renunciation kept martyrdom visible for Christians throughout their lives; even for the catechumen Arnobius of Sicca in the opening years of the fourth century, martyrdom remained a defining paradigm of Christianity: "For nothing is promised to us in this life, nor for accommodations in the husk of this bit of flesh; no help is offered or aid decreed: but indeed, we have been taught to reckon and esteem lightly every menace of fortune, whatsoever they be."[1] Arnobius denies that Christian faith has any import for worldly concerns; corporeal things are to be shunned as irrelevant to salvation. This is an especially striking attitude for a catechumen to reveal after four decades of toleration by the Roman government. Even after the opening of the Diocletianic persecution in 303, Christianity still relied on the most traditional concepts of martyrdom to contend with the external pressures of the time. These traditions are summarized neatly in the *Thessalonikan Martyrs*, composed in 304: "Now from this place they were taken together, and led before the one directing the persecution, so that, having fulfilled the remainder of the [divine] injunctions and having loved their master even unto death, they might crown [themselves] with the crown of immortality."[2]

There are four elements in this passage that call for examination. First, the martyrs spoken of here "loved their master" and fulfilled the divine commands for Christian living; that is to say, they lived according to the ideal of renunciation prior to the outbreak of persecution. Second, they accepted martyrdom as "the remainder" and the culmination of the divine command, following Christ "even unto death." Third, they expected to have a chance to fulfill that command. Fourth, they lived and died "together," as part of a community sharing the same ideals.

Martyrdom as Renunciation

As we have seen, renunciation underlay basic Christian attitudes and behaviors, even when the ideal itself was not fully actualized. As one could expect, then, renunciation also supported the ideal of martyrdom in times of crisis; Justin Martyr argued this explicitly in his *First Apology:*

> And consider that we say these things on your behalf, because when we are tested we could deny that we are [Christian]. But we do not want to live, telling a lie. For desiring eternal and unblemished life, we exert ourselves for the way of living according to God, the Father and Creator of all things; and we hurry to confess, we who trust and believe that they can possess these things, who through their works have persuaded God that they followed him and loved his way of life, in which evil is resisted. These, to speak briefly, are the things which we await, and have learned through Christ, and teach.[3]

Justin here argues that the distinctive characteristic of separatist Christians is their "exerting themselves" to live "according to God." This he describes further as "persuading God through works" that one "follows him and loves his way of life"; in short, Justin once again speaks of living a distinctly Christian life in a state of renunciation from the world. The goal of this disengaged life is "eternal and unblemished life." Those who desire this, and live accordingly, concomitantly "hurry to confess" their Christianity, knowing full well the worldly penalty for that confession. Because Christians live a disengaged life, Justin argues, they are uniquely prepared to accept martyrdom. Dying for Christ is not fundamentally different from living for Christ; both are a profound denial of Roman cultural ideals. Christians "resist" the "evil" of these Roman ideals, not merely because of the idolatry of paganism, but also because Roman ideals idolatrously pursue material goods, which the ideal of renunciation defines as opposed to God.

This same message was promoted by Clement of Alexandria in his disciplinary *Stromata:*

> And the Gnostic[4] now makes progress in the Gospel, not only using the law as a step, but understanding and observing it, as the Lord who gave the Covenant delivered [it] to the Apostles. And if he governs himself rightly—just as it is impossible to pursue knowledge by sloth—[and if] further, he becomes a martyr out of love, confessing most rightly, achieving the greatest honor among men, not thus will he first be acclaimed perfected in the flesh; since the conclusion of life justifies this appellation, when the perfected deed of the gnostic martyr has first rightly been revealed and exhibited, when [his] blood has been shed in thanksgiving through gnostic love, when he has given up his spirit. For this he will be blessed, and acclaimed perfect in truth.[5]

Like Justin, Clement insists that renunciation, "understanding and observing" the divine law set forth in the Gospel, is the true manner of Christian living. Those who "live rightly" in renunciation prepare themselves to "confess rightly" in martyrdom; those who do not live rightly prepare themselves poorly for martyrdom, just as a lazy student learns less than a vigorous one. Nevertheless, Clement argues, it is not by living that Christians achieve the greatest perfection, but by dying, since only martyrdom can conclusively prove the full worth of Christ's followers. Renunciation, then, is, as it were, a course of study that prepares the Christian to graduate through martyrdom into the fully Christlike state.

It is highly significant that these two passages are *not* from martyrial sources. One might expect that sources that are not explicitly urging either renunciation or martyrdom ought to be largely devoid of these ideas. As these passages show, however, even the apologetic and disciplinary literatures of the separatist period—even in times of toleration by Roman officials—make strong use of the related themes of renunciation and martyrdom, thus reinforcing these ideals. Moreover, these genres do so in precisely the same way as martyrial sources, including, for example, the *Martyrdom of Apollonius,* contemporaneous with Clement:[6]"The disciples of the Logos which is among us die each day to pleasures. Proclaiming this the purpose of life, proconsul, we do not find it hard to die in service to the true God."[7] In this passage, as in the nonmartyrial passages above, renunciation stands out as the distinguishing characteristic of Christians. Christians "die each day to pleasure," following the teaching of the Logos. Also as in the previous passages, this renunciation makes the acceptance of martyrdom easier. Since it is "the purpose of life" to "die each day," Christians "do not find it hard to die" in a more literal sense, still obedient to God.

This close connection between renunciation and martyrdom is a source of conviction for Christians in crisis situations, as for Justin before his martyrdom:

> The eparch said to Justin, "If you are scourged and beheaded, do you believe that you will ascend into heaven?" Justin said, "I hope [for this] because of my endurance, if I endure; and I also know that the divine favor awaits those who live rightly, even unto the conflagration." The eparch Rusticus said, "And so do you surmise this, that you will ascend?" Justin said, "I do not surmise, but am precisely persuaded." The eparch Rusticus said, "If you will not obey, you will be punished." Justin said, "We believe that we are saved through prayer when we are punished." The eparch Rusticus proclaimed, "Let those who refuse to sacrifice to the gods be scourged and executed in accordance with the laws."[8]

During his judicial examination, Justin expresses his hope for a martyrial opportunity. He has "lived rightly" as a separated Christian; by dying rightly in a "conflagration," he seeks to secure absolutely the "divine favor" which is likely but not assured for him. Martyrdom would assure his entry into Heaven; this Justin does not "surmise," as the magistrate asks, but rather "believes," because he is "persuaded" of it. The punishment of sacrilege by the Roman authorities—martyrdom—is for Justin a salvific action.

Precisely the same connection between renunciation and martyrdom is still being made in later, third-century martyrial texts, as for example in the *Martyrdom of Montanus and Lucius*, dating from the Valerianic persecution:

> Then, since the Lord opposed [him], his intention was destroyed; he commanded us to be put into prison. We were escorted there by sol-

diers, but we were not terrified of the loathsome darkness of that place; and soon the shadowy prison shone with resplendent spirit, against the odious and blind night-veil of obscurity, the shining devotion of faith clothed us with light as if it were day. And we were ascending to the summit of penalties as if we ascended into heaven. . . . For it is easy for servants of God to be killed, and therefore death is nothing; the Lord, crushing the stings of death and subduing contention, has triumphed through the victory of the cross.[9]

In this passage, the martyrs have just been examined by the Roman magistrate and are being returned to prison. Here the martyrs console themselves against the spiritual terror and isolation of their predicament with "the shining devotion of faith." Their disengaged life as Christians facilitates the choice they must each now make; "it is easy for Christians to die," since Christians are already disengaged from worldly ties. Thus to the martyrs "death is nothing"; they anticipate their martyrdoms in the same spirit as they have lived: they follow the example of Christ, despising death as they have despised life.

Finally, this connection between martyrdom and renunciation accentuates the fundamental contrast between Christian and Roman worldviews. Christians, like the third-century bishops Agapius and Secundinus, who both fully accept worldly renunciation and have the opportunity for martyrdom, throw the contrasting values of Christians and Romans into sharp relief:

Among them, therefore, Agapius and Secundinus were led out of their exile to the prefect: commendable bishops, both harmonious with spiritual love, and one with the sanctity of fleshly continence. They were led, I was saying, not from penalty to penalty (as it seemed to the pagans), but rather "from glory to glory,"[10] from battle to battle, so that those who have driven under the deceptive displays of the world in acquiring the name of Christ, might trod underfoot even the stings of death by the perfect strength of faith. For it was not right that those whom the Lord was hastening to have with himself should seek more slowly victory in earthly struggle. And it happened, brothers, that the glorious martyrs Agapius and Secundinus, because of their illustrious priesthood, while they were going by the earthly power of the prefect but by the choice of Christ to the combat of their blessed suffering, deigned to enter our dwelling. So great in them was the life-giving spirit of grace that it was not enough that they devote their precious blood to glorious martyrdom, unless by so holy and so glorious witnesses to God they should make other martyrs by the inspiration of their faith.[11]

These two bishops are "commendable" because of their commitment to renunciation; they conform in exemplary manner to the separatist ideal, rejecting "the deceptive displays of the world," and also, in the case of Secundinus, marital union. In their martyrdoms, they emphasize this exemplary nature in direct contrast to Roman expectations: where the Christian author wants his audience to believe that the Roman magistrate intends to act punitively, forcing the two bishops "from penalty to penalty," they in contrast believe themselves to be forced "from glory to glory," being both more Christian and more exemplary as a result of martyrdom. Moreover, both in life and in death, Agapius and Secundinus intend their action to be models for their followers. As world-renouncing Christians and as martyrs, they are to be imitated just as they imitate Christ.[12]

Thus martyrs' examples served a fundamental role in separatist Christianity *even* in moments of toleration. Martyrdom was portrayed as the culmination of renouncing the world; renunciation was not merely discipline for Christians, but underlay the most basic understanding of Christ's importance. Both martyrial and nonmartyrial sources consistently demonstrate this relationship between renunciation and martyrdom.

Martyrdom as Divine Command

In the separatist Christian worldview, martyrdom was also required by divine command: martyrdom was enjoined by God according to the example of Christ. Not all Christians had the opportunity to embrace martyrdom, but those who did were obliged to accept it as the most secure path to salvation established by Christ, and as the opposite of idolatry. This can again be seen in both martyrial and nonmartyrial sources.

The rigorist Tertullian in his *Antivenom against the Gnostics* developed a rather extensive argument concerning the necessity of martyrdom for salvation:

But nothing must yet be learned concerning the good of martyrdom, without first [something concerning] the obligation [of martyrdom], nor concerning its utility, before [something] concerning its necessity.

Divine authority comes first, whether God has wished and ordered anything of the sort. . . .[13]

Nor do I think it [needful] to discuss, whether God rightly prohibits his name and honor to be added to a lie; whether he rightly does not want those whom he has torn away from the error of superstition to return again into Egypt; whether he rightly does not suffer those whom he has chosen for himself to stand away from him. And so, no one will expect it to be reconsidered by us, whether he wished the teaching which he instituted to be followed, and whether the abandonment of what he wanted followed is punished deservedly. . . .[14]

Therefore, if it is evident from the beginning that this [abandonment], prohibited by so many precepts and never committed with impunity, according to so many examples, is considered by God nothing other than the most extreme offense—[the avoidance of] which sort of transgression, moreover, we should understand [to be] the purpose of divine declarations and punishments, and also now [to be] defending the martyrs, not only [because they] do not doubt, but also, indeed, [because they] endure; for which [martyrs], namely, he has prepared a place by prohibiting idolatry; for otherwise martyrdoms would not take place—then assuredly he [God] has made his authority unassailable, desiring those things to happen for which he has prepared a place. For if following the precept entails violence, this will be as it were a command about following the precept: that I suffer that through which I may be able to follow the precept, namely, whatever violence threatens me while I guard against idolatry. And assuredly he who imposed the precept enforces obedience. Therefore I cannot not want those things to occur, through which he [God] maintains obedience.

Therefore you have the will of my God. And so his will is good, who is not God if not good. This will prove the goodness of the thing which God wants—I mean martyrdom—since good wants only good. I contend that martyrdom is good before God, the same [God] by whom idolatry is both prohibited and punished. For martyrdom struggles against and opposes idolatry; for it frees from idolatry.[15]

Tertullian's argument runs as follows: among the principles that God has taught Christians is the absolute necessity of avoiding idolatry in any form, both pagan ritual and corporeal pursuits; this principle is at the core of Christian identity in Tertullian's time. In contrast, Tertullian continues,

Roman society demands both participation in civic affairs, including festivals and circus events,[16] and—since virtually all Roman civic events included some form of recognition or invocation of civic gods—concomitant actions that by Christian standards are idolatrous. Therefore, God cannot desire Christians to participate in Roman society: this is the ideal of renunciation. When Christians conform to this ideal, pagans naturally pressure them to conform instead to the cultural norms of the majority; this pressure can at times escalate into physical violence. Christians, however, are enjoined to do whatever it takes to renounce idolatry. If they must suffer violence for this, then so be it; God obviously wills them to suffer this violence for His own reasons.[17] God, then, has foreseen the need for martyrs, both to uphold Christian constancy and to demonstrate Christian conviction. Thus, concludes Tertullian, martyrdom is a necessary element of Christianity, and as such, it must be good in and of itself, for God, the source of goodness, cannot command an evil action to his followers. Martyrdom, moreover, is not only good and necessary, but also absolutely opposed to idolatry, which God commands Christians to avoid. By embracing martyrdom, Christians absolutely reject idolatry in a manner pleasing and obedient to God. For Tertullian's rigorist Christianity, these considerations make martyrdom an absolute command to Christians.

For other, less rigorist Christians, martyrdom may not be an absolute command, for the opportunity may not always exist. When it does exist, however, martyrdom must be embraced; within the limited context of a violent crisis situation, martyrdom becomes an unavoidable necessity:

> If the ancient examples of faith were arranged in letters in order to bear witness to the grace of God and to foster the edification of men, so that by reading them, as if by manifesting the deeds, God is honored and man comforted, why are new examples suitable to both causes also not equally written down, so that neither weakness nor hopelessness of faith may consider that divine grace was conferred only on ancient [holy ones], in worthiness either of martyrdom or of visions? God always achieves what he promises, as a witness to the non-believing, as a gift to the believing.[18]

In this passage from the *Acts of Perpetua and Felicity*, contemporaneous with Tertullian, the author states why he has recorded these martyrdoms. Just as the biblical stories are read by Christians as examples of and exhortations to virtue, so too martyrs' deeds should be remembered, lest Christians believe that "God's grace" and the "gift" of martyrdom are no longer enjoined upon them in their own day. Just as Perpetua showed herself "worthy," other Christians should believe themselves "worthy" of visions and martyrdom, of the secure path to the salvation promised by God. Such an attitude inclines Christians to accept martyrdom when the opportunity arises, as it did in Carthage for Perpetua, Felicity, and others.

Many such examples of martyrdom were recorded with the explicit purpose of encouraging others to embrace the ideal. Christian writers regularly demanded that the audiences of the *Acta,* which recorded these events, conform to the examples being provided, and accept martyrdom either as necessary for salvation or in the event of persecution. This demand is explicit in the *Acts of Marian and James:*[19] "When they were about to have their combat—so sublime a battle, which they joined by the inspiration of the heavenly spirit—against the afflictions of a cruel world and [against] the pagan assault, they wished it to come through us to the notice of the brotherhood, not because they wanted the glory of their crown to be preached throughout the earth through boasting, but so that by these preceding testings, a multitude of the flock and people of God might be armed in the example of faith."[20] Martyrdom here is explicitly "the example of faith." The author touches on several points we have examined: martyrdom as the test of faith, martyrdom as inspired by Christ, martyrdom as extension of renunciation; but these familiar themes then introduce the core understanding of martyrdom provided by this text: all Christian faith leads to martyrdom. This is the message of the martyrial literature. Martyrdom was not peripheral to Christian identity, despite the fact that the majority of separatist Christians encountered no opportunity for martyrdom. The mere possibility that such an opportunity might arise was sufficient to maintain the importance of martyrdom in separatist Christian teaching until the fourth century.

Separatist Christian thinkers consistently argued and preached that the present world was an impediment to salvation, corrupted from its spiritual heritage by the devil, and not to be returned to grace until the Parousia. The ideal of renunciation, with its culmination in martyrdom, was God's commanded standard of behavior for Christians. Ideally, Christians were prepared to accept martyrdom when the opportunity arose, following the example of Christ.

Martyrdom as Fulfillment of Christian Expectation

Separatist Christians also promoted martyrdom as a fulfillment of specific Christian expectations. By opposing (even passively) Roman norms, separatist Christianity often predisposed itself to expect violent events, which could easily be interpreted as apocalyptic.[21] The ideal of renunciation created considerable external social pressure on Christian communities; when these pressures occasionally escalated into violent confrontations, such violence merely reinforced the expected contrast between Christian and Roman worldviews. Martyrdom as a Christian ideal fit neatly into this pattern of social differentiation.

Tertullian's *Apologetic* demonstrates just how well the idea of martyrdom did fit the separatist ideal:

> Indeed, malefactors desire eagerly to lie hidden, avoid appearing in public, fear being caught, deny when they are accused, do not confess always or easily even when tortured; they certainly grieve when they are condemned; they reckon among themselves the violent impulses of [their] evil minds, which they impute to fate or to the stars; for they do not want what they recognize as evil to be in themselves. Among Christians, however, it is not at all the same; he is ashamed of and suffers from the name [of Christian] in no way, except, to be sure, not to have been [Christian] formerly. If he is denounced, he rejoices; [if] he is accused, he does not defend himself; [if] he is interrogated or worse, he confesses; [if] he is condemned, he gives thanks. How is this [a thing] of evil, whose defendant rejoices, whose accusation is a vow, and [whose] penalty a happiness?[22]

Tertullian in this passage contrasts the attitudes of Christians and of non-Christian criminals when arrested and tried by Roman authorities. Criminals, says Tertullian, don't want to believe themselves evil, and seek to avoid the consequences of their criminal actions. Christians, in contrast, expect to be believed evil by others, and embrace the consequences of their Christianity. Christians expect to be denounced, arrested, interrogated, and condemned by the hostile society in opposition to which they define themselves. Because they expect these things, Tertullian claims, Christians are prepared to confront antagonism with martyrdom, as they are taught to do by authoritative texts such as this one.

This expectation—present, as the previous passage proves, even in apologetic literature—is again most clearly seen in the martyrial texts. The second-century *Acts of the Scillitan Martyrs* expressed this expectation clearly:

> Saturninus the proconsul recited the decree from the tablet: "Speratus, Nartzalus, Cittinus, Donata, Vestia, Secunda, and the others, who have confessed that they live according to the Christian rite, since they obstinately persist when the opportunity to return to the usage of the Romans is offered to them, are condemned to death by the sword."
>
> Speratus said, "We give thanks to God."
>
> Nartzalus said, "Today we are martyrs in Heaven. Thanks be to God."[23]

This rather sparse account of the martyrs' judicial examination records the responses of these Christians to the sentence of death. They see their execution as a positive thing; they are thankful that their expectations have been fulfilled. They understand themselves to have achieved something that not all Christians can achieve; by dying as martyrs, they believe themselves to have reached the pinnacle of Christian obedience.

The same expectation is likewise evident from the third-century martyrial texts. The *Acts of Cyprian,* for example, describe how Cyprian's response to his sentence inspired his Christian followers present at the time to demand to be killed along with him: "And he recited the decree from the tablet: 'Thascius Cyprian is condemned to death by the sword.' The bishop Cyprian said, 'Thanks be to God.' After his sentencing the crowd of brothers said, 'Let us be beheaded with him.' Because of this, an uproar sprang up among the Christians, and a great disturbance followed him away."[24] Cyprian's response to being sentenced to death is identical to that of Speratus and Nartzalus in the previous passage: he gives thanks to God that his expectations have been fulfilled. The author of Cyprian's *Acta* takes no chances that his audience might miss the exhortatory point of Cyprian's example; when the Christian observers of Cyprian's examination realize what has happened, they too want to fulfill expectations by undergoing execution along with their beloved bishop.

Similarly, in the contemporary *Acts of Montanus and Lucius,* the soon-to-be-martyred author, writing from prison, quite poetically lauds the instruments of persecution for their role in fulfilling violent expectations: "That same day we were suddenly taken before the procurator, who was governing in place of the dead proconsul. O happy day, O the glory of bonds! O the hoped-for chains, desired by all! O iron, more honorable and precious than the best gold! O the clang of iron, that rattled when drawn over other iron! To speak of the things that would happen to us was our consolation."[25] Here the author clearly expresses the ideal response of separatist Christians to persecution: embracing martyrdom as the fulfillment of expectation. The martyrs are "happy" to have an opportunity to undergo judicial torture; their bonds are "glorious," "hoped-for," and "desired by all." These martyrs look forward eagerly to this opportunity; they talk amongst themselves, describing what they will have to endure as a "consolation." The imminence of death, of the fulfillment of expectations of a violent confrontation between Christian and Roman values, forces a conscious embracing of martyrdom as a core value of separatist Christianity.

This expectational aspect of martyrdom could also be drawn upon to widen the circumstances under which separatist Christians recognized a martyrdom to have occurred. As Cyprian argued during the Decianic persecution, not only those Christians who die as a result of torture are martyrs; those who die as a result of any aspect of persecution are likewise martyrs, if they were willing to be martyrs in the stricter sense:

> Let a more willing attention and care be bestowed on the bodies of all those who are not tortured, but [who] in prison die the glorious departure of death; for neither their strength nor their honor is less than that of the least of those also gathered together among the blessed martyrs. What is in them has endured whatever they were prepared and ready to endure. He who submitted himself to torture and death under the eyes of God suffered whatever he wished to suffer; for he was not lacking to the tortures, but the tortures rather to him. When by our confession and will in prison and in chains the end of dying approaches, the glory of the martyr is perfected.[26]

Cyprian here makes use of the expectation of confrontational violence to promote a rigorist response to that violence. Because Christians expect violence to erupt, as it did in the Decianic persecution, they should be "prepared and ready to endure" the consequences of that violence. By "submitting" themselves to persecution, Christians embrace the martyrial ideal, even when this submission does not necessarily lead them to a public and defiant death under torture or execution. It is for Cyprian as much the *desire* to embrace martyrdom—a desire created out of prior expectations of violence—as the reality of a violent death which qualifies a Christian as a martyr.

Martyrdom as Communal Salvation

The fourth and most important reason for martyrdom's prominence to Christians throughout the separatist period was its role in the salvation of the whole Christian community. We have already seen its individual salvific role in separatist sources; but a wider, communal aspect was also attached to martyrial salvation in this period. Examples of martyrdom were not seen by separatist Christians as random, isolated events. Rather, martyrdom actively supported the coherence of Christianity as more than simply a collection of disparate urban communities. Martyrdom was one way in which Christians in Carthage (for example) could irrefutably identify themselves as "the same" as Christians in Alexandria; and more importantly, as we have seen, as following the example that Christ provided.

Because martyrdom embodied a positive community dynamic for separatist Christians, it perpetuated itself quite effectively through the examples remembered in the martyrial *Acta*.[27] In part this is true because Christians were rarely singled out *as individuals* for persecution by either pagan mobs or Roman authorities, but were rather attacked *as a group* that was failing to meet Roman cultural norms.[28] This had the beneficial (for Christians) side effect of making it easier to accept martyrdom, since martyrs were rarely in the position of having to die alone. In the extant martyrial texts, martyrdom as part of a group is clearly more desirable than martyrdom in isolation:

> Concerning Felicity also, the grace of God touched her in this way. Since she was in her eighth month (for she had been pregnant when arrested), when the day of the spectacle [i.e., when her companions were to be martyred] drew near, she was in great grief, lest on account of her pregnancy she should be postponed (since it is not legal for pregnant women to be exposed to [physical] penalties) and lest afterwards she should pour out her holy and innocent blood among others [who were] miscreants. Her fellow martyrs also were gravely saddened along with her, lest they leave behind so good and loving a companion, alone on the same road of hope.[29]

Felicity's inability to embrace the opportunity provided for martyrdom, even though it is merely postponed, disrupts the coherence of the group. In addition, her martyrdom would be less noteworthy, less a public statement of her rejection of Roman values in favor of Christian, if her death were confused among other more mundane penalties, rather than occurring in the company of a particular group of dissidents.[30] To underscore this aspect of communal salvation, Felicity miraculously gives birth to her child early, in time to be martyred with the rest of her prison group.[31]

But the communal efficacy of martyrial salvation is not limited to those who themselves become martyrs, even in groups. All the martyrs stand in a "sacerdotal" relationship between God and Christians in the world, making possible through their "sacrifice" more extensive forgiveness of sin for nonmartyrs, and hence more generous salvation for the whole Christian community. Origen made this clear in his tenth homily on Numbers:

> But concerning martyrs, the Apostle John writes in the *Apocalypse* that "the souls of those who are sacrificed[32] because of the name of Jesus the Lord stand at the altar";[33] but he who "stands at the altar" is shown to fill a sacerdotal function; and the sacerdotal function is to supplicate for the sins of the people. Therefore I fear lest perhaps, since there are no more martyrs and the sacrifices of the saints are no longer offered for our sins, remission of our sins no longer occurs. And therefore also the devil, knowing that remission of sins occurs through the suffering of martyrdom, does not desire to encite against us the public persecutions of the pagans.[34]

Origen here explicitly ascribes an intercessory function to martyrs; they plead before God for the sins of Christians still living in the world. Not only does martyrdom expunge the postbaptismal sins of the martyr, it can also help expunge sins for nonmartyrs. The entire community of Christians gains from every martyrdom. At the time Origen wrote this homily, probably about 240,[35] there had been little persecutive activity anywhere in the Empire for roughly three decades. Origen—not now widely regarded as a rigorist Christian on this issue[36]—laments that the lack of martyrial "sacrifice," to which the devil has cunningly avoided giving occasion, threatens the most central and secure avenue for salvation open to all Christians. So central is the ideal of martyrdom for salvation in separatist Christianity that even toleration by the Empire serves the devil's purpose!

The wider salvific properties of martyrdom are also explicitly called upon to promote martyrdom. The audience is exhorted to martyrdom, not only for their own salvation, but for the salvation of their fellow Christians who lack either the opportunity or the fortitude to endure: "There is also a battle for us among you, most beloved brothers, that nothing other must be done by the servants of God and those dedicated to his Christ, than to think of the multitude of brothers; this love, this duty impels us by force and by reason to these letters, so that we may leave behind for later brothers a faithful witness to the magnificence of God, and in our memory struggles and endurance on behalf of the Lord."[37] In this epistolary introduction to the *Martyrdom of Montanus and Lucian*, written in Carthage during Valerian's persecution in 258–59, this larger appeal to communal martyrial salvation is plain. The priests and bishops imprisoned by Valerian's edicts express here their "love" and "duty" in considering the continued welfare of their community; which duty they undertake by leaving a written example of their own steadfastness and willingness to embrace the martyrial ideal. The audience is thus exhorted to martyrdom for a more significant goal than only individual salvation. The salvation of the entirety of Christianity, it is implied, is within reach of every individual Christian who chooses martyrdom.

The intercession of martyrs has long been an object of study for modern scholars. Delehaye's treatment of the topic remains indispensable. He argues that the most fundamental aspect of the cult of martyrs before Constantine was the "honor offered to a venerable memory."[38] This memory took the form of a communal celebration of the martyr's "anniversary," or rebirth in Heaven; the principle elements of this celebration were a mass, a public panegyric on the martyrdom, and some form of communal feast or *refrigerium*.[39] The underlying salvific reason for this memory is tacitly acknowledged by this argument, but the emphasis on "rendering honor" to the dead for their *individual* bravery or piety obscures the *communal* significance of the martyr's memory. Salisbury's recent treatment of the reception of Perpetua's martyrdom follows Delehaye, arguing that only "heterodox" Christians remembered Perpetua's act as an explicit appeal for further martyrdoms.[40]

This argument partly obscures the importance of the martyrial ideal in all forms of Christianity before Constantine. The martyr is more than a hero; she is in fact a Christlike savior, an intercessor for her community. For both rigorist and nonrigorist Christians (including Montanists), the memory of previous martyrs was revered and perpetuated primarily because of the salvific benefits for the whole Christian community which martyrs provided. As the next chapter will demonstrate, martyrs brought the Parousia—and the ultimate reward of all Christians—closer to actualization through their imitation of Christ's Passion, because their victory was pleasing to God and in accordance with divine commandments. Their intercession for nonmartyred Christians would only be effective after this event.

Conclusions

Martyrdom and its various meanings formed a dominant theme in every genre of separatist Christian writing, including disciplinary and apologetic as well as strictly martyrial literature. Martyrdom could not easily be separated from the promise of Christian salvation for both individuals and the entire community, even by the least rigorist writers. Martyrdom was a formative element of Christian identity in the separatist period, one which supported the separation of Christian and Roman and their inherent opposition to each other. As the next chapter will show, this opposition also perpetuated strong apocalyptic expectations.

CHAPTER SIX

Apocalyptic Expectations

The guiding principles of renunciation of worldly affairs in times of tacit toleration and martyrdom in times of persecution were explicitly reinforced in the separatist community by expectations of Christ's return (Parousia). Throughout the second and third centuries, three themes can be found, separately and together, in all separatist genres: the *imminence* of the Parousia; the *violence* accompanying the Parousia; and the *transformation* of creation following the Parousia.

Some scholars have acknowledged these apocalyptic expectations, but use apparent pro-world and pro-state evidence to attenuate both the importance and the strength of the expectations in the third and even the second century. It is commonly argued that the failure of the Parousia actually to happen, coupled with the increasing size of Christian communities and the improving social status of its members from the mid-second century on, made such expectations increasingly marginal, so that by the reign of Marcus Aurelius, "mainstream" Christianity had largely abandoned such expectations.[1] If this is true, then one expects apocalyptic imagery to be preserved more by marginal groups, such as the mystical Gnostics or the ultradisciplined Montanists.[2]

In contrast, this chapter argues that apocalyptic expectations remained potent throughout the separatist period. Some attenuation of such expectations did occur during the second and third centuries, but this attenuation was neither as early nor as strong as typically depicted. Apocalyptic expectations remained as important for Arnobius in the first decade of the fourth century as they were for Hermas in the early second; they are evident even in nonmartyrial sources. The continued employment of this theme in exegetical and apologetic material reinforces these expectations, and their soteriological relationship with renunciation and martyrdom.

Imminence of the Parousia

The first expectation to be considered is that Christ's return would happen soon. Christians of the mid-first century expected the Parousia to occur during their lifetimes, as the letters of Paul reveal: "We who are still alive, who are left till the coming of the Lord, will certainly not precede those who have fallen asleep. For the Lord himself will come down from Heaven, with a loud command, with the voice of the archangel and with the trumpet-call of God, and the dead in Christ will rise first. After that, we who are still alive and are left will be caught up together with them in the clouds to meet the Lord in the air."[3] Paul identifies himself and his audience with "we who are still alive." Even though he can't be sure when Christ will return, he still expects to see the Parousia within his lifetime.

In the last years of the first century, almost fifty years after Paul's first letter to the Thessalonians, the imminence of Christ's return was still expected in the immediate future, as *Revelations* indicates: "Behold, I am coming soon! My reward is with me, and I will give to everyone according to what he has done. . . . Blessed are those who wash their robes, that they may have the right to the tree of life and may go through the gates into the city. Outside are the dogs, those who practice magic arts, the sexually immoral, the murderers, the idolaters and everyone who loves and practices falsehood."[4] Christ relates to John in this vision that he will "come soon." Here, the imminence of the Parousia is reason to renew one's commitment to the ideals of renunciation and martyrdom. Christ promises to come "with his reward": this is to be given to the "blessed" who have "washed their robes," that is, accepted martyrdom as the only alternative to Roman idolatry. Those who are in any way concerned with corporeal affairs, which are but "falsehood," will not be rewarded; they will be left "outside" of God's salvation and consigned to eternal damnation.

A century after the writing of *Revelations*, the rigorist Tertullian demonstrates the same expectation of the imminence of the Parousia and its significance for Christian behavior:

> But as the conquering power of evil is increasing—which is characteristic of the last times—good things are not now allowed to be born, so corrupted are the seminal principles; or to be trained, so deserted are studies; or to be enforced, so tired are the laws. In fact, the modesty of which we are now treating is by this time grown so obsolete that it is not the abjuration but the moderation of the appetites which modesty is believed to be: and he is held to be chaste who has not been chaste. But let the world's modesty see to itself, together with the world itself and its inherent nature . . . except that it would be even more unhappy if it had remained only to prove fruitless, in that it was not in God's household that its activities were exercised. I should prefer no good to a vain good. It is good things whose position is now sinking; it is the system of modesty which is being shaken to its foundation, which derives its all from Heaven, its nature from the laver of regeneration,[5] its discipline from preaching, its censorial rigor from the judgements which each Testament exhibits, its subjection to a more constant compulsion from apprehension of the eternal fire or from desire for the kingdom.[6]

Tertullian in this passage deplores the failure of proper Christian virtue, because of the imminence of the Parousia. In these "last times," evil increasingly seeks to subvert Christians from the path to salvation. One such ploy, Tertullian argues, is the belief that "modesty" is not the "abjuration" but merely the "moderation" of corporeal participation. As we have established, Tertullian equated proper Christian virtue with renunciation; his evocation of that ideal in this passage is clear from his distinction between "worldly" modesty, which he calls "a vain good," and that practiced "in God's household," which reveals "desire for the kingdom" and fear of damnation. Thus the modesty of which he writes in this tractate is a facet of renunciation. Renunciation requires the "abjuration" of corporeal pursuits; moderation by itself neither demonstrates sufficient commitment to God nor excludes idolatry. The most fully committed Christians display proper modesty and renunciation; they are "in God's household."

The laxity of virtue noted elsewhere by Tertullian demonstrated the imminence of the Parousia and the judgment of mankind that would follow.

The apocalyptic expectation of Tertullian in this work cannot be attributed only to his extreme rigor or his Montanist sympathies.[7] A generation earlier, Irenaeus (whose orthodoxy has never been questioned) could evoke precisely the same expectation:

> As, at the beginning of our formation in Adam, that breath of life which proceeded from God, having been united to what had been fashioned, animated the man and manifested him as being endowed with reason, so also in the end, the Logos of the Father and the Spirit of God, having become united with the ancient substance of Adam's formation, rendered man living and perfect, receptive of the perfect Father, in order that, as in the natural [Adam] we all were dead, so in the spiritual we may all be made alive. For never at any time did Adam escape the Logos of God, to whom the Father speaking said, "Let us create man in our image, after our likeness." And for this reason in the last times, not by the will of the flesh nor by the will of man, but by the good pleasure of the Father, his Logos formed a living man, in order that Adam might be recreated after the image and likeness of God.[8]

Irenaeus here contrasts the creation of man "in the beginning" with the parallel second creation of man "in the end" implied by the Incarnation of Christ. This makes little sense if Irenaeus expects the Parousia to be delayed any significant amount of time; it must happen soon for the Incarnation to balance creation as approximating the two end points of time. Moreover, although Irenaeus does not draw any disciplinary conclusions from this imminence in his exegetical text, his statement that "Adam never escaped the Logos" evokes the whole nexus of obedience to God's will as the path to salvation; this, in separatist Christianity, implies the ideal of renunciation.[9]

Clement of Alexandria likewise indicates his expectation of the imminence of the Parousia, and links it to the necessity of renunciation:

> As is right, then, knowledge (*gnôsis*) loves and teaches the ignorant, and instructs the whole creation to honor God Almighty. And if one teaches to love God, he will not hold virtue as a thing to be lost. . . . Thus also the Lord enjoins "to watch,"[10] so that our soul may never be perturbed with passion, even in dreams; but also to keep the life of the night pure and

stainless, as if spent in the day. For assimilation to God is preserving, as far as we can, the mind in its relation with [virtue]. . . . But the variety of disposition [toward virtue] arises from inordinate affection for material things. For this reason, it seems, they have called the night good thinking (*euphronē*), since then the soul, released from the perceptions of the senses, turns to itself and has a truer grasp of thinking (*phronēsis*). . . . "For blessed are those that have seen the Lord,"[11] according to the apostle, "for it is time to wake out of sleep. Now our salvation is nearer than when we first believed. The night is spent, the day is at hand. Let us therefore cast off the works of darkness and put on the armor of light."[12] By day and light he designates figuratively the Son, and by armor of light the promises [of salvation].[13]

Clement here explicitly links the ideal of renunciation as the core of Christian discipline with the expectation of an imminent Parousia. It is precisely because Christians expect Christ's return to occur soon that they "know" and "think" virtuously, avoiding "inordinate affection for material things." The corporeal world in which Christians now live is "the night" which precedes the Parousia, "the day" when Christ will return. In this night, Christians "dream unperturbed with passions," that is, live according to the ideal of renunciation. They also "watch" for Christ's coming as the Gospels order, preparing themselves through renunciation to receive the salvation promised by Christ. But no one who fails to "think rightly" about these things, and to treat the world as "night," remaining engaged with corporeal pursuits, will receive this promise.

In the course of the second century, then, the imminence with which the Parousia was expected attenuated only very slightly, from "within our lifetime" to "soon."[14] Regardless of the rigor of one's discipline, the imminence of Christ's return was motivation to adhere to the ideals of renunciation and martyrdom, which lead to salvation.

Violence Accompanying the Parousia

The second salient characteristic of the Parousia was that it would be accompanied by considerable violence through both human and natural agents. In the letters of Paul, written before the First Jewish Revolt, this violence is a side effect of Christ's return, since the worldly powers opposed to God would not easily give up the old order:

But Christ has indeed been raised from the dead, the firstfruits of those who have fallen asleep. For since death came through a man, the resurrection of the dead comes also through a man. For as in Adam all die, so in Christ all will be made alive. But each in his own turn: Christ, the firstfruits; then, when he comes, those who belong to him. Then the end will come, when he hands over the kingdom to God the Father after he has destroyed all dominion, authority, and power. For he must reign until he has put all his enemies under his feet. The last enemy to be destroyed is death. . . . When he has done this, then the Son himself will be made subject to him who put everything under him, so that God may be all in all.[15]

For Paul, the providential goal of creation is the return of Christ, "so that God may be all in all."[16] Since, however, death (that is, human and angelic pride)[17] is opposed to God, this goal will not be attained without a conflict. Those whose wills are not in accord with the divine will must be forced to conform. Christ will conquer them, "putting his enemies under his feet." In the course of this conflict, then, mankind will suffer all the usual calamities of war.

Paul does not here imply the necessity of death for salvation. In the *Apocalypse* of John, however, written after the destruction of the Temple, the failed First Revolt has changed the expectation of violence accompanying the Parousia. For John, this violence will specifically be aimed at Christians, as demonic forces attempt to compel Christians to abandon Christ: "When he opened the fifth seal, I saw under the altar the souls of those who had been slain because of the word of God and the testimony they had maintained. They called out in a loud voice, "How long, Sovereign Lord, holy and true, until you judge the inhabitants of the earth and avenge our blood?" Then each of them was given a white robe, and they were told to wait a little longer, until the number of their fellow servants and brothers who were to be killed as they had been was completed."[18] In this passage, expectations of the Parousia's attendant violence have become more acute. Those Christians already in Heaven because of martyrdom demand of Christ how much longer he will delay his Parousia. There are two actions involved with this return: that of judging and that of avenging. The unjust persecutors of Christians will be judged guilty of their idolatry, and their damnation will avenge the injustice of their previous actions. This Parousia, however, cannot happen until a sufficient number of Christians have been "given white robes," that is, martyred as those already in Heaven were martyred.[19] The heightened expectation of violence thus implies that those who are to be saved must first die as Christ died, and will only afterwards be raised and rewarded:

> After this I looked and there was before me a great multitude. . . . They were wearing white robes and were holding palm branches in their hands. . . . Then one of the elders asked me, "These in white robes — who are they, and where do they come from?"
>
> I answered, "Sir, you know."
>
> And he said, "These are they who have come out of the great tribulation; they have washed their robes and made them white in the blood of the Lamb."[20]

The "great tribulation" is the conflict between Christ and Anti-Christ. Roman worldly authority, directed by the "Prince of Darkness,"[21] will be set against Christianity, and will employ violent and fatal methods to destroy the people of God. There is here a clear implication that the only method of salvation for Christians is martyrdom; we have already seen how more rigorist Christians, well into the third century, strongly maintained the absolute necessity of martyrdom for salvation. Because, therefore, of the imminence of the Parousia, Christians must utterly reject all that concerns corporeal affairs, and embrace the literal martyrdom that that rejection implies.

Violence in Rigorist Christianity

Expectation of specifically anti-Christian violence accompanying the Parousia tended to reinforce more rigorist ideas within separatist Christianity. If Christians were to be increasingly persecuted as Christ's return approached, then this must be providential and hence necessary. The rigorist position regarding the necessity of martyrdom was standard in the first half of the second century, as in the *Shepherd of Hermas:*

> And when I wished to sit on the right side, it was not permitted; but she indicated to me with her hand that I should sit on the left side. And as I was considering [this], and sorrowing that she did not allow me to sit on the right side, she said to me, "Hermas, why are you sorrowful? The place on the right side belongs to those who have already served God, and suffered for the sake of his name [i.e., martyrs]. But much remains

for you, in order for you to sit with them. Continue to abide in your innocence, and you, and whoever will perform the sacrifice which they have
performed and endure what they have endured, will sit with them."

I said to her, "Lady, I wish to know what things they endured."
"Listen," she said; "wild beasts, and beatings, and prisons, and crosses,
for the sake of his name. Because of this, the right-hand portions of
holiness belong to them, and to whomever suffers because of God's
name; but the left-hand portions belong to those who remain. To both of
them, those sitting on the right and those sitting on the left, are given
gifts and promises; it is just that those who sit on the right have [their]
reward also. Now you desire to sit on the right with them; but your
shortcomings [i.e., sins] are many. Yet you will be purified of your
shortcomings, and everyone who will not doubt will be purified of all
their sins on that day.[22]

This passage describes the future movement of Christians from the "left"
to the "right" side of God. This movement implies not the hoped-for
worldly victory of Christianity,[23] but the worldly destruction of Christians
and their salvation. The angel of Hermas's vision makes clear what separates the right- and left-hand groups; both have received "gifts and promises"[24] because of baptism, but those on the right have "reward" also.
These are the martyrs, who have "endured wild beasts and beatings and
prison and crosses because of Christ's name"; they have "sacrificed" themselves to the world for the sake of salvation. Among the promises made to
those on the left, however, is that they will be given the opportunity to join
those on the right; by "sacrificing, enduring, and suffering" just as the
martyrs have already done, they will all be "purified of sin." All right-
thinking Christians, then, who reject the world and embrace martyrdom,
will be saved "on that day," that is, the day of Christ's return.

This rigorist attitude toward the Parousia, which makes martyrdom
absolutely necessary for Christian salvation rather than required only
when the sole alternative is idolatry, persisted throughout the separatist Christian period. Tertullian's *Apologetic* provides an excellent example
from the early third century:

The reason which composed the universe out of diversity . . . has also
fitted time itself by so fixed and distinct a making that this first part,
which we inhabit, flows down through a temporal lifetime from the
creation of things to the end; but the following [part], for which we

hope, is extended into an infinite eternity. When, therefore, the medial end and limit [i.e., of the first part], which opens between [the two parts], occurs, so that even the form of this temporal world will be transformed . . . then the entire human race will be revived, in order to reckon up what it has merited of good and evil in this age, and then to pay [the reckoning] throughout the immense perpetuity of eternity.[25]

Here Tertullian describes the judgment aspect of the Parousia. God has appointed a fixed date to the end of creation's purpose; when that date is reached—a moment that Tertullian himself "hopes" to see—the flawed, material nature of created matter will be perfected and transformed, so that matter will no longer in itself be unspiritual. Humans too will be transformed, so that the physical body that will be resurrected with the soul will no longer weigh down the soul. Not all humans, however, will live eternally in the perfected world; only those who have merited God's favor will attain this, while the rest will suffer eternally in flame. That those who have earned God's favor are all martyrs is clear from this further passage: "Who [among Christians] does not hope to suffer, in order to procure the full reward of God, [and] in order to obtain complete favor from him by giving in exchange his blood? [B]ecause there is opposition between divine and human affairs, we are absolved by God when we are condemned by you."[26] For Tertullian and other rigorist Christians, it is only by "giving in exchange one's blood" that one can obtain "complete favor" and "full reward" from God. Martyrdom is necessary for every Christian's salvation; Christ, the first martyr, remains unimpressed with unmartyred Christians.

Violence in Nonrigorist Christianity

For separatist Christians less rigorist than Tertullian, however, it was not strictly necessary for every Christian to be a literal martyr in order to be saved. In the works of these Christians, there is some attenuation in the apocalyptic expectation, but this does not affect their belief in either the imminence of the Parousia or its transformative significance; rather, what is attenuated is the level of the attendant anti-Christian violence they expect. Since in this less rigorist view not all Christians need be martyred, it follows that not all Christians living on the day of Christ's return need die on that day. This kind of attenuation of apocalyptic expectation is evident in the works of Tertullian's contemporary Clement of Alexandria:

For those who strive after perfection,[27] according to the same Apostle [Paul], must "give no cause for offence in anything, but in everything associate themselves not with men, but with God."[28] And as a consequence, [they must] also submit to men, for there is also right reason in these things because of slanders which have threatened abusively. . . .[29] "Let us, then," he says, "perfect holiness in the fear of God."[30] For if fear begets pain, "I rejoice," I say, "not that you were made to feel pain, but that, having suffered rightly, you were [moved] to repentance."[31] These things are the preparatory exercises of the gnostic mode of life. And since God himself, the Pantocrator, "gave apostles and prophets and evangelists and workers and teachers, for the restoration of the saints, for the work of the ministry, for the building up of the body of Christ, until we all return to the oneness of the faith and of the knowledge of the Son of God, to a perfect man, to the measure of the age of the fullness of Christ,"[32] one must strive to become mature in the gnostic manner.[33]

Clement sees Christian teaching as the striving after Christ's perfection, the union of humanity with divinity. In the world, however, this can only be achieved by renunciation, by "associating oneself with God" and spiritual pursuits rather than "with men" and corporeal pursuits. Literal martyrdom is implied in renunciation, but only when circumstances warrant; one must be willing to accept martyrdom "because of the slanders" against God, that is, idolatry, "which have threatened abusively" to condemn a Christian soul to eternal punishment. Martyrdom is only an absolute necessity in the particular circumstances that make it the only alternative to idolatry. The Christian, then, seeks perfection in this "gnostic manner," renouncing the world and prepared to accept martyrdom at need. Full perfection, however, will never be reached in this world. The martyrs reach their individual union with Christ through martyrdom, but all other Christians, living and dead, must await "the restoration of the saints" and "the building up of the body of Christ," when all Christians will be joined to "the oneness of the faith and of the knowledge" of Christ, the perfect man.

For Origen as for Clement, the attenuation of apocalyptic expectations was limited to the level of violence necessitated by the Parousia. Origen expressed precisely the same idea of Christian striving after perfection as his predecessor: "The one who prays for the kingdom of God to come, prays rightly about this [in praying that] the kingdom of God spring up in him, and bear fruit, and be perfected; for all the saints are ruled by God, and obey the spiritual laws of God, [and] live in themselves as in a well-ordered city."[34] For Origen as for Clement, the Parousia, the coming of the "kingdom of God," is for individual Christians in this world a process of seeking perfection. This seeking consists in the completely traditional ideals of renunciation and martyrdom at need, "obeying the spiritual laws of God" rather than the corporeal, worldly laws of the Roman state. The "well-ordered city" in which committed Christians live within themselves is modeled on the Heavenly Jerusalem, but is not a replacement for that city. The true Jerusalem will be established only with the Parousia and the transformation of the material world into a perfect and spiritualized world: "We follow the road to perfection, if, reaching towards what lies ahead, we abandon what lies behind;[35] and so for the kingdom of God in us who make progress incessantly, the highest point will be established when what was spoken by the Apostle[36] will be fulfilled, when Christ, with all his enemies made subject to him, will give over the kingdom[37] to God the Father."[38] Only with Christ's return will the goal of perfection toward which Christianity leads its adherents be achieved; just as for Clement, so for Origen that event will include the transformation of un-martyred Christians both living and dead from the state of striving after perfection to the state of being perfected.

For Clement and Origen, this teaching about perfection through re-nunciation and martyrdom is the whole purpose of Christianity in the world. Indeed, Origen himself makes it clear that Christians, truly to be Christians, must understand this and accept the consequences of their choice to be Christian: "Each member of the Church must pray that he may make way for the Father's will in just the same way in which Christ made way [for it], who came to do the will of his Father and accomplished it completely."[39] In seeking to be like Christ, the perfect man, Christians must submit themselves to the will of God, just as Christ did. Christ, how-ever, did not merely submit to the will of God; he "accomplished it com-pletely," that is, he died an unjust death, the first Christian martyr in the final stage of God's plan for the world. This implies that, even in Origen's nonrigorist anticipation of the Parousia, expectations of anti-Christian violence are not entirely attenuated. Origen is in fact fully aware of the rigorist tradition, and while not himself excessively rigorist, he makes ready use of that theme when it suits his purposes:

Paul also, in the second Epistle to the Thessalonians, declares in what way will be revealed then "the man of lawless conduct, the son of perdition, the adversary, and the one who is raised above all which is called 'god' or [is] an object of worship, such that he sit in the temple of God, proclaiming himself to be God. . . ."[40]

And there is also, for him who wants [it], to be extracted from Daniel the prophecy[41] concerning the Antichrist.[42]

Origen is here making reference to precisely the same set of apocalyptic Old and New Testament texts on which the rigorist tradition of Hermas and Tertullian is based. Origen cannot reject these canonical texts; he cannot, therefore, completely eliminate the expectation that the Parousia will be accompanied by some violence and the martyrdom of some Christians. Like Clement and other nonrigorists, however, Origen makes it clear that while some violence and some martyrdoms will accompany the Parousia, this is not the only, or perhaps even the most significant, means of salvation for Christians. Martyrdom, during both the wait for the Parousia and the Parousia itself, is necessary only as a defense against idolatry: "But he [i.e., Celsus] seems to advocate forcefully for those who witness for Christianity even unto death, where he says, 'And I do not say that he who has embraced a teaching of good, if about to be in danger from men because of it, must renounce the teaching, either pretending that he has renounced it or becoming [in fact] a renouncer.' He condemns indeed those who rightly understand what concerns Christianity but pretend not to understand or renounce [their Christianity], when he says that one must not pretend to have renounced the teaching or become [in fact] a renouncer of it."[43] In this apologetic text, Origen clearly upholds the importance of martyrdom in the nonrigorist manner. Even the pagan Celsus, Origen claims, agrees that "teachings of good" must not be abandoned in the face of "danger from men"; renunciation of Christianity, whether actual or feigned, in moments of crisis is in fact idolatry, and must be avoided at all costs.

Thus, alongside the rigorist tradition of martyrdom as necessary for salvation, there existed a less rigorist expectation of violence accompanying the Parousia. For Clement, Origen, and others,[44] the conflict that Christ's return would spark would target some, but not all, Christians. All Christians needed to be ready to accept martyrdom for this reason, but unmartyred Christians were not excluded from salvation.

Violence outside of Persecution

If the attenuation of apocalyptic expectations in separatist Christianity was in fact limited, then one should expect strong apocalyptic imagery to surface in nonpersecutive crises for Christian communities as well. Indeed, such imagery is commonly evoked; for example, in the wake of natural disasters such as the severe plague of the mid-250s,[45] Christians resorted to expectations of parousial violence to explain the significance of the crisis. The apocalyptic nature of Christians' deaths from plague is the central theme of Cyprian's tract *On Mortality:*

> For he who serves God should acknowledge himself, most beloved brothers, as one who, placed in the heavenly camp, already hopes for the divine [reward], so that there be in us no agitation, no disturbance, at the tempests and whirlwinds of the world, since the Lord himself foretold that these would come about; by the encouragement of his foreseeing word, instructing and teaching and preparing and strengthening the people of his Ecclesia for the endurance of all future things, he foretold and predicted that wars and fires and earthquakes and pestilences would erupt in every place. And lest a new and unexpected fear of infestation disturb us, he forewarned [us] that adverse conditions would increase more and more in the last times. Behold, the things which were spoken are happening.[46]

In this treatise, Cyprian tries to explain why Christians who have just survived the imperial persecution of Decius are now dying, unmartyred, from a severe epidemic. His explanation is entirely apocalyptic. The plague, like the persecution, is one of the signs of the "last times." Christ forewarned Christians, in his own words and in those of prophets like Daniel and John, that they would be especially afflicted by both evil men and the material world just preceding his return. Christians must take courage from the imminence of the Parousia implied in these events, and not fear to die by disease rather than martyrial torture. Both torture and disease are inspired by the devil, who seeks to turn Christians away from God and earn for them God's punishment rather than his favor; therefore, there is in fact a martyrial aspect to dying from this epidemic while resisting the despair inspired by the devil.[47]

Even in the early fourth century, after four decades of toleration by Roman government, the newly-converted Arnobius of Sicca, whose grasp of the full implications of Christian teaching was certainly not equal to that of Origen or Clement, could say precisely the same things regarding the Parousia as his predecessors: "Therefore, men, refrain from obstructing with futile investigations[48] your hope [for salvation]. The times, full of perils, beset [us], and fatal punishments threaten; let us flee for refuge to the saving God; let us commit ourselves to God, and let not our incredulity be given more weight in ourselves than the greatness of his name and power, lest the last day take [us] by surprise, and we be found in the jaws of death [our] enemy."[49] Arnobius understands no differently from Clement or Origen or Cyprian the salvific "refuge" in God and "commitment" to God that separatist Christianity claims. God will protect from the "perils" and "threatening punishments" of the world—here including both potential persecution and more recent natural afflictions—those who obey him according to the ideals of renunciation and martyrdom, not by ensuring that they are not hurt by these perils, but rather by saving their souls from the effects of these perils.[50] This commitment and obedience is the whole purpose of Christianity in the world. For Arnobius as for Origen or Clement, Christ in the Incarnation inaugurated the final phase of creation, which will therefore soon end; the "last day" remains imminent. Those who wish to be saved must therefore follow the precepts given by Christ, that is, renunciation and martyrdom at need, in order to avoid "the jaws of death," that is, eternal punishment, when the Parousia actually comes.

It is highly significant that Arnobius can make such a claim in the first years of the fourth century. Expectations of the Parousia do not seem to have faded significantly in the two centuries separating Arnobius from the author of *Revelations*. There has been attenuation in the level of expected violence among nonrigorist Christians, but no significant attenuation of the *imminence* of Christ's return.

Transformation Following the Parousia

The third salient characteristic of early Christian apocalyptic expectations was the idea that the Parousia would transform the fallen, sinful nature of matter, restoring it to the state of spiritual perfection in which it had been created. The Gospels gave a glimpse of that transformation in the story of Christ's transfiguration.[51] Paul describes how all the saved will receive a body, transformed and perfected as Christ is perfect: "Now we know that if the earthly tent[52] we live in is destroyed, we have a building from God, an eternal home[53] in Heaven, not built by human hands. Meanwhile we groan, longing to be clothed with our heavenly dwelling, because when we are clothed, we will not be found naked. For while we are in this tent, we groan and are burdened, because we do not wish to be unclothed but to be clothed with our heavenly dwelling, so that what is mortal may be swallowed up by life."[54] The "destruction" of the "earthly tent" is death, possibly but not necessarily martyrdom. Paul claims that Christians who die before the return of Christ will still have the reward of salvation, and will be "clothed" with a new "home" to house the soul. This "heavenly dwelling" will not be a "mortal" or corruptible body, but a "living" one, in the sense in which Christ was the first to live since Adam's fall.

The incorruptibility of transformed matter was a crucial idea in separatist soteriology, differentiating Christian orthodoxy from Gnostic denials of material goodness. Since in this world it is sin that separates man from God, the promise of sinlessness for the saved restores the paradise God once meant for mankind; God and man would once more live together, as the *Revelations* of John claim: "Then I saw a new heaven and a new earth, for the first heaven and the first earth had passed away, and there was no longer any sea. I saw the Holy City, the new Jerusalem, coming down out of Heaven from God, prepared as a bride beautifully dressed for her husband. And I heard a loud voice from the throne saying, 'Now the dwelling of God is with men, and he will live with them. They will be his people, and God himself will live with them and be their God. He will wipe every tear from their eyes. There will be no more death or mourning or crying or pain, for the old order of things has passed away.' "[55] In the "Heavenly Jerusalem," mankind and God will dwell together. Not only human bodies but all matter will be transformed to a perfect, spiritual state. There will be no corruption, "no death or mourning or crying or pain," because the possibility of human will transgressing the divine will won't exist. The "old order," that which was established when Lucifer and Adam first sinned, will have passed away entirely, and only perfection will remain.

This perfection is the same as that of which martyrs have a foretaste in their martyrdom. We noted in chapter 4 that Christ could be present and suffering in the martyr even before death; and in some cases, such as that of Sanctus in Lyons, Christ's perfect presence effected miraculous healings of previous tortures before the martyr died. The same *gloria* or *dóxa* of

Christ's presence infuses the Heavenly City: "I did not see a temple in the city, because the Lord God Almighty and the Lamb are its temple. The city does not need the sun or the moon to shine on it, for the glory ($\delta \acute{o} \xi a$) of God gives it light, and the Lamb is its lamp."[56] The Heavenly Jerusalem does not need a physical temple to be rebuilt in it, because Christ is the temple;[57] his "glory" shines throughout the city, illuminating everything, just as his "glory" shines, visible in the martyrs. The perfect Christ is the symbol of the transformation expected for Christians and for the world.

Thus, by pinning the hope for material salvation on a coming transformation, separatist Christianity was able to accommodate both sides of Paul's ambiguous relationship to the world. Matter was inherently good because created by God, but had *become* evil through sin. Because of the Parousia, however, that sinfulness could be removed, and matter again restored to good. Moreover, this expectation was held by both rigorist and nonrigorist Christians. The rigorist Tertullian, for example, described how matter would be restored from its fallen state through divine providence:

> Shall that flesh not rise again, which the Creator formed with his own hands in the image of God, which he animated with his own breath, after the likeness of his own vital vigor, which he set over all the works of his hand, to dwell among and enjoy and rule over, which he clothed with his sacraments and instructions, whose purity he loves, whose mortifications he approves, whose sufferings for himself he deems precious? God forbid that he should abandon to everlasting destruction the labor of his own hands. . . . As he requires from us love for neighbor after love for himself, so he himself will do what he has commanded. He will love the flesh which is his neighbor, although infirm, since his strength is made perfect in weakness;[58] although disordered, since they that are whole need not the physician;[59] although not honorable, since we bestow more abundant honor on the less honorable members;[60] although ruined, since he came to save what was lost;[61] although sinful, since he desired the salvation, not the death, of the sinner;[62] although condemned, since he says, "I will wound, but also heal."[63] Why reproach the flesh with these conditions that wait for God, that hope in God, that receive honor from God, that God succors? Indeed, if such casualties as these had never befallen the flesh, then the bounty and grace and mercy and beneficent power of God would have been lacking.[64]

In this passage from the tract *On the Resurrection of the Flesh,* Tertullian ascribes the transformation of matter, and especially human bodies, to God's providential plan from the moment of creation. God created men and angels with free will. In order the better to demonstrate both his mercy and his omnipotence, God allowed men and angels to fall through free will, but also restored them through the same free will, when Christ accepted his death on the cross. Christ's death made the salvation of souls possible for the first time since Adam's fall; his Parousia will likewise make possible the salvation of bodies, through the expected transformation of sinful matter into sinless matter. Humans in paradise will be complete humans, having both body and soul as God first made Adam and Eve in paradise.[65]

Precisely the same argument is made late in the third century by Methodius, in his *Banquet of the Ten Virgins:*

> For man also was created without corruption, that he might honor the king and maker of all things, responding to the shouts of the melodious angels which came from heaven. But when it came to pass that, by transgressing the commandment, he suffered a terrible and destructive fall, reduced to a state of death, for this reason the Lord says that he came from heaven into life, leaving the ranks and armies of the angels. . . . For with this purpose the Word assumed the nature of man, that, having overcome the serpent, he might by himself destroy the condemnation which had come into being along with man's ruin. For it was fitting that the evil one be overcome by no other than him whom he had deceived, and whom he was boasting he held in subjection, because not otherwise was it possible that sin and condemnation be destroyed.[66]

Methodius here links Christ's Incarnation, the fall of man, and parousial transformation, just as Tertullian does. The intended purpose of man in creation required that he be "without corruption"; man's fall necessitates some means of "overcoming" the subsequent "destruction" and "condemnation." This means is Christ, whose own crucifixion restored the possibility of salvation for mankind. The transformation that will ensue after the Parousia will thus return man to a state of being "without corruption" once again.

For nonrigorist Christians in the separatist period, the same expected transformation was likewise linked with providence and Incarnation. No difference existed in this aspect of apocalyptic expectations between rigorist and nonrigorist traditions. Irenaeus in his *Against Heresies*, for example, says much the same thing as Tertullian and Methodius: "But vain in every respect are they who despise the entire dispensation of God, and disallow the salvation of the flesh, and treat with contempt its regeneration, maintaining that it is not capable of incorruption. But if this indeed does not attain salvation, then neither did the Lord redeem us with his blood, nor is the cup of the Eucharist the communion of his blood, nor the bread which we break the communion of his body."[67] Irenaeus here attacks those Gnostic groups that maintain salvation for the soul only. He claims for Christianity an "entire dispensation," according to which God providentially arranges for the salvation of both the soul and the body of humans, through the Incarnation of Christ. By dying as a man, Christ "redeemed" man from Adam's sin. The Eucharist, like martyrdom, is a symbol and an instance of that "regeneration," which will allow complete humans to live "incorruptibly" in paradise after the Parousia: "Our bodies, being nourished by it [i.e., the Eucharist], and deposited in the earth and decomposing there, shall rise at the appointed time, the Word of God granting them resurrection to the glory of God."[68] The soul is saved at the time of death, but the body is saved only with the Parousia, at "the appointed time." When the soul has been reclothed with the new, incorruptible body, both ascend to the "glory" of God, dwelling in God's presence in the Heavenly Jerusalem eternally.

Origen likewise, in his *Commentary on the Gospel of John*, when treating of the passage in which Jesus says, "Destroy this temple, and in three days I will raise it up,"[69] evinces precisely the same set of ideas about parousial transformation:

Both of these two things, the temple and the body of Jesus, appear to me to be types of the Church, and to signify that it is built of living stones,[70] a spiritual house for a holy priesthood, built on the foundation of the Apostles and prophets, Christ Jesus being the corner-stone; and it is, therefore, called a temple. Now from the text, "You are the body of Christ, members each in his part,"[71] we see that even though the harmonious fitting of the stones of the temple appears to be dissolved and scattered, as it is written in the twenty-second Psalm that the bones of Christ are, by the plots made against it in persecution and afflictions on the part of those who war against the unity of the temple in persecutions, yet the temple will be raised again, and the body will rise on the

third day after the day of evil which threatens it, and the day of consum-
mation which follows. For the third day will rise on the new heaven and
the new earth, when these bones, the whole house of Israel,[72] will rise in
the great Lord's day, death having been overcome. And thus the resurrection of the Savior from the passion of the cross contains the mystery
of the resurrection of the whole body of Christ.[73]

Origen again insists on the salvation of man in both soul and body. Christians are martyrs who await the return of Christ, so that they may take
their place in the "new heaven and the new earth," the Heavenly Jerusalem described in *Revelations*. Christ allowed the salvation of the soul in
his crucifixion, and his return will transform the world into paradise, into
which the bodies also of the saved will be raised.

The expectation of a worldly transformation following the Parousia
was a constant in separatist Christianity. The physical world was not
currently the same as God had made it; it was corrupt through sin. After
Christ's return, however, matter would be purified to a state of incorruptibility, such as God had first created. In this new world, the saved would
live as complete humans, having both body and soul, in the presence of
God. Sin would not exist in this Heavenly Jerusalem, and none would
again be separate from God.

Conclusions

Some scholars have seen a significant attenuation of apocalyptic expectations in the second and third centuries. They argue that apocalyptic
expectations undermined the successful expansion of Christianity and its
recognition as a legitimate religious tradition within the Empire; these expectations were thus quickly abandoned by most Christians, who sought
precisely those goals. But, as this chapter has shown, apocalyptic themes
do *not* anticipate a Christianized Roman Empire. The Heavenly Jerusalem awaited by separatist Christians would *replace* the Empire (a corrupt tool of corrupting Satan) with the *temple*, not the imperial governance, of Christ. There will be no politics in paradise.

Thus, I argue, Christians maintained strong apocalyptic expectations
until the conversion of Constantine. These expectations concerned the
imminence of, the violence accompanying, and the transformation following Christ's return. Only in nonrigorist Christianity was there attenuation

of the expected levels of violence, since in this tradition the necessity of literal martyrdom for salvation was circumvented. In all other respects, apocalyptic expectations were a key component of separatist Christian understanding of the world. Such expectations reinforced the ideal of renunciation, since Christ's return was imminent; they also supported the ideal of martyrdom in both rigorist and nonrigorist traditions, since Christ's return would entail some violence and persecution against Christians, both by men and by nature under demonic forces. More importantly, moreover, apocalyptic expectations supported the development of theology and soteriology during our period, underpinning ideas that would remain imbedded in Christianity to the present day.

Furthermore, the preservation rather than the decline of these apocalyptic expectations had much to do with the ultimate success of Christianity. Apocalyptic expectations both supported Christians in times of crisis (especially the persecutions of Decius, Valerian, and Diocletian), and spurred the development of theological speculation; both these factors would enable the politicization of Christianity during the fourth century. The final two chapters, therefore, will examine the apologetic tradition in separatist Christianity and its reinterpretation by Constantine and his supporters after 312.

CHAPTER SEVEN

The Apologetic Evidence

While acts of the martyrs and bold exhortations to uphold the ideal of separation could be effective in rallying committed Christians, such uncompromising responses to the material and political world might rather reinforce among marginal Christians a lack of commitment. For these Christians, especially in moments of crisis for the community, the ideal of separation and its demand of martyrdom at need had to be presented in another way. Apologetic texts tried to offer a less intransigent version of renunciation's consequences.

Apologists employed the same separatist definitions of spiritual and corporeal as other genres, conflating as "corporeal" the expected threesome of matter, empire, and paganism. They included fairly strong anti-Roman sentiment that cannot be explained as opposition to paganism only. This anti-Roman sentiment focused on rebutting the crucial Roman accusation that Christians failed to support the fortuna of the Empire, an accusation very likely to convince Christians not committed to the ideal of separation to apostatize under duress. Rather than seeking to persuade Roman officials not to persecute Christianity, the apologists—who in fact welcomed persecution as an opportunity for martyrdom[1]—sought to prevent apostasy among marginal Christians by showing that Christians did support imperial fortuna, while pagans in fact did not. Apologetic texts thus served the same general purpose as martyrial texts, but for a different segment of the Christian audience.

The Problems Posed by Apologetic Evidence

The apologetic material presents an extremely consistent argument about the nature of Christianity's relationship with the world and with the Roman Empire. This argument runs essentially as follows: Romans accuse Christians of various sorts of crimes, most especially of treason and injury to imperial fortuna, the protection, aid, and enhancement offered to Romans by the gods in return for proper fulfillment of traditional rituals.[2] They then demand that Christians abandon their exclusive religion, at least to the extent of temporarily conforming to the pagan norms of Roman civic society. The apologists declare in rebuttal that these Roman accusations are false. Christians are not treasonous, because they do offer prayers on behalf of the emperors to their own God, similar to those the pagans offer to their gods. Moreover, because the Christian God is the only God truly capable of affecting events within and in favor of the Empire, the Christians actually do more than the pagans to support imperial fortuna by their prayers. Indeed, because the pagan gods are in reality malicious demons, the pagans themselves are the ones who injure imperial fortuna by praying to them. Pagans, then, are guilty of the very charges they level at Christians, while Christians are entirely innocent.

This argument appears naturally tailored to Augustinian-like distinctions between use and enjoyment, and especially between state and religion. Hence the apologetic evidence has generally been read as intended entirely for an external, pagan audience. Most scholars accept that apologists like Justin, Theophilus, and Tertullian addressed their works to the highest level of Roman officials and to the emperors themselves, but that these appeals went unheeded by these rulers.[3] Grant goes so far as to argue that apologies ought to be classed as imperial *libelli,* that is, as official documents addressed to the emperor or his representative whose purpose is to bring attention to some case of injustice in the imperial government, and thus gain redress of wrong.[4] In this view, the purpose of the apologies was to prove to persecutive, anti-Christian Romans that

Christians did not represent a threat to the Roman civic order, and thus to win some semblance of official toleration.

It is the Roman accusation that Christians fail to support imperial fortuna, and the apologetic claim that this accusation is false, which define the problem. Only if apologists intended an Augustinian-like distinction between state and religion could Christians participate in the governance of the Roman Empire while still completely rejecting idolatrous paganism. But such a distinction, as we have seen, is at odds with the attitude toward the world and the Empire presented in every other genre of early Christian writing. Moreover, the Christian retaliation that Romans actually injure fortuna is suspicious if these texts are intended to conciliate Roman antipathy; even as a purely rhetorical device to unseat Roman prejudice, this argument still increases rather than decreases anti-Christian sentiment in a Roman reader. Both these objections are removed, however, if apologetic texts are read with a separatist definition of renunciation underlying their basic themes.

Separatist Definitions of Spiritual and Corporeal

The apologetic material, exactly like the martyrial, disciplinary, and exegetical sources already considered, conflated under "corporeal" affairs the expected trio: the world and its material goods, the Roman state, and Roman paganism. Opposed to these things in all apologetic sources are the "spiritual" ideals that separate Christians from Romans. The late-second-century apologist Athenagoras, for example, clearly defines everything relating to matter in any way as demonic: "To the good of God . . . is opposed the spirit that is concerned with matter, [a spirit] created by God just as the other angels were created by him, and entrusted with the management [of things] concerning matter and the forms of matter."[5] The "spirit concerned with matter" is the devil, the fallen angel; once created by God to govern the created world, the devil has turned against God. This renders material concerns ungodly, demonic; for the devil still has power over these things, and uses them against God and the followers of God. Christians, therefore, cannot make any use at all of material objects or concerns, even for spiritual ends; all such things are under the devil's authority. This is precisely the same separatist understanding of the spiritual/corporeal dichotomy which previous chapters have already established.

Athenagoras's contemporary Theophilus expresses the same alienation of the material world from God: "Show, then, the eyes of your soul seeing, and the ears of your heart hearing. For just as they who see with the eyes of the body perceive the earthly business of life . . . just so also it is regarding the ears of the heart and the eyes of the soul, to be able to perceive God." [6] Here again the spiritual is clearly opposed to the corporeal in a non-Augustinian way. Even the manner of perceiving reality, Theophilus states, is different for Christians than for Romans. Romans perceive with the eyes and ears of the body, and so they perceive only material things; Christians, however, perceive with the "eyes of the soul" and the "ears of the heart," and so are able to apprehend the divine in unique ways. It is from this spiritual perception of reality that Christians derive un-Roman conclusions regarding proper civic behavior.

This perception is not arrived at by Christians independently of God, however; souls must be guided by the divine Logos to the proper understanding of reality. Tatian, another late-second-century apologist, makes this point explicitly:

> The Logos is the light of God, but the ignorant soul is darkness. Because of this, if it [i.e., the soul] continues alone, it tends downward towards matter and perishes along with the flesh; but if it obtains union with the divine Spirit, it is not helpless; it ascends to the place whither the Spirit leads it. For the dwelling-place of the Spirit is above, but the origin of the Soul is from below. . . . For the souls which heed wisdom attract to themselves the cognate Spirit; but the souls which do not heed [wisdom] and reject the minister of the God who has suffered, are revealed to be God-fighters rather than God-fearing.[7]

For Tatian, the soul's union with the Logos is the criterion that distinguishes spiritual from corporeal perception and wisdom. Salvation can only be achieved through the Logos; without the Logos, the soul is unable to escape its corporeal perception of reality, and thus "perishes with the body," condemned after death to the same separation from God it endured during life. With the Logos, however, the soul can transcend the corporeal to the spiritual perception of reality, and can apprehend true wisdom. Only those souls that heed this divine wisdom can hope to be saved, to be accounted "God-fearing" and not "God-fighting."

Origen's *Against Celsus* once again makes the same point, contrasting the divine wisdom which saves with a worldly wisdom which damns. The pagan Celsus had made the claim that Christians call all wisdom foolishness; Origen objects to this claim on that grounds that Christians only consider foolishness that wisdom which hinders salvation:

> Since Celsus quoted as being said by many Christians, "In life, wisdom indeed is evil, but folly good,"[8] I must respond that he merely quibbles about the teaching, for he does not bring out this [passage] which is found in Paul, and which reads like this: "If anyone among you thinks himself wise, let him become a fool in this age, so that he may become wise; for the wisdom of this world is foolishness before God." And so the Apostle does not say simply, "Wisdom is foolishness before God," but rather, "the wisdom of this world." And moreover, [he says] not, "If anyone among you thinks himself wise, let him become a fool" absolutely, but rather, "let him become a fool in this age, so that he may become wise." And so we call "the wisdom of this age" every philosophy which hinders and teaches falsely, according to the Scriptures; and we call foolishness a good, not absolutely, but when anyone becomes a fool in this age.[9]

Origen's reply is at the heart of the separatist definitions of spiritual and corporeal: the spiritual "wisdom of God" saves, but the corporeal "wisdom of this age" damns. Previous chapters have already established, however, what specific behaviors Origen and others promote as the path to salvation: namely, renunciation and martyrdom at need. Christians must live according to the spiritual wisdom, rejecting the corporeal things Romans consider wise to pursue: wealth, rank, authority, safety, and so forth. The ideal of renunciation, which is salvific wisdom for separatist Christians, precludes any Augustinian-like use/enjoyment distinction; not even use for good purposes can justify a desire for more material goods than strictly necessary to maintain life in expectation of the Parousia. All such desires are formulated according to worldly wisdom, which Christians must consider to be foolish, because fundamentally opposed to God.

In this apologetic description of the difference between Roman and Christian, the only real division is in one's point of view. This can be changed relatively easily, requiring only right use of the human intellect. Indeed, for Melito of Sardis in the late second century, pagan worship was merely a symptom of separation from the divine, not the root cause of damnation:

But why this world was made, and why it will pass away, and why there is a body, and why it perishes and rises again, will not be given to you to know, unless you shake off the madness in which you are sunk, and, opening your eyes, perceive God to be One, the Lord of all things, and devote yourself to him with all your heart. Then he will grant you to know his will. For those who are far from the knowledge of the living God, already are dead and buried. Vainly with prayers you seek after demons and shadows, who can grant you nothing. . . . Give thanks to God, who created you endowed with a free mind, so that you can direct [yourself] according to your judgement; for if you choose evil, you will lie in damnation for works of evil, but if [you choose] good, you will enjoy many good things along with eternal life.[10]

For Melito, as for other apologists, spiritual wisdom implies a true perception of reality. When one, as a Christian, is associated with and "fully devoted" to the Logos, one gains an unimpeded understanding of creation, providence, and salvation; one is "granted knowledge" of the "will of God," and one can thus begin to see what one must do to gain salvation. Without the Logos, however, one is "sunk in madness," unable to perceive reality truthfully, condemned to be "dead and buried," "far from the knowledge of God." In this untruthful perception of reality, paganism seems reasonable. One is easily convinced that paganism is both right and righteous, because one can never understand the true nature of divinity according to worldly wisdom. But, Melito continues, all men by nature have free will; the example and knowledge of Christ have been made known to all, and all are free to choose the truer perception of reality. Those who so choose will be saved and rewarded, but those who choose the worldly understanding, and thus oppose themselves to God, will be punished.

Fully in keeping with the implications of separatist Christianity's demand for renunciation from the corporeal, the rewards for those who choose to perceive and behave spiritually are also spiritual, not corporeal. So fundamental is the ideal of renunciation that Cyprian can argue, even in an apologetic tract, that these spiritual rewards do not preclude worldly suffering. The fact that Christians suffer in the world does not imply a lack of truth in Christian convictions; worldly suffering, like worldly pleasure, is an illusion:

And no one indeed should think that Christians are not avenged by the things which occur, just because they also seem to be wounded by the onset of accidents.[11] He feels the penalty from a hostile world, for whom all happiness and glory are in the world; he grieves and weeps if it is ill for him in this life, for whom it cannot be well after this life; all his enjoyment of living is found here; all his solace is ended here; his brief and perishable life counts here some sweetness and pleasure, but when it has departed hence, there remains only punishment upon pain. But to these others, for whom there is assurance of future goods, there is no pain from the attack of present evils. Indeed, by adverse things we are not prostrated, nor broken, nor do we suffer [from them], nor do we complain in any misfortune of affairs or condition of bodies. Living more for the spirit than for the flesh, we overcome weakness of body with strength of soul. Through those things which torture and torment us, we know and believe that we are tested and approved.[12]

Cyprian here argues that the misfortunes that befall Christians in the world, both the persecution of Christians by Romans and the natural persecution of famine and plague, are not unavenged by God. Christians must endure all these things from time to time, because providence requires a testing of faith.[13] But in truth, Cyprian claims, the Christian only appears to suffer from these afflictions. The Christian—whom a true and spiritual understanding enables to ignore as irrelevant both sorts of suffering—is buffered by association with the divine from the mere bodily effects of that suffering. The Roman, however, whose purpose, whose pleasure, and whose values are entirely corporeal, firmly grounded in this world, stands exposed to these persecutions, both by nature as the Christian, and by God for unjust persecution of Christians. It is the spiritual wisdom and behavior of the spiritual Christian that distinguish him clearly from the corporeal Roman.

The significance of the contrast between spiritual and corporeal is thus no different in apologetic literature than in other kinds of separatist Christian writings. Rather than supporting pro-imperial attitudes within Christianity, apologetic texts strongly argue that Christians must never compromise their sanctity by participating in the corporeal and idolatrous civic life of the Roman Empire.

Justification of Anti-Roman Attitudes

If apologetic texts were not intended to employ Augustinian-like state/religion or use/enjoyment distinctions, then they may be read as quite consistently anti-Roman. This anti-Roman attitude is most explicit in language about pagan cultic practices; but because separatist Christianity did not make any distinction between the state and pagan religion, this anti-Roman attitude must be understood as being broader than simply anti-pagan. Nor are the apologetic sources devoid of explicitly anti-imperial language, though this sort of language is much rarer than the other.

Both these sorts of language, the explicitly anti-pagan and the explicitly anti-imperial, were intended to justify the anti-Roman stance implied by renunciation. Nonparticipation in Roman civic society naturally exposed Christian communities to societal pressure, at times severe pressure, to conform. Christian leaders wrote apologies in an effort to mitigate the effects of these pressures on Christian communities, by arguing that conformity to Roman norms was undesirable because these norms themselves were wrong, ungodly, and violent.

The external pressure on Christian communities to conform often took the form of accusations of immoral and criminal behavior. Christians were accused of two broad kinds of deviation from Roman norms: one moral (promiscuity, incest, and cannibalism), and the other political (religious innovation or *superstitio*, illegality of association, treason, atheism, and injury to fortuna).[14] Of these, the most seriously damaging from the Christian leaders' point of view was the accusation of injury to fortuna, because this charge exposed most clearly the divergence of Christian and Roman worldviews, and consequently was the most likely to induce marginal Christians to apostatize.[15] This charge therefore required special treatment in the apologetic literature, and it will be dealt with separately in the next two sections. The remaining charges, being easier to deal with, were often handled together in the apologetic literature; apologists dismissed these less persuasive accusations, and even reversed them against the Roman civic order. They did this not out of concern for Christians' reputation within the Empire, but rather to prove to marginal Christians that the norms they were being pressured to conform to were themselves ungodly, and therefore had to be rejected.

The late-second-century apologist Theophilus lumps several of these accusations together in order to dismiss them all as false rumor:

For we didn't need to demolish these things, except that I still see you doubting the teaching of truth. For you, although prudent, endure fools gladly. Otherwise you would not have been moved by mindless men to yield yourself to empty words and to heed the prevalent rumor of godless mouths falsely calumniating us, who are called god-fearers and Christians, saying that the wives of all of us are [held in] common and cause [us] to participate in corrupt intercourse; and that we even have intercourse with our own sisters; and, the most godless and savage [rumor], that we partake of all human flesh. But also, [they say] that the teaching being spread among us is recent, and that we have nothing to say in support of the truth of the teaching among us; but they say that our teaching is foolishness. And so I greatly marvel at you—who in other things are serious and demand an account of every affair— because you listen to us carelessly.[16]

Theophilus here contemptuously dismisses the charges of promiscuity, incest, cannibalism, and religious innovation. Such things are simply absurd, Theophilus implies, mere "empty words" in the "godless mouths" of "mindless men." These rumors are heeded only by those who fail to pay careful attention to what it actually means to be a Christian; and Theophilus is "amazed" that there might be such careless people in the audience of his work.

What it actually means to be a Christian is, in the apologetic sources, defined in terms having as little relation as possible to civic society. Even for the recently converted Arnobius, this distinction is crucial: "We Christians are nothing other than worshipers through Christ our teacher of the highest king and prince; if you consider it, you will find that nothing else is circumstanced in this religion. This is the sum of [our] every action; this is the stated end and totality of sacred duties."[17] In the first decade of the fourth century, Arnobius can still claim that Christians are only worshiping God rightly, as they have been taught to do by Christ; this, and only this, is what Christianity is about. Christians therefore need not fear Roman antagonism; because Christianity is entirely centered on God, Romans must either accept Christianity or defy God in rejecting it.

Moreover, the apologists are able to define precisely *how* Romans fail to worship the divinity in a godly manner. In demanding that the Christians both worship what is not God and worship wrongly, Romans, claim the apologists, are manifestly making unjust use of their imperial authority. In the words of Justin Martyr:

> But since we do not think it just, to ask to be acquitted on account of the name if we are convicted as evil; [then,] if we are not found to commit injustices regarding this appellation of the name and regarding our daily living as citizens, all the more must you strive, lest, punishing unjustly those who are not convicted, you be judged with just punishment. . . .
>
> Wherefore we demand that the deeds of all those accused before you be judged, so that the one who is convicted be punished as unjust, but not as a Christian. But if anyone is clearly unconvicted, let him be released, since the Christian commits no injustice at all.[18]

Based on a law issued by Hadrian,[19] Christians could be sentenced merely for being Christians; no other accusation or proof was necessary. This, Justin and other apologists claimed, was patently unjust. Everyone else was granted the right to be tried on a specific charge, not on a categorical nomenclature the nature of which is scarcely understood: "We also, therefore, claim the right accorded to all, to be hated and punished not because we are called Christians (for what does the name matter for us concerning badness?), but to be judged on the charge if any accuse us, and either to be acquitted of the calumny and be released, or to be punished for the crimes if we are convicted; not because of the name (for no Christian is a criminal, unless he feigns the teaching), but because of the injustice."[20] Christians *qua* Christians, both Justin and Athenagoras argue, commit no actions contrary to Roman law; the only crime a Christian can commit is apostasy, feigning to follow the teaching of separatist Christianity regarding renunciation and martyrdom, while actually conforming to Roman societal norms. In punishing Christians as Christians, rather than as criminals guilty of a specific crime, the Roman authorities are unjustly punishing those who are inherently most just, and are thus preparing themselves to be punished in turn by God.

However, Justin and Athenagoras are not entirely accurate in claiming that Christians never break Roman law. A number of anticonspiracy laws were occasionally enforced during the separatist period; these laws banned, among other things, secret or nocturnal meetings, which were sometimes interpreted so as to include Christian meetings.[21] Origen in his *Against Celsus* addressed this issue specifically:

First and chiefly, [it is objected] by Celsus, desiring to calumniate Christianity, that "Christians make among themselves secret conventions contrary to what is lawful. . . ." To this I must reply that, if someone found himself among the Scythians (who have unlawful customs), and had no opportunity of returning, and were forced to live among them, he would do this rightly on account of the law of truth, which for the Scythians is lawlessness: he would make a convention with those of like mind, against what is for them lawful. In the same way, judging according to truth, the laws of the nations concerning images and godless polytheism are the laws of the Scythians; and [this law] is more irreverent than any [law] of the Scythians. And so it is not unreasonable to make a convention on behalf of truth, against what is lawful. For, just as, if certain ones make a secret convention on behalf of the removal of a tyrant who has seized control of a city, they do so rightly; just so the Christians, when they are tyrannized by falsehood and by the one they call the devil, make conventions contrary to what is for the devil lawful, against the devil and for the sake of the salvation of those whom they may be able to persuade to free themselves from the law of a tyrant and, as it were, of Scythians.[22]

Celsus, Origen says, has charged that Christians form secret "conventions," contravening the various anticonspiracy laws that the Roman government maintains and sometimes enforces. But, Origen argues, the position of a Christian in the Roman Empire is comparable to the position of an educated Hellene among the Scythians, the fiercest and least Romanized of the various trans-Danubian tribes that raided Roman provinces in the second and third centuries.[23] To these savage barbarians, the norms of civilized Roman society seem uncustomary or even illegal; but the Hellene, from his superior cultural perspective, recognizes that Scythian custom and law ought not apply to himself. In just this way, Origen claims, while Christian communal meetings may technically be against the law, such a law is "unreasonable," and ought not apply to Christians. Indeed, making such laws apply to Christians is "more irreverent" than anything the Scythians may ever have thought of doing; and in fact this is done only at the instigation and "tyranny" of the devil, who seeks to prevent proper Christian behavior and to hinder Christian salvation.

Moreover, the injustice of the Romans in attempting to curtail Christian worship and to force Christian conformity to Roman norms recurs strongly throughout apologetic sources. This is in fact a crucial piece of the apologetic argument for separatist Christianity: Roman injustice justifies rejection of Roman authority. No claim made on Christians by Roman authorities is to be considered legitimate by the audience of apologetic texts; this is bitingly clear in, for example, the *Octavius* of the third-century apologist Minucius Felix: "It is now the common lesson of other and later kings and leaders, learned with Romulus, to drive their neighbors from their land; to overthrow nearby cities with their temples and altars; to gather captives; to grow by others' losses and their own offenses. Therefore, whatever the Romans hold, cultivate, and possess, is the plunder of shamelessness; it is from the booty of every temple, from the destruction of cities, from the despoiling of the gods, from the murder of priests."[24] Anti-imperial language could hardly be more explicit than this; Minucius Felix rejects all Roman imperial authority as tainted from the very earliest beginnings, the foundation of Rome by Romulus, by the violently aggressive actions of Roman leaders. Not even other pagans are safe from the rapacity of Rome! In conquering and despoiling cities and temples, the Romans have clearly demonstrated what sort of authority they hold. It is not the authority granted to kings and rulers by God, to maintain peace and judge justly, which Paul claims for the Empire in his letter to the Romans; it is rather the tyranny of demonic violence, the piling up of worldly goods for their own sake, which, as has been shown, is antithetical to separatist Christian ideals.

First Rebuttal of the Accusation of Injuring Fortuna

Although apologists rejected Roman authority and claimed that Christians worshiped God rightly, the implications of separatist Christianity—namely renunciation, martyrdom, and apocalyptic expectations, which are made explicit in the disciplinary and exegetical sources of the period—were left undeveloped in these apologetic sources. The apologetic response to the political accusations, especially the accusation of injury to imperial fortuna, hinged on this.

The audience for these sources was composed of marginal Christians; the goal of the apologetic literature was to keep these marginal members as Christian as possible. Because they were potentially more susceptible to believing the Roman accusation of injury to fortuna, the apologists needed to convince them that the Christians support fortuna rightly, and the Romans wrongly. The audience, therefore, was not supposed to draw the inferences that previous chapters have sketched, because this might cause them to reject the Christian rather than the Roman worldview. The audience was supposed to understand only that Christians worship God rightly, according to God's own teaching, and that pagans worship wrongly, contrary to God's teaching. This was the root of the apologetic sources' misleading portrayal of Christians as wanting to support the imperial fortuna; for, if marginal Christians wanted to support the imperial fortuna and understood fully what separatist Christianity really entailed, they would more likely apostatize than uphold renunciation. The apologists therefore set out to convince this marginal audience that truly supporting the imperial fortuna meant being a Christian (because the Romans try to support fortuna wrongly); they did this by displacing the full implications of renunciation behind generalities of "right worship."

The anti-imperial theme in apologetic sources was crucial to this purpose. The connection between the proper observance of paganism and the success of the state underlay the Roman worldview in all matters; Rome was great because Romans were especially pious. It was to support this piety that Romans tried to force Christian participation in civic rituals, since Christians, from the Roman point of view, were utterly impious in their deliberate rejection of those religious forms that had made Rome what it was.[25] The Christian reply to political accusations, therefore, had to demonstrate that Rome was not great because of Roman piety. Instead, Christian apologists argued, Roman dominance came from the accident of Roman military supremacy; and this military domination, which Romans considered to be the greatness of Rome, was considered tyranny by God. Tertullian squarely confronted this issue in his lengthy apology:

Since, however, mention of the Roman name in particular occurs [here], I do not neglect the attack which that prejudice invites, which says that the Romans, for the merit of most diligent religion, have been raised to such loftiness that they occupy the world, and [which says] that so truly godlike are [their] gods, that they who beyond all others worship them, flourish beyond all others. . . . But how groundless it is to attribute the exalted rank of the Roman name to religious merits, since after her empire . . . her religion advances. . . . Therefore the Romans were not religious before they were great; and thus not great because of religion. But how could they be great because of religion, whose greatness comes rather from what is contrary to religion?[26]

Tertullian here summarizes neatly the Roman ideal of fortuna: Rome is great because of the exceptional religious merit of the Romans. But, he objects, this "prejudice" is simply not true. Rome became great before the by now traditional, anthropomorphic, Olympian cults were firmly established there; and Rome became great from "irreligious" merits, by violent and aggressive expansion against her neighbors. Roman fortuna is merely a myth proposed after the fact to justify the rapaciousness of an insatiable and militant people. To succumb to this myth, Tertullian implies, is to abandon the truth revealed by Christ.

Because of this truth, Tertullian argues, both paganism and the political entity it supports must be rejected: "You say, 'You do not worship the gods, and you do not offer sacrifices for the emperors.' That we do not sacrifice for others follows from the same reason that we do not for our own selves: the gods must not be worshiped [even] once. And so we are accused of sacrilege and treason. This is the chief, or even the entire, charge, and so it is worth being investigated, if neither prejudice nor unfairness judge, the one of which has no hope of truth, the other of which objects against truth. We leave off worshiping your gods because we know that they do not exist."[27] Tertullian voices the Roman accusation clearly: "You do not worship the gods, and you do not offer sacrifices for the emperors." This is true, Tertullian acknowledges; Christians do not do these things, because Christ has taught that these things ought not be done. The result is that Christians are denounced as traitors and atheists, whose presence within the Empire threatens the material success of the whole community. This accusation is the "chief charge" by Romans against Christians; but this charge for Tertullian is "prejudicial" and "unfair," for the simple reason that Christians are right and Romans wrong: the pagan deities "do not exist." These nonexistent deities have no power to make Rome great; neither have they power to punish Romans for the Christians' refusal to offer sacrifice.

Since the pagan deities have no power to punish the Christians' refusal to worship them, it follows that the Roman attempt to force Christians to this act is unjust and contrary to the will of God:

> I think that kingdom may peaceably be governed, whose king knows and fears the true God, so that he cause his people to understand [God], and [so that] he always judge rightly, as a man who never forgets that even he himself must be judged in the eyes of God. Then, because of

God, his subjects abstain from injury to their king and from doing violence to each other. So through knowledge and fear of God evil is eradicated from the kingdom; for if a king rule his subjects justly, they will act justly toward him among themselves, because he [i.e., the king] indeed reveals a realm living in peace and enjoying many good things, since all praise the name of God. For if a king recalls his subjects from deception, what is more worthy of praise? Thus is he pleasing to God, for deception introduces every evil. But the source of deception is this: if a man is ignorant of God, and in place of God worships what is not God.[28]

A true emperor, Melito here argues, would not force the most right-minded of his subjects to abandon the truth; he would rather embrace that truth, and propagate it throughout his realm. A king who "knows and fears the true God," who "justly judges" his subjects (as he will be judged by God in his turn), who spreads the true knowledge of God, so that all his subjects deal "justly" with him and with each other, fulfills the role God intends kings to play in the world. This king's kingdom is peaceful and prosperous, or in other words, has uninjured fortuna.

When a king does otherwise, however, as Roman officials have done in persecuting Christians,[29] then God is not pleased, and the fortuna of that realm is injured, not by Christians but by those who seek to prevent their being Christian. These anti-Christian kings are advancing "deception," paganism, errors contrary to Christian truth; they serve the devil, who has power over the material world and who seeks to cause the perdition of Christians.[30] These demonic kings, Melito argues by implication, must not be obeyed by Christians.

In these passages Tertullian and Melito were not advocating a future Christian empire in the world, because they did not distinguish between the Roman Empire and its pagan underpinnings; the only future "Christian empire" they anticipated was the postparousial "kingdom of God." Instead, Tertullian and Melito argued that the Roman Empire was unjust in its use of authority, and that this injustice inhered in the Empire's very nature as a corporeal (nonspiritual, ungodly, and demonic) institution. Christians must not heed the illegitimate authority of the Empire, however persuasive the Romans' arguments about fortuna may seem. Such compromise with corporeal institutions threatened Christians with loss of salvation; it was far better to undergo martyrdom and ensure salvation, they argued, than to accept such a risk.

This core apologetic argument would have been all the more persuasive to Christians when apocalyptic expectations were brought into play. Cyprian, for example, argued that the misfortunes attributed by Romans to the Christians' injuring *fortuna* were in fact the signs of the impending Parousia:

> But that wars continue more frequently, that drought and hunger pile up cares, that health is broken by raging diseases, that the human race is devastated by ravaging plague, you know to have been foretold, and [you know] various evils and afflictions to be multiplied in the last times; and, when the day of judgement now approaches, [you know] the censure of an angry God to befall more and more for the slaughter of the human race. For these things occur, not, as your false complaining and ignorance of the truth vaunt and bawl, because your gods are not worshiped by us, but because God is not worshiped by you.[31]

Cyprian here acknowledges that the mid-third century sees more than its share of wars, famines, plagues, and so forth; but these things, he argues, are signs of God's wrathful judgment on the Romans.[32] They do not come about because Christians have injured imperial *fortuna*; they come about because the Romans have done so, by refusing to heed the truth proclaimed by Christ. These obstinate persons continue to rebel against God, and thereby contribute to the impending "censure" of God, which will "slaughter the human race."

Second Rebuttal of the Accusation of Injuring Fortuna

In addition to the line of argument just described, there was also a second, independent rebuttal of the accusation of injury to *fortuna* employed in the apologetic sources. While the first rebuttal denied the validity of the Romans' concept of *fortuna*, the second admitted *fortuna* but denied that Christians injured it by their actions. Because separatist Christians conflated (and rejected) the Empire and paganism together, Christian apologists were not advocating the Christianization of the Roman Empire. In claiming that Christians prayed for the emperors, the apologists sought only to prevent apostasy among marginal Christians. This was considered a far greater evil than failure to live up to the ideal of renunciation; a Christian imperfectly disengaged from the world might still hope for salvation, but a Christian who apostatized and committed an idolatrous act was (almost surely) damned.³³

Tertullian was once again the clearest exponent of the second argument:

> For we pray for the well-being of the emperors to the eternal God, the true God, the living God, whose favor also the emperors themselves prefer above all others for themselves. . . . We, all of us, always pray on behalf of every emperor, for extended life for them, for secure rule, for a protected house, for strong armies, for a loyal senate, for a virtuous populace, for a peaceful world, for whatever things pertaining to man and Caesar are desired. . . . There is also another, greater necessity for us in praying for the emperors, and even for the complete stability of the empire and for [all] Roman affairs; namely, that we know that a great power, threatening the whole world and [even] the very end of the world, threatening horrendous afflictions, is delayed by the toing and froing of the Roman Empire. And so we pray that the things which we do not want to know by our own experience, may still be put off: we are in favor of Roman durability.³⁴

Tertullian here makes the explicit claim of positive Christian support for imperial *fortuna*. Christians are said to pray for the health and well-being of the emperors, the armies, the senate, the populace as a whole; in short, for "whatever pertaining to man and Caesar is desired." Christians pray all the more, Tertullian continues, because they know about the "threatening horrors" that will signal and accompany the Parousia. The Christians do not want to endure those "afflictions," and so they pray that the calamities may be postponed, and that the Empire may continue in its strength and stability yet longer.

Much the same idea was also expressed by Theophilus, though without Tertullian's added rationale concerning apocalypse: "And thus I will rather honor the king, not worshiping him, but praying on his behalf. I worship God, the existing and true God, for I know that the king is made by him. And so you say to me, 'Why do you not worship the king?' Because he is not made to be worshiped, but to be honored with lawful honor; for he is not a god, but a man appointed by God, not to be worshiped, but to judge justly."³⁵ Theophilus here claims that Christians are willing to pray *for* the emperor, as long as they are not required to pray *to* him. The emperor is merely a man, like any other; but he has been given a superior position by God, in order to promote justice in the world. This position does not justify worship of the emperor, for no worship not of God is justifiable; Christians do, however, honor the emperor as an emperor, to the extent that he fulfills his role of justice giver.

Athenagoras likewise made explicit claims about positive Christian support for imperial fortuna:

> Now you, who are in all respects, by nature and by learning, excellent and moderate and philanthropic and worthy of rule, since I have dismissed the accusations, and shown that we who have been punished are God-fearing and good and spiritual, bend your royal head. For who are more justified in having what they request, than those who pray for your rule, that the son may receive the kingdom from the father, according to what is most just, and that your rule be upheld with increase and largess, all men becoming subject [to you]? And this is for ourselves as well, for thus we may lead a gentle and peaceable life, and may ourselves willingly render every service asked of us.[36]

It is now proven, Athenagoras argues at the conclusion of his *Apology*, that the various accusations raised against the Christians have no basis in fact; therefore, he asks, ought not the Christians be given the same treatment and favor as the adherents of every other cult within the Empire? Indeed, he continues, they ought to be given more favor, for Christians pray for imperial fortuna just like everyone else; but the Christians pray to the only God who is actually capable of affecting fortuna. They are therefore most worthy of imperial gratitude. Yet, Athenagoras notes, hinting where Tertullian expounds, Christians do not pray merely for the emperors' benefit; they themselves are also benefited by imperial stability, for peaceable living and the propagation of their faith.

It is highly significant that the clearest expression of the inverse relationship between fortuna and Parousia is that of the rigorist Tertullian. We have already seen the importance of apocalyptic expectations, both for the martyrial ideal and, even in the apologetic context, for the justification of anti-Roman ideas. It is thus most unusual to have such a strong mitigation of apocalypticism from the pen of the most rigorous of all the third-century Christian writers.

Nevertheless, this second argument is accepted at face value by many scholars. Grant, for example, in part bases his arguments specifically on the passage from Theophilus cited above. Christian objections to Roman rule, these scholars argue, derived not from the illegitimacy of the Empire but from its illegitimate *religious* demands of emperor worship and pagan sacrifice; it is these demands which are to be considered "unjust" and hence ended by just emperors. Furthermore, if Christians prayed for the Empire, resistance to imperial authority could have derived only from idolatrous demands that Christians found unacceptable.[37]

However, this argument is plausible *only* if Christians such as Tertullian, Theophilus, and Athenagoras differentiated between the Empire (to which they seemed to profess loyalty) and paganism (which they clearly rejected). I argue that this Augustinian-like church/state distinction was *not* being made by separatist Christians. As we have seen, none of these Christian authors considered the Roman Empire as something separate from the traditional trio of corporeal things (material things, empire, and paganism). Because of this conflation, the emphasis on "just rule" noted above takes on greater significance. For separatist apologists, the demonization of worldly authority meant that a pagan emperor could never be truly just. This implication only reinforced the conclusion that marginal Christians were intended to draw from these texts: that all Roman demands were to be rejected.

Moreover, the statement by Tertullian, hinted at also by Athenagoras, that Christians pray for the continued stability of the Empire *because they do not want the Parousia to happen,* is completely disingenuous. The expectation of the Parousia—that event which will both punish all those who have denied and resisted God and reunite with God both all those who have obeyed his will and the balance of creation—is an indispensable part of the single most important Christian tenet of belief: that Christ died for the salvation of mankind.[38] Any argument posited on a hope of delaying the Parousia *must* be suspect. Tertullian, who considered any attempt to avoid the opportunity for martyrdom idolatry, could not have been seeking an end to martyrdom; further, because martyrdom hastens the Parousia, toleration by the Roman government (which reduced the opportunity for martyrdom) was a demonic plot to prevent salvation, as Origen argued. Therefore this apologetic claim simply cannot be accepted at face value.

Why would Tertullian have made such an absurd claim about the intent of Christian support for imperial fortuna? Why could he not simply have said, as Paul had done, that Christians supported the Empire because the Empire was a divine institution, providentially provided for humans to live more justly? I believe Tertullian made this absurd claim ironically; this absurdity underscores the further absurdity of Roman demands for Christian participation. As Arnobius reveals, even a catechumen could be expected to realize the importance of parousial expectations, and to see irony in such a claim.

But if this is true, must one also reject less absurd apologetic claims that Christians supported imperial fortuna? Can it be literally true that Christians prayed for the health of the emperor? Everything that we have seen thus far indicates that this was not true. First, separatist Christianity consistently conflated the Roman state with Roman paganism, and the emperor, as head of the Roman state, was also Pontifex Maximus, the chief priest of all the pagan cults—or rather, from the Christian point of view, of all the demonic cults opposed to God's plan for salvation. Second, the authority of the Empire embodied in and wielded by the emperor was not considered by separatist Christians—and particularly by these same apologists—to be a legitimate, godly authority. Rather, Roman imperial authority was corrupted and made illegitimate by its association with corporeal affairs; it had utterly failed to remove itself from the demonic control under which matter had fallen when the devil turned against God, as the unjust persecution of Christians proved. Third, according to the ideal of renunciation, Christians were not supposed to pray even for their own health, much less for someone else's.[39] Fourth, by this same ideal, Christians were not supposed to support the Empire with their actions—as for example through military service—but only through the payment of taxes in money and in kind, goods of which the Christians considered themselves well rid.

In contrast, the only grounds on which I find it plausible that separatist Christians were praying for the emperors is that of the New Testament injunction to "pray for your enemies."[40] These biblical injunctions to pray for one's enemies can be read two ways: that the enemies might be converted to Christian truth, and thus be saved, or that God might not count the act of persecution itself against them at the Last Judgment. In either case, Christians are not praying for imperial success as Romans understand such prayers; a successful divine response to either possibility would result in the conversion of the Roman being prayed for, and thus his ceasing to conform to the Roman norms Christians have already rejected. It is not, I therefore believe, reasonable to hold that apologetic claims about Christians praying for the emperors imply active Christian support for imperial fortuna or loyalty to the Empire.

It is, nonetheless, significant that this rationale is not an important one in the apologetic literature, either in this context or in any other. In short, I believe, the statements of the apologists just quoted make sense only if they were intended to prevent apostasy among marginal Christians at moments of potential or ongoing crisis; for no possible argument could be left unused that might convince those marginal Christians that Romans were wrong, both in their religion and in their demands on Christians, while Christians were justified because of their religion to refuse those demands.

Christian or Pagan Audience?

This chapter has repeatedly stated that the intended audience of apologetic literature was not a pagan one, but a marginal Christian one: those new or imperfectly socialized Christians most "at risk" of being persuaded by the potent Roman accusation of injury to imperial fortuna. In part, this assertion is a logical consequence of rejecting any reading of the apologetic corpus which distinguishes between state and religion in an Augustinian-like manner. Separatist Christianity's conflation of state and religion makes the apparently pro-imperial apologetic arguments stand out in sharp contrast to other separatist sources. The most straightforward way to harmonize this apparent contradiction between apologetic and nonapologetic sources is to posit an internal but marginal audience[41] for the apologetic material.

There is, moreover, evidence within the apologetic material itself which suggests that marginal Christians were indeed the intended recipients of this literature. This is stated in no uncertain terms in, for example, Origen's Preface to his *Against Celsus:* "[I have attached this preface] so that he who will read our reply against Celsus will find it first of all, and see that this little book was written, not for the wholly faithful, but for those who have not wholly tasted the faith of Christ,[42] or those whom the Apostle[43] names 'weak in faith.' "[44] Origen here explicitly states for what audience he intends his apologetic work. This audience is specifically those Christians whose attachment to the separatist ideals of renunciation and martyrdom is weakest, who are susceptible to be convinced that Christianity does indeed injure Roman imperial fortuna, and so to apostatize under duress.

Justin Martyr affords the same evidence in his *Second Apology*. He places himself in the context of the marginal Christian, by referring to his own previous conversion: "For I also, myself, when I was enjoying the teachings of Plato, heard the Christians being calumniated, and saw [them] fearless even unto death and [unto] all the other things accounted fearful, [and] perceived that it was not possible that they be devoted to evil and to love of pleasure. For what pleasure-loving or immoderate man, who also thinks it good to eat human flesh, could welcome death and thus be deprived of his pleasures; but would not preferably live always in this life, escaping the attention of the rulers—not that he could even denounce himself, indeed, being liable to be killed?"[45] Justin here describes how he became convinced of the truth of Christian teaching regarding salvation—and, by implication, renunciation and martyrdom—when he was only passingly acquainted with that teaching. The ability of Christian martyrs to die happily for their faith proved, for Justin, that these Christians could not be guilty of the accusations raised against them by the Romans. So, Justin argues, should the audience reading this work—an audience likewise imperfectly understanding Christian teaching, likewise pressured to conform to Roman norms—likewise be convinced by the examples of martyrdom available within the community, and, indeed, within the same text.[46]

Clement of Alexandria offers a similar argument in his apologetic *Exhortation*, though instead of placing himself in the position of the marginal audience, he emphasizes the threat of damnation which Christianity teaches how to avoid:

Come, come, my band of youths. For if you do not become again like children, and be born again, as the Scripture says, you will not receive the truly existent Father, nor ever enter into the kingdom of Heaven. For how is it permitted for a stranger to enter? . . . For this is the first-born Church, composed of many good children; these are "the first-born, enrolled in Heaven, celebrating with so many myriads of angels."[47] We are the first-born children, nourished by God, genuine friends of the First-born, we who first among [all] other men have known God, who first have been freed from sins, who first have been separated from the devil. But now the more certain ones are ungodly, the more philanthropic is God; for he desires us from slaves to become sons, but they scorn to become sons. O the enormous senselessness! Do you deny the Lord out of shame? He offers freedom, you run into slavery. He grants salvation, you submit to a man. He will give eternal life, you await punishment; and the fire approaches, which the Lord[48] "has prepared for the devil and his angels."[49]

Clement here assumes a cajoling, avuncular tone toward his audience of "youths." Like all youths, Clement's tone implies, these don't submit easily to discipline; and like all paternal figures, Clement tries to tell them that discipline is for their own good. The reason for this, Clement argues, is the imminence of the Parousia, with its "approaching fire" that threatens all those who refuse God's "philanthropic" offer of freedom and heavenly patrimony.

In addition to such direct references to a marginal Christian audience, there is also indirect evidence that supports this argument. If the audience of the apologetic literature were indeed a pagan one, one would expect a more conciliatory tone throughout. However, we have seen that the apologetic evidence is in fact strongly anti-Roman, denigrating both Roman paganism as vacuous and demonic and Roman imperial authority as inherently unjust; and that seemingly pro-imperial passages occur only in the context of claims for Christian support for imperial *fortuna*, a context that renders such pro-imperial claims highly suspect. Apologetic literature depicts the Romans as acting wrongly, not just in the active persecution of Christians (which one would expect, if the purpose of apologetic text were to mitigate persecution), but indeed in every aspect of their civic lives. In contrast, Christians are depicted as acting rightly, always and in every way—unless, specifically, a Christian apostatizes.

This vindication of Christian truth is explicit, for example, in Aristides's late-second-century *Apology:* "And these are they who more than any other nation of the earth have found the truth; for they know God, the builder and creator of all things through the only-begotten Son and the Holy Spirit, and they fear no other god than him. They have the commands of the Lord Jesus Christ himself engraved on their hearts, and they guard them, looking for the resurrection of the dead and life in the age to come."[50] The truth as known by Christians, Aristides argues, is superior, more complete, than truth as known by any other group, Hellenic, Barbarian, or Jewish. The Christians alone know the true nature of divinity; the Christians alone fully follow the will of God; the Christians alone understand the imminence of worldly destruction and the sole manner of avoiding destruction along with the world.

Tertullian likewise asserts the supremacy of Christianity, not just in matters of theoretical knowledge but in the everyday practice of piety: "But it is not part of religion to compel religion, which should be taken up freely, not through force; since even the sacrificial victims are required of free mind. And so you compel us to perform sacrifices, [but] thereby you distinguish yourselves not at all to your gods; for they do not desire sacrifices from the unwilling, unless they are contentious; but what is contentious is not god."[51] In contrast to the Christian truth, Tertullian bluntly asserts, the Romans are not merely wrong; they are so totally wrong that, even if their gods did exist, the Romans would still be worshiping them wrongly, since a sacrifice offered under duress rather than by free will could not properly propitiate the gods.

Furthermore, as Minucius Felix argues, one must not be swayed by mere rhetorical skill into believing what is not true according to Christian teaching: "And in however great a measure your oration has pleased me with subtle variety, yet I am more highly moved, not concerning the present activity, but concerning the whole category of disputing, because, to a considerable extent, the state of truth is changed by the force of speaking and the power of very clear eloquence. This is well known to occur through the facility of the listeners, who, while they are diverted by the allurement of words from attention to the things [themselves], consent without distinction to everything said; nor can they discern false from true."[52] Minucius Felix's *Octavius* is the only apologetic work that puts the Roman accusations against Christianity into the mouth of a pagan character. In the first thirteen chapters of the work, Caecilius is made to enumerate the various charges against Christianity. The narrating character (also named Minucius) now speaks decisively, without yet having heard the second half of the debate: Caecilius's discourse was skillful and pleasing to hear; it was not any more true thereby. The narrating character speaks directly to the audience: you know that what you have just heard is not true; now listen to what you already know is true. This intermediate passage between Caecilius's pagan discourse and Octavius's Christian reply serves to undercut everything Caecilius has just said. The audience is not supposed to give equal consideration to both sides; the conclusion of the debate is foregone from this point in the work.

These two sorts of evidence make it clear that apologetic material was intended for a marginal Christian audience. The direct evidence, such as the passage quoted from Origen, states this explicitly; the indirect evidence, such as the passage from Aristides, emphasizes the great contrast between Christian truth and Roman falsehood, both in knowledge of the divine and in practices which act on that knowledge. Finally, as the quotations from Justin, Clement, and Aristides have shown, both kinds of evidence refer to apocalyptic expectations as a justification for enforcing adherence to Christian truth. This last is extraordinarily telling; in the final analysis, it is highly illogical to base any argument intended to convince pagan Romans not to persecute Christians on the expectation of an event that will destroy the Roman Empire.

Conclusion

This chapter has sketched how apologetic evidence should be read in light of the ideals of renunciation and martyrdom. The apologetic sources present these ideals no differently than do other kinds of separatist Christian literature. Anti-Roman motifs and reliance on apocalyptic expectations to prove Christian truth make apologetic arguments unlikely to persuade any non-Christian. Apologies, I therefore conclude, were anti-Roman, making no distinction between Roman state and Roman paganism; were intended for a marginal Christian audience; and tried to prevent apostasy among marginal Christians in times of crisis.

CHAPTER EIGHT

Constantine, Eusebius, and the Triumph of Christianity

We have seen how the failure of the Zealot movement in the early second century altered Pauline Christianity's ambiguous attitudes toward the world and the Roman Empire. Christians increasingly viewed both world and state negatively, while the ideal of separation, and its related expectations of martyrdom and apocalypse, came to overshadow Christian attitudes for most of the second and third centuries. But this ideal did not remain unchallenged within Christian communities. We have already noted the divisions that arose over discipline (rigorist and nonrigorist traditions), and over the status of apostates (especially between Cyprian and Novatian in the 250s). Throughout the third century, a related problem became increasingly acute: what to do with those who sought admittance to the Christian community but had not entirely given up ties to the Roman world.

At the end of the separatist period the emperor Constantine's conversion and support for Christianity necessitated a reinterpretation of the renunciation traditions of the previous two centuries. The historian of Christianity, Eusebius, in order to resolve new tensions within Christianity, successfully redefined the spiritual and corporeal categories that had supported renunciation. Whereas the ideal of renunciation conflated matter, empire, and paganism together as corporeal and opposed to God, Eusebius defined the corporeal only as paganism. This allowed him to make three extraordinary changes in the tradition we have been examining: he now could, first, portray the martyrial tradition as a rejection solely of idolatry; second, define renunciation as asceticism, in keeping with established pagan philosophical traditions; and third, link Constantine's conversion with the Parousia. These changes allowed the spiritual category to include the nominally Christian Empire.

Eusebius's revisionist history effectively turned traditional Christian communities inside out. Those imperfectly socialized Christians who had maintained Roman ties—increasingly numerous in the last decades of the third century, as we shall see—now provided a practical foundation on which to build a newly pro-imperial Christianity. Christians who had fully supported the ideal of renunciation, and who had nonetheless survived the persecution of Diocletian (which lasted in the East for more than ten years, from 303 to 313),[1] either accepted the changes, upheld renunciation through asceticism, or turned to (now heterodox) traditions like Montanism and Donatism.[2]

Erosion of the Ideal of Disengagement Prior to Constantine

The decade of the 250s was a critical period for early Christianity, presenting two imperially ordered persecutions (Decius's in 250–51, and Valerian's in 258–59), a severe plague, and a resulting famine. Christian communities suffered significant loss of leadership and unprecedented pressure to abandon their convictions.[3] With these challenges, the problem of discipline became paramount for Christian leaders. How could they maintain traditional norms of renunciation in the face of such community fragmentation?

This problem was compounded by the Roman reaction to the two imperial persecutions in the last four decades of the century. From the Roman point of view, insisting that Christians toe the party line on pagan ritual was a way to protect the Empire from the disasters besetting it.[4] But the very public Christian rejection of those Roman norms had not appreciably worsened the situation; on the contrary, Decius was killed and Valerian was captured on campaign in the East, each within a year or so of issuing the order for universal sacrifice.[5] Faced with more pressing issues of succession, the emperors of the 260s largely ignored the Christians.[6] As the economic and political fortunes of the Empire slowly brightened, few imperial leaders saw much advantage in renewing imperial persecution. As a result, Christian communities could operate with little fear of governmental restriction, as long as they remained relatively discreet.[7]

In this climate, Christian communities began to expand more rapidly. Many pagans had been impressed with the Christians' cohesion during the 250s, especially their response to the terrifying plague.[8] The Christians' vigorous proselytism found a more receptive audience than ever before, and the lack of government interest lowered the physical and social risks for converts.

But as Christian communities increased in size, community mechanisms for enforcing the traditions of renunciation failed to keep pace. More and more Christians were able both to participate in their new community and to remain involved in Roman social and political life. There was often little repercussion from either set of leaders for this fence-sitting. The vigorous disciplinary tradition of the early third century, led by Tertullian, Cyprian, Clement of Alexandria, and Origen, were not renewed as strongly in this new generation. In the last decades of the third century, only Arnobius and Methodius wrote extensively about separatist discipline.

Thus, as the third century drew to a close, more and more Christians remained imperfectly socialized to renunciation. While there had been some Christians in the army and in municipal or imperial government perhaps as early as the late second century,[9] their numbers had always been small, and they had regularly been under pressure from Christian leaders to conform to the ideal of separation.[10] By the end of the third century, however, their numbers were no longer so insignificant, and conformist pressure was usually very slight indeed. Bishops struggled to shore up separatist boundaries, but lacked the resources appropriate to their larger communities.[11]

This dilution of renunciation made the Diocletianic persecution that much larger a crisis for Christianity. There was still a vigorous core of committed Christians, as the large number of martyrs attributed to those years shows. Yet incompletely socialized Christians were less likely to accept martyrdom than fully committed separatists, even with strong examples confronting them. Even some priests and bishops avoided martyrdom during this persecution, which did not help to enforce the ideal.[12]

In 313, therefore, when persecution finally ceased entirely, the division between rigorist and nonrigorist over the status of apostates was much more acute than it had been in 251 or 259. The rigorist, committed separatists were able to argue that the erosion of renunciation had *caused* the persecution to take place,[13] and thus that the apostates (most of whom, one supposes, had been among the incompletely socialized Christians) had to be excluded from surviving Christian communities.[14] The nonrigorists were able to lean on Cyprian's inclusive tradition, made all the stronger by the numbers involved in this instance, to encourage (eventual) readmittance of the lapsed.[15] These lines would soon entrench themselves theologically: the rigorist position hardened into the heterodox Donatist tradition, while the inclusive tradition successfully co-opted imperial interest in Christian unity.[16]

Constantine's Conversion

In this situation, the rapid rise of Constantine and his support for Christianity had remarkable consequences.[17] Constantine was the son of Constantius, one of the four emperors under Diocletian's Tetrarchy.[18] He grew up in and around the imperial courts, and was trained from youth to rule. In 305, when Diocletian abdicated for reasons of health, Constantius was promoted and Constantine expected to move into his father's former position, but was passed over by Diocletian in favor of another imperial scion, Severus, nephew of Diocletian's eastern emperor Galerius. Constantine left Galerius's court and returned to his father in Britain. When his father died some months later, Constantine was acclaimed by the British legions and assumed imperial rank.

During the persecution begun in 303, it seems that Constantius interested himself very little in uncovering Christians in his legions and bureaucracy.[19] Constantius may have had very few Christians to contend with in Britain at this date; or he may have been sympathetic to their monotheism. It is possible he somehow identified Christianity with Mithraism's solar cult, so popular among the legionnaires; it has also been speculated that

Constantine's mother Helena was already a Christian by this date.[20] Whatever the reason, only one famous Diocletianic martyr is now remembered from Britain, Albanus,[21] and the dating of his death may be incorrect.[22]

Thus, when Constantine began maneuvering to eliminate his main western rival Maxentius about 307, he was able to claim a "traditional" support for religious unity in his propaganda.[23] This unity does not yet seem to have included Christianity; instead, it evoked the long-standing theory that Roman piety was the source of Roman greatness. Constantine's propaganda promoted syncretistic monotheism, usually under the guise of solar cult. This move seems clearly calculated to appeal to both the army (his own and Maxentius's), and the populace, and was in no way unusual.

In 312, the two rivals provoked each other to active war. Constantine fought his way south through Italy, eventually meeting and routing Maxentius at the Milvian Bridge, just north of Rome on the Tiber. Constantine triumphantly proclaimed himself the restorer of peace and unity in the West, declared the civil war at an end, and consolidated his gains. Consolidation was necessary, because while Constantine had eliminated his western rivals, Licinius was accomplishing the same in the East.[24] In 313, therefore, the two emperors met at Milan to arrange concord between themselves. The result of this meeting was a marriage between Licinius and Constantine's half-sister Anastasia, and a document, soon published throughout the Empire, now known as the Edict of Milan. The concord, however, lasted only three years; by 316, armies were skirmishing along the Italian-Illyrian border, and in 318 Constantine attacked Licinius and pushed him out of Illyria, Thrace, and Macedonia entirely. After a brief pause, hostilities resumed, and in 320 Constantine defeated and captured Licinius in Asia Minor, and ruled as sole emperor until his death in 337.[25]

The document now called the Edict of Milan is a remarkable one, and is preserved for us by both Eusebius (in Greek) and Lactantius (in Latin).[26] Its significance lies in its treatment of Christianity; in effect, it extends Constantine's concern for religious unity to a group previously considered outside the boundaries of licit Roman religion:

> Thus when I, Constantine Augustus, and I, Licinius Augustus, had met at Milan and were discussing all those matters which relate to the advantage and security of the state, among other things which we saw would benefit the majority of men we were convinced that first of all

those conditions by which reverence for the Divinity is secured should
be put in order by us to the end that we might give to the Christians and
to all men the right to follow freely whatever religion each had wished,
so that whatever of Divinity there be in the heavenly seat may be favor-
able and propitious to us and to all those who are placed under our
authority.[27]

This passage clearly demonstrates, not that Constantine is now a Christian—he is not, as Grant's study of his coinage from this decade showed[28]—
but that the imperial policy of forcing Christians to conform to Roman
religion has failed. Constantine and Licinius capitulate to Christian resistance; they admit that they cannot compel Christians to support Roman
fortuna in traditional pagan forms. But they do not wish Christians to
continue practicing their religion outside the boundaries of Roman religion, where their prayers cannot support imperial success. Their solution
to this dilemma is eminently Roman: they co-opt Christianity as a licit
religion, by legislating away all the anti-Christian precedents of the past
two centuries.

This solution owes a great deal both to the earlier impetus toward
syncretism, especially of Constantius's and Constantine's solar variety,
and to the erosion of renunciation in previous decades. A great deal of
Constantine's success against Maxentius had already depended on deliberately vague monotheism, which encompassed both military traditions
and the loyalty of upper and lower classes of many cultural backgrounds.
With incompletely socialized Christians holding positions in the army and
bureaucracy in larger numbers, their monotheism could also be included.
Thus, despite the weight of tradition against Christianity, it was logical to
extend Constantine's ideal of religious unity to this group.

But it is a far cry from Constantine offering legitimacy to Christianity,
to Constantine actually becoming a Christian. We do not know exactly
when or why Constantine's syncretism became more exclusive.[29] For our
purposes, however, it is most significant that his new policy of official
recognition for Christianity polarized the division among Christians between rigorists and nonrigorists. As a licit religion, Christianity came
under the authority of the *pontifex maximus,* the head priest of all Roman
religion—a position that, as emperor, Constantine claimed.[30] Constantine
used his priestly authority to interfere in this internal dispute, attempting
to impose unity for the sake of *fortuna.*[31] The tools available to him to

achieve this end were legislation, money, and force. He used all of these aggressively.

Immediately after his defeat of Maxentius, and even before his conference with Licinius, Constantine undertook to subsidize several of the more important Christian bishops.[32] Among these was the bishop of Carthage, Caecilian, whose tenure was disputed by a rival, Majorinus.[33] Those who supported Caecilian were the less rigorist. Those who opposed him claimed that he had been consecrated by a *traditor* bishop, that is, one who had apostatized by surrendering copies of Scriptures to Diocletian's officials during the persecution, and that therefore his appointment was invalid. This group was more rigorist. Constantine's generosity made this dispute much more significant, since imperial recognition of one claimant would imply illicit status for the other. Constantine initially sided with Caecilian, naming him as bishop in his instructions to Anulinus, proconsul of Africa.[34] Majorinus petitioned for the dispute to be settled by other Latin-speaking bishops, a traditional—and internal—mechanism; Constantine agreed, but two successive councils found in favor of Caecilian. Majorinus, and his successor Donatus, insisted the affair be decided by Constantine himself, but without success, since an imperial investigation ruled that Caecilian's consecrating bishop had not in fact given over Scriptures during the persecution.

When Donatus and his supporters refused to accept even this third decision, Constantine attempted to suppress them with force, ordering arrests and forbidding them to meet together.[35] This, however, allowed the rigorist Donatists to invoke the traditional defenses against persecution, and, in their view, only further delegitimized Constantine's interference. They entrenched themselves ever deeper in the separatist, anti-imperial traditions we have already examined, and henceforth little could be done to reconcile them with the pro-imperial party.

But successful intervention in favor of Caecilian's party had the opposite effect on these less rigorist Christians. It established a significant precedent for imperial control of Christian communities, while obligating those communities to Constantine for his benefaction. This precedent implied a positive connection between the Roman Empire and Christianity, something that contradicted traditional views. Such a contradiction underscored the tension between Christians' daily experience and the ideal of renunciation still officially proclaimed. It was this implicit tension that Eusebius attempted to resolve with his revisionist writings.

Eusebius on Martyrdom

By 324, the date of completion of the first nine books of Eusebius's *Ecclesiastical History,*[36] much of traditional, separatist Christianity had already changed. Eusebius could no longer fully maintain separatist definitions of spiritual and corporeal. The cessation of persecution removed one of the strongest supports from the separatist tradition; without at least the possibility of martyrdom, renunciation became a much more difficult ideal to justify. Thus, for Eusebius to resolve the new tension between renunciation and an imperial demand for Christian unity, he must address the relationship between martyrdom and renunciation.

In the separatist tradition, as we have seen, martyrdom had many positive connotations. Martyrs imitated Christ by dying for him, following his teachings to the greatest possible extent. Martyrs linked the past of Christ's historical presence with both the present of the martyr and the future of Christ's return. Martyrs increased the chance for salvation for their whole community, and thus also linked Christian communities across the Empire. Eusebius neither can nor intends to deny these aspects of martyrdom, but he strongly downplays them in favor of a much more limited view of martyrdom solely as a defense against idolatrous demands.

This view is also part of the separatist tradition, as we have seen. But as part of that tradition, martyrdom as defense against idolatry implied a whole range of anti-imperial concepts. Idolatry had been seen as part of the corporeal category that Christians ideally sought to renounce; and so rejecting idolatry necessarily entailed rejecting the other two parts of the corporeal category: matter and empire. By limiting the significance of martyrdom *only* to defense against idolatry, Eusebius was able to suppress the anti-imperial implications.

Eusebius draws on the established, separatist texts for these martyrial accounts. Thus he can't simply rewrite the story to satisfy his rhetorical agenda. What he can do, however, is influence the reader's interpretation of the text with contextual clues. For example, in presenting Polycarp's famous martyrdom in book 4, Eusebius precedes his account with a lengthy discussion of theological disputes at that time, and the role that Polycarp played in them; and then he concludes with an assurance of Polycarp's orthodoxy.[37] He then immediately opens the martyrial account: "At this time, when the greatest persecutions were embroiling Asia, Polycarp ended his life by martyrdom."[38] So few years after the end of Diocletian's persecution, Eusebius's original audience would need little imagination to understand Polycarp's situation. Eusebius implies that Polycarp's orthodoxy singles him out for the enemies of Christ. Polycarp is being attacked not only because he is a Christian but because he is a true-thinking Christian. Thus, when Polycarp is faced with an angry mob in the arena, their demands for his conformity to pagan norms are now read without the connotations of Smyrna's *fortuna* (which we noted in chapter 2): "And when he was led forward, there was a great tumult. . . . The proconsul . . . endeavored to persuade him to deny [to swear by the *genius* of Caesar], saying, 'Have regard for your age,' and such like."[39] When we examined this confrontation in the context of second-century, separatist expectations, we noted that the text's main focus was Polycarp's salvific example in imitation of Christ. This example increased cohesion of the Christian community in the face of resentment for their renunciation of pagan norms, thus reinforcing that ideal. Avoiding idolatry, while of course important in itself, was more profoundly a means to maintain the ideal of renunciation. In Eusebius's presentation, the context invites the reader to focus on pagan resentment of Christian truth, not Christian separatism. Polycarp's refusal to offer the imperial sacrifice demanded of him, Eusebius implies, is thus prompted primarily by his desire to avoid idolatry. Avoiding idolatry is now the sole goal of Polycarp's actions. The famous martyr's view of the Empire is no longer negative.

This treatment of martyrdom is even more striking in Eusebius's accounts of the martyrs in Palestine during Diocletian's persecution, for which no well-established, separatist textual tradition existed. These accounts fill the whole of book 8 of the ten-book *Ecclesiastical History*. Eusebius explicitly claims that the purpose of the persecution was to make Christians commit idolatry.[40] Thus successful martyrs include not merely those who die to avoid sacrificing, but also those who avoid it in other ways:

> Thus one, while those around him pressed him on by force and dragged him to the abominable and impure sacrifices, was dismissed as if he had sacrificed, though he had not. Another, though he had not approached [the altars] at all, nor touched any polluted thing, left when others said that he had sacrificed. . . . Another . . . was cast aside as if dead, and a certain one lying on the ground was dragged a long distance by the feet and counted among those who had sacrificed. One cried out loudly and testified his rejection of the sacrifice. Another shouted that he was a

Christian . . . another protested that he had not sacrificed and never would. But they were struck in the mouth and silenced by a large band of soldiers who were drawn up for this purpose . . . and they were driven away by force, so important did the enemies of truth regard it, by any means to seem to have accomplished their purpose. But these things did not avail them against the holy martyrs.[41]

Here Eusebius can claim explicitly that the purpose of martyrdom is to avoid idolatry. The last three examples, who publicly display their Christianity, upheld the traditional ideal of separation. Yet Eusebius presents their martyrdoms only in terms of the sacrifice they were ordered to perform; the soldiers silence them, not for refusing to sacrifice, but for disrupting the illusion of unity in the Roman community. This interpretation of their martyrdom is reinforced in the first two examples, who escape without injury despite their refusal to sacrifice. By the standards of separatist Christianity, these two did not uphold fully the ideal of renunciation, because they did not proclaim their devotion to Christ explicitly. Yet Eusebius ignores this previously crucial difference in describing the scene; these two, for Eusebius, are no less martyrs than those who are beaten and killed.

Eusebius thus redefines the relationship between martyrdom and renunciation. Where the separatist tradition employed a wide range of meanings for martyrdom, which enforced the ideal of renunciation in a variety of ways, Eusebius limits martyrdom's significance to avoiding idolatry. This removes negative attitudes toward the Empire from martyrial contexts, and thus avoids implications of an anti-imperial tradition in martyrdom.

Eusebius on Asceticism

Eusebius's second task was to redefine the ideal of renunciation in daily life. We have examined how that ideal was interpreted by separatist Christians like Clement and Origen. Having as little as possible to do with the material world, these authors argued, trained one in the practice of renouncing, both as a preparation for literal martyrdom and as metaphorical martyrdom if literal opportunities never arose. Eusebius once again alters this tradition, placing Christian asceticism instead in the tradition of pagan philosophical asceticism.

For example, in describing Origen's living habits throughout his life, Eusebius relates:

> Then, for the good reason that he might never be in need of others' assistance, he disposed of all the volumes of ancient literature which he formerly so fondly cherished. . . . For many years he lived like a philosopher, putting aside everything that might lead to youthful lusts. All day long, his discipline was to perform labors of no light character, and most of the night he devoted himself to studying the sacred Scriptures. He persevered . . . in the philosophic life, at one time disciplining himself by fasting, at another measuring out time for sleep, which he was careful to take, never on a bed, but on the floor. And above all he considered that those sayings of the Savior in the Gospel ought to be kept, which exhort us not [to have] two coats nor to use shoes, nor indeed to be worn out with thoughts of the future.[42]

We have already seen what such practices signified in separatist tradition. Here, however, Eusebius describes Origen's motivations as independence from others and avoidance of "youthful lusts." Such physical discipline still imitates Christ, but there is no other hint of martyrdom in this renunciation of the world. Even when Origen's example inspires others to follow him, and when some of these students are accused of being Christians and martyred, the connection isn't drawn out by Eusebius: "By displaying such proofs of a philosophic life to those who saw him, he naturally stimulated a large number of his pupils to a like zeal. . . . By his agency these people received the faith of the divine word [Logos] in the depths of their soul, and were conspicuous at the persecution then taking place, such that some of them were arrested and perfected by martyrdom."[43] Origen's renunciation does help convince others of the rightness of Christianity; but once they accept this, their impetus to accept martyrdom is in no way the teaching of renunciation; instead, it is their faith in the Logos. Unlike in the separatist tradition, for Eusebius there is no continuing connection between the discipline enjoined by the ideal of renunciation and one's willingness to accept martyrdom.

Eusebius limits the significance of ascetic discipline to imitation of Christ. This limitation undermines the martyrial implications of renunciation. Since discipline is now dissociated from martyrdom, it also implies nothing about one's attitude toward the Empire. Among the pupils of Origen martyred on one occasion was a woman named Potamiaena. As she is being led away to execution, one of the soldiers guarding her is moved to pity, and later converts. He too is then martyred: "Not long afterwards, when Basilides was asked by his fellow-soldiers to swear [by the pagan gods] for some reason or another, he stoutly affirmed that swearing was absolutely forbidden in his case, because he was a Christian."[44] Basilides is then arrested and beheaded. In the separatist tradition, as we have seen, a soldier who converted to Christianity could not continue to be a soldier, and Tertullian and other separatist writers strongly encouraged martyrdom in such cases. Here, however, Eusebius implies strongly that Basilides would have been perfectly willing to continue serving as a soldier, had he not been required to perform an idolatrous act.

We have lost all sense of the connection between ascetic renunciation and martyrdom in this case. The causal chain from Origen to Potamiaena to Basilides, which in the separatist tradition would have provided such a wealth of material for expounding on the ideal of renunciation, is here obscured behind various ascetic and martyrial imitations of Christ. Eusebius is thus able to uphold the *forms* of renunciation, but to remove from ascetic practices the anti-imperial content supplied by separatist tradition. This "philosophical" asceticism is consonant even with military service, although not of course with idolatry.

Constantine as Parousia

The third idea that Eusebius revises is that of the Parousia. This is perhaps the most radical of the three; linking Constantine's conversion and the superficial Christianization of the Empire in the 320s and 330s to traditional expectations of Christ's return and rule over the transformed world was a masterstroke of political propaganda.

In the separatist tradition, Parousia implied political violence against Christians and a physical deterioration of the world, prior to Christ's return and spiritual renewal of the world (both physical and political). The natural disasters of the second half of the third century, from plagues to earthquakes, provided plenty of evidence of these physical aspects,[45] while Diocletian's persecution seemed tailor-made to fulfill expectations of anti-Christian violence. But in casting the recent past in this light, Eusebius must also supply a transformation of the world after these disasters.

This transformation, Eusebius claims, was the rise of Constantine. This claim is a radical departure from separatist tradition. Even in its eroded state in the late third century, the ideal of renunciation could not support so unambiguously positive an attitude toward the Empire. Eusebius, however, sidestepped the limitations of separatist traditions, by insisting that Constantine ruled not merely as a providential emperor (a traditional idea that could be contained within the ideal of separation),[46] but as a prophesied savior, directly inspired by the Logos:

> The only begotten Word [Logos] of God reigns [eternally] . . . the partner of his Father's kingdom; and [our emperor] beloved of him, who derives the source of imperial authority from above . . . has controlled the empire of the world for a long period of years. The Preserver [Logos] of the universe orders . . . the earth and the celestial kingdom consistent with his Father's will; even so our emperor whom he loves renders those whom he rules fit subjects . . . by bringing them to the . . . Savior. And as the Savior of mankind . . . drives far from his flock [corrupting spirits], so too his friend . . . subdues and chastens the adversaries of truth. . . . The pre-existent Word [Logos] . . . imparts to his disciples the seeds of true wisdom and salvation . . . [just as] our emperor, his friend, acting as interpreter to the Word, aims at recalling the whole human race to the knowledge of God.[47]

In this series of parallels between Constantine and the Logos, Eusebius emphasizes how the emperor emulates divine rulership. Just as God rules all things eternally and providentially, so too Constantine has been given a long rule in order to teach his Roman subjects salvific Christian truth; just as Christ defeats demonic enemies, Constantine has defeated paganism.

This claim must shock an audience still thinking about the Parousia in separatist terms, even heavily eroded. Separatist tradition clearly included expectations of rule by the Logos after the transformation of the world; but this rule specifically excluded imperial rule, as we have seen. When Christ came to rule in his own right, the Empire would become obsolete; there would be no more need for an emperor. Eusebius's claim that Constantine *is* in some sense the rule of the Logos thus departs radically from traditional expectations.

At the time of Constantine's death in 337, Eusebius pushed the parallels just described even further, presenting Constantine simultaneously as a martyr and as a heavenly emperor: "To whatever quarter I direct my view, whether to the east, or to the west, or over the whole world, or toward heaven itself, everywhere and always I see the blessed one yet administering the self-same empire . . . still . . . endowed with the same imperial dwellings and honors and praises. . . . But [then] I raise my thoughts to the arch of Heaven, and there contemplate his thrice-blessed soul in communion with God himself . . . shining in a refulgent robe of light . . . and honored with an ever-blooming crown."[48] In this description, the attributes of the dead emperor are precisely those normally awarded to martyrs. Constantine, of course, was a martyr in none of the traditional senses when he died in 337. Eusebius's presentation of him as a martyr justifies the claim that he "yet administers the self-same empire." Constantine as martyr imitates Christ, not in dying, but in ruling. Now in heaven, Constantine continues to serve as Christ's deputy, ruling the Empire in a still more godly way from his permanent throne. This role, strictly speaking, is Christ's; yet Constantine can fill this position because of his personal relationship with the Logos.

By thus linking Constantine's memory with Christ, the Logos, and martyrdom in these ways, Eusebius heavy-handedly implies that Constantine's rise and conversion fulfilled the spiritualizing transformation of matter promised at Christ's return. He thus re-creates the proper Christian life as pro-imperial, with Constantine himself as the God-given exemplar: "The lives of pious men . . . bear witness to posterity of the same; and . . . in our own days, Constantine . . . has appeared so clear an example of a godly life."[49] The godliness of Constantine's life consisted in his support for the Church and his concern to promote unity and orthodoxy; this he himself summed up in styling himself "bishop for external affairs" at the Council of Nicea in 325.[50] The martyrial allusions demand imitation of Constantine by Eusebius's audience, just as Constantine imitates Christ in Eusebius's portrayal.

Conclusions

Eusebius successfully resolved the tensions between imperial involvement in Christian communities after 312 and the traditional, separatist ideals of renunciation, martyrdom, and apocalyptic expectation. Separatist traditions had presented renunciation as the basis of Christian living in a pagan world, and martyrdom and apocalypse as the fulfillment of renunciation. Eusebius brilliantly recast renunciation as merely ascetic discipline, and limited martyrdom to a response against idolatry. Moreover, he overturned traditional expectations of Christ's Parousia, instead casting Constantine in the role of Logos-ruler. The imperial inclusion of Christianity as a licit religion afforded an opportunity to claim that paganism had been defeated as Christ's resurrection foretold; hence Constantine's Christian Empire (regardless of how superficially Christianized) fulfilled biblical prophecies of a new age of divine rule for the world.

The tone of Christian sources from the mid-fourth century is thus excessively triumphalist. But Eusebius's solution to the question of imperial interference in Christianity was not complete. The separatist tradition of rejecting material means to spiritual ends could not be ignored completely. A century after Eusebius, Augustine provided the lasting resolution of this dilemma with his two distinctions between church and state, and between use and enjoyment. With these tools in hand, the separatist ideal could finally be successfully rewritten, along the lines outlined by Eusebius. The middle way between excessive Donatist rigor and heterodox Manichaean dualism, embraced by Augustine in his own conversion and famously recounted in his *Confessions*, proved the enduring path.

Conclusions

Throughout this work, we have examined how the ideas of martyrdom, apocalypse, and separation from the Roman social and political world developed distinctively in the second and third centuries. These ideas formed a nexus of consistently anti-Roman sentiment, which supported a distinctive spiritual-corporeal dichotomy in Christianity of this period. The corporeal category included not just paganism for its idolatrous content, but also Roman imperial government and worldly society: Romanitas in its fullest social, political, religious, and material sense. Antithetically opposed to this is Christianitas, the spiritual pursuit of Christian salvation.

These ideas showed up consistently in all the main genres of early Christian writing. We expected to find them in martyrial texts, since these were the most directly opposed to pagan, Roman actions — namely, persecution of Christians for religious reasons. But we also found them in exegetical, disciplinary, and even apologetic texts, which are generally seen as not supporting anti-Roman ideas.

The coherence and ubiquity of the anti-Roman, separatist ideals in second- and third-century Christian writing therefore challenge us to see

Christianity in this period as different from that of later periods. Yet there
is nevertheless an essential continuity between the second century and the
fourth and later centuries. Constantine and Eusebius reinterpreted many
of the separatist ideas to suit the changing circumstances of the fourth
century, but they did not reinvent Christianity in its entirety. The changes
of the fourth century capitalized on possibilities created in the margins of
third-century Christian communities, among Christians less well socialized to the separatist ideals.

The distinctiveness of the second and third centuries should alert us
against anachronistic understanding of key terms and ideas. The influence of Eusebius and Augustine is especially difficult to avoid in early
Christianity, but we should strive to separate what comes before from its
later interpretations. Eusebius's key historical theme of reducing the significance of martyrdom to a simple defense against idolatrous demands of
pagan government is commonly read back into the period before Constantine. Augustine's compelling distinctions between church and state
and between use and enjoyment are likewise commonly read backwards
in time. Because we know what the dichotomy between spirit and matter
means in the fourth century and later (largely on the basis of these two
authors), it is easy to assume that this meaning was current prior to the
fourth century.

This work has shown that this assumption does not in fact fit the
separatist period. Because the social and political contexts of Christianity
changed noticeably after 312, it is necessary to recognize the achievement
of fourth-century thinkers in that period, without applying them to earlier
centuries. The ways in which ideas about martyrdom, apocalypse, and
separation were connected before Constantine were not the same as those
of Eusebius or Augustine. Eusebius unhinges martyrdom from its apocalyptic and separatist links, while Augustine liberates social and political
ideas from their demonic, corporeal associations.

The boundaries between spirit and matter were therefore not the same
in the two periods. For Eusebius and Augustine, society and politics could
be Christianized at some level, and therefore could be attached to the
spiritual category in some way. For Christians before Constantine, however, society and politics could not be removed from an essentially demonic (because idolatrous) influence, and were therefore embedded in
the (negative) corporeal category.

In two other significant areas, we should avoid anticipating the fourth century in earlier Christianity. First, it is especially easy to minimize the level of expectation of apocalyptic violence after the middle of the second century, when apologetic texts start appearing in large numbers. The most common view of historians, that apologetic texts are addressed to non-Christian audiences, includes the assumption that Christians *wanted* to support and be part of Roman society. The reduction of apocalyptic expectations is usually included in this argument, as proof of attitudes toward Romans that are, if not positive, at least neutral. But this work has shown how the consistency of anti-Roman attitudes, even in apologetic texts, makes it difficult to believe that a Roman audience was targeted by this genre. If Christians do not seek to support Roman norms, then there is no reason to infer from apologetic texts that apocalyptic expectations were waning throughout the second and third centuries. We thus saw how other genres, especially disciplinary works, supported the separation of Christians from Roman society on apocalyptic grounds throughout the whole period ending in 312. There was some attenuation of apocalyptic expectations over time, but primarily in the levels of violence associated with the Parousia; the expected nearness of that event attenuated very little.

Second, we should avoid marginalizing the significance of martyrdom in this period. Eusebius gives a much more limited view of what martyrdom achieves than his predecessors. If we accept Eusebius's ideas in the earlier period, we fail to understand why martyrdom was accepted as commonly as it was, and how martyrdom could be conceived of as bringing the Parousia closer. In particular, the Christological and community-building meanings of martyrdom were central to separatist conceptions of the spiritual-corporeal dichotomy. These crucial connections were consistently used during the second and third centuries to promote not only martyrdom itself but the whole nexus of separatist, anti-Roman ideas. These connections occur in every genre from martyrial to apologetic, and their frequency underscores their centrality.

Yet despite the distinctiveness of the separatist period, we must also recognize the continuity between the third and the fourth centuries. Most profoundly, the daily experience of the community of Christians in liturgy and prayer remained intact. The purpose and structure of Christian communities was not fundamentally altered by Constantine's conversion. Salvation was still understood and pursued in much the same way. Although martyrdom was no longer literally available (at least for most Christians most of the time), the traditional extensions of metaphorical martyrdom into discipline ("dying to the world") could still be used. Indeed, asceticism in the fourth century became the preeminent form of metaphorical martyrdom, on the model of hermits like Antony of Egypt. Antony's example was vigorously promoted by as powerful and high-profile a bishop as Athansius of Alexandria, and influential for such dominant western figures as Ambrose of Milan and Augustine. Many of the Christological and community-building ideas that had been attached to literal martyrdom could remain attached to asceticism, even as Eusebius's reinterpretation of martyrdom as defense against idolatry limited their traditional relevance.

On this basis, the cult of the saints expanded rapidly from the late fourth century on, expanding the criteria for sanctity from literal to metaphorical martyrs. The salvific intercession of martyrs was thus expanded to nonmartyrs, and in so doing was strengthened by including increasingly worldly forms of miraculous intervention. This increasing worldliness could be accepted, however, because Augustine's redefinition of the spiritual category now included material objects and actions with ultimately spiritual ends.

Again, the sacramental life of Christian communities seems to have remained intact. The three earliest clearly defined sacraments (baptism, Eucharist, and ordination) had many of the same Christological and community-building aspects as separatist martyrdom. In the second and third centuries, these aspects reinforced the separateness of Christian communities from Romans, as in the case of the martyr Perpetua and her pagan father. The fourth-century shift from literal to metaphorical martyrdom may paradoxically have strengthened the sacramental meaning of these events, by realigning distinctiveness in opposition to idolatry rather than Romanitas. In other words, Christianity may have become more popular in the fourth century because the demand that converts—still the larger proportion of the Christian population—give up their non-Christian past became implicit (separate from demons) rather than explicit (separate from Romans).

Moreover, the idea of grace in the sacraments was certainly strengthened by the loss of literal martyrdom. We have seen how the Christological significance of martyrdom included the presence of Christ suffering in and with the martyr. In the second and third centuries, this most crucial moment of identification with Christ overshadowed "ordinary" moments of the same grace. But once martyrdom becomes primarily metaphorical, this "extraordinary" idea of grace is downplayed, both by the absence of literal martyrdom and by the extenuation in time of disciplinary motifs. Thus sacramental grace (Christ's presence in the sacraments, and by extension in those receiving the sacraments) emerges in the fourth century as the most important aspect of Christian ritual.

Finally, the salvific purpose of Christians in following Christ did not change in the fourth century. The redefinition of martyrdom by Eusebius, and of the spiritual-corporeal dichotomy by Augustine, were secondary to the more crucial content of Christianity. The salvation of individuals and communities from sin, the understanding of the person and role of Christ, and participation in sacraments all require *some* definition of spirit and matter. But that definition can shift over time according to the needs of the community for effective cohesion and identity.

The significance of this study, then, is not the fact itself that these categories changed over time, but rather how and why those changes occurred. The pressure on Christianity in the first century, especially after the destruction of the Temple in 70, to define itself clearly both within and against the scriptural story of God's salvific purpose in human history forced a more radical interpretation of spiritual-corporeal definitions than Paul himself created for Christians in the 40s and 50s. This radical nexus effectively limited pro-Roman attitudes to acceptance of Roman conversion, and linked paganism, Roman imperial government, and demonic control of the material world as the essential elements of the corporeal category. In the late third century, the rapid expansion of Christian communities beyond the ability of bishops to enforce traditional norms created new stresses, which were exploited by Constantine and Eusebius to create a pro-imperial Christianity. This exploitation ultimately redefined traditional separatist categories of martyrdom and the spiritual-corporeal dichotomy in enduring ways.

These changes thus developed for particular reasons at particular moments. In each case, the root cause of change was adaptation to new circumstances. The core content of Christianity was not fundamentally altered by these changes, yet the modes of understanding that the community used to identify itself, and to cohere against the conflicting demands of nonmembers (especially nonmembers who were family members of converts), did significantly change. This flexibility within Christianity to find successful forms of community identity and cohesion in changing circumstances without altering core meaning must be considered one of the fundamental causes of its long-term success.

Notes

Abbreviations

ANF	*Ante-Nicene Fathers*
CSEL	*Corpus Scriptorum Ecclesiasticorum Latinorum*
NCE	*New Catholic Encyclopedia*
NPNF	*Nicene and Post-Nicene Fathers*
PG	*Patrologia Graeca*, ed. Migne
PL	*Patrologia Latina*, ed. Migne
SC	*Sources Chrétiennes*

ONE: The Origins of Separatist Christianity

1. Jgs 4:1–23.
2. Origen, *Homilies on Judges*, 5.4–6; C. Mondésert, ed., *Sources Chrétiennes*, 430 vols. (Paris: Edition du Cerf, 1968–98), 389:138–47. Henceforth *SC*.
3. E.g., Rom 13:1–7; this passage is described in detail below, chapter 3.
4. E.g., 1 Cor 2:6–10.
5. Augustine, *On Christian Doctrine*, 1.2–5, esp. 1.3; *On the City of God*, bks. 9, 14, 18.
6. Wayne A. Meeks, *The First Urban Christians: The Social World of the Apostle Paul* (New Haven: Yale University Press, 1983), 85–94, 183–89.
7. *Homilies on Numbers*, 2.1.3; *SC* 415:56–59; see below, chapter 2.
8. Augustine, *On the City of God*, 14.11; Paul, Rom 1:21–32.
9. Paul, Rom 2:1–16.
10. Augustine, *On the City of God*, 14.13.
11. Ibid., 15.5.
12. James C. VanderKam, "Messianism and Apocalypticism," in *The Encyclopedia of Apocalypticism, Vol. 1: Origins of Apocalypticism in Judaism and Christianity*, ed. John J. Collins (New York: Continuum, 1998), 222–23.
13. Jacob Neusner, "Varieties of Judaism in the Formative Age," in *Jewish Spirituality from the Bible through the Middle Ages*, ed. Arthur Green, vol. 13 of *World Spirituality: An Encyclopedic History of the Religious Quest* (New York: Crossroad, 1994), 194–95.
14. E.g., Justin Martyr, *First Apology*, 31.

15. Yarbro Collins, "The Book of Revelation," in *Encyclopedia of Apocalypticism*, ed. Collins, 409–10. This opened a debate within Christianity on the nature of the spiritual kingdom *after* Christ's return; see chapter 6.

16. These might be called "Early Apostolic" (33–70) and "Later Apostolic" (70–135), to distinguish them from the separatist period. On the events of these years and their significance for Christian and Jewish development, see S. G. Wilson, *Related Strangers: Jews and Christians 70–170 C.E.* (Minneapolis: Fortress Press, 1995).

17. On the growing division between the followers of James and of Paul before 70, see Norbert Brox, *Kirchengeschichte des Altertums*, trans. J. Bowden, *A Concise History of the Early Church* (New York: Continuum, 1996), 4–7.

18. Neusner, "Varieties," 193.

19. Ibid., 190–95. It is of course a gross oversimplification to identify all accommodationist Jews as Pharisees; both Sadducees and Hellenistic Jews outside Palestine also desired accommodation, for different reasons. Nevertheless, as Neusner claims, it seems clear that the Pharisees were most instrumental in uniting the various Diaspora communities behind the emerging rabbinical ideal in the second and third centuries.

20. Neusner, "Varieties," 183–86.

21. R. Eisler, *Iēsoûs basileùs où basileúsas*, 2 vols. (Heidelberg, 1929–30), trans. A. H. Krappe, *The Messiah Jesus and John the Baptist* (London, 1931), and more recently, S. G. F. Brandon, *Jesus and the Zealots* (New York: Scribner, 1967), argue strongly for the conclusion that Jesus was, if not a Zealot leader, at least an agitator against Roman rule in Palestine. Oscar Cullmann, *The State in the New Testament* (New York: Scribner, 1956), rejects such precise conclusions but admits that some observers may have interpreted Jesus's message along those lines, and that Zealots were among Jesus's followers. I prefer to follow Cullmann in this (even though I disagree with his conclusions on some points), because he is more cautious in treating the extremely difficult and confused evidence for the events surrounding Jesus's condemnation and death. Eisler and Brandon are convincing that, after Jesus's death, stories about him acquired messianic elements (both political and apocalyptic), which would influence Christianity, Judaism, and Gnosticism after the destruction of the Temple in 70; but their reconstruction of Jesus's historical role before his death is only one possible solution to the evidentiary problems.

22. The most detailed treatment of persecution in the Roman Empire is W. H. C. Frend, *Martyrdom and Persecution in the Early Church: A Study of Conflict from the Maccabees to Donatus* (Oxford: Blackwell, 1965).

23. The role and nature of apologetic material is discussed in detail below, chapter 7.

TWO: The Ideal of Separation after A.D. 135

1. Such is the division for Clement of Alexandria; see below.

2. For an excellent and succinct summary of the varieties of pagan ritual in

Roman government, see Joyce Salisbury, *Perpetua's Passion: The Death and Memory of a Young Roman Woman* (New York: Routledge, 1997), 9–32; for more extensive coverage, see F. Millar, *The Emperor in the Roman World* (Ithaca, N.Y.: Cornell University Press, 1977); J. Bayet, *Histoire politique et psychologique de la religion romaine* (Paris: Payot, 1957); J. Beaujeu, *La Religion romaine à l'apogée de l'Empire* (Paris: Société d'Edition "Les Belles Lettres," 1955).

3. For more on Christians' inability to separate pagan ritual and Roman governmental forms, see below, chapter 7.

4. See below, chapters 4 and 5.

5. Tertullian, *To the Martyrs*, 2; J. P. Migne, ed., *Patrologiae Cursus Completus, series Latina,* 217 vols. (Paris: Garnier, 1844–64), 1:695–96; henceforth *PL.* The Christians addressed in this tract, as some have speculated, may have been Perpetua, Felicity, and their companions, who were martyred, probably in Carthage, and almost certainly during Tertullian's own lifetime. See H. Musurillo, *The Acts of the Christian Martyrs: Introduction, Texts, and Translations* (Oxford: Clarendon, 1972), xxvi; Hippolyte Delehaye, *Les Passions des martyrs et genres littéraires,* 2d ed., *Subsidia Hagiographica* 13B (1921; Brussels: Société des Bollandistes, 1966), 50–51.

6. On the demands of military service, see A. H. M. Jones, *The Later Roman Empire* (Oxford: Blackwell, 1964), 61ff, esp. 65. Because taxation in labor, including military service, was calculated according to the head-tax (*capitatio*), independent of the land-tax (*jugatio*), urban Christians were not exempt from this claim by the state.

7. On this event, see E. F. Osborn, *Tertullian, First Theologian of the West* (Cambridge: Cambridge University Press, 1997), 84–85; D. Rankin, *Tertullian and the Church* (Cambridge: Cambridge University Press, 1995), 69–70; R. Braun, "Christianisme et pouvoir impérial," in *Approches de Tertullien: Vingt-six études sur l'auteur et l'oeuvre, 1955–1990,* ed. R. Braun (Paris: Institut d'Etudes Augustiniennes, 1992), 64; T. D. Barnes, *Tertullian: A Historical and Literary Study* (Oxford: Clarendon Press, 1971), 132–35.

8. Mt 26:52.

9. 1 Cor 6:1–11.

10. Mt 5:38–42; Lk 6:28–29.

11. Tertullian, *On the Crown*, 11. See M. Sordi, *I cristiani e l'impero romano,* trans. A. Bedini, *The Christians and the Roman Empire* (Norman, Okla.: University of Oklahoma Press, 1986), 74–90; J. Danielou, *L'Eglise des premiers temps: des origines à la fin du troisième siècle* (1963; Paris: Editions du Seuil, 1985), 102; R. M. Grant, *Augustus to Constantine: The Thrust of the Christian Movement into the Roman World* (New York: Harper and Row, 1970), 88–96; Peter Brown, *The Rise of Western Christendom: Triumph and Diversity, A.D. 200–1000* (Cambridge, Mass.: Blackwell, 1994), 23; Frend, *Martyrdom,* 397–406.

12. *Acts of Maximilian,* 2.1; Musurillo, *Acts of the Christian Martyrs,* 244, 246.

13. On the isolation of Maximilian's martyrdom, see Musurillo, *Acts of the Christian Martyrs,* xxvii; Delehaye, *Passions,* 77–81. According to the current evidence, only one other military martyr conceivably dates from between 261

and 303, namely Marcellus, whose conversion, which resulted in death after he publicly threw off his military insignia (*balteus*), took place during his period of service. Musurillo accepts the date of 298 for this event, but Delehaye more cautiously refuses positively to claim Marcellus's martyrdom for the period before 303.

14. On the significance of late-third-century toleration, as distinct from accommodation, between Christians and pagans, see chapters 5 and 8.

15. On the imperial cult, see J. H. W. G. Liebeschuetz, *Continuity and Change in Roman Religion* (Oxford: Clarendon, 1979), 64–70; G. Bowersock, *Augustus and the Greek World* (Oxford: Clarendon, 1965), 117ff; S. R. F. Price, *Rituals and Power: The Roman Imperial Cult in Asia Minor* (Cambridge: Cambridge University Press, 1984); Ramsay MacMullen, *Paganism in the Roman Empire* (New Haven, Conn.: Yale University Press, 1981), 100–105; A. Wardman, *Religion and Statecraft among the Romans* (Baltimore, Md.: Johns Hopkins University Press, 1982), 81ff; D. R. Edwards, *Religion and Power: Pagans, Jews, and Christians in the Greek East* (New York: Oxford University Press, 1996), 7–17, 92ff.

16. For a detailed discussion of this relationship, see chapter 3.

17. *Passion of Polycarp*, 8.2; Musurillo, *Acts of the Christian Martyrs*, 8. See Wardman, *Religion and Statecraft*, 127–31; Grant, *Augustus to Constantine*, 86–87; Barnes, "Pagan Perceptions of Christianity," in *Early Christianity: Origins and Evolution to 600 A.D.*, ed. I. Hazlett (London: Abingdon, 1991), 237; Price, *Rituals and Power*, 42.

18. On the persecution in Asia Minor in the mid-second century, see Frend, *Martyrdom and Persecution*, 268ff; Sordi, *Christians*, 70–72; Barnes, "Pagan Perceptions," 234. The suggested dates for Polycarp's death range from the late 140s to the late 170s, though most scholars generally accept a date about 156/57; see Musurillo, *Acts of the Christian Martyrs*, xiii; T. D. Barnes, "Pre-Decian *Acta Martyrum*," *Journal of Theological Studies*, n.s., 19 (1968): 512–13.

19. On mob violence in persecutions of Christians in the separatist period, see Frend, *Martyrdom and Persecution*, 270–73; Grant, *Augustus to Constantine*, 86–87; Barnes, "Pagan Perceptions," 237.

20. Swearing by the emperor's *genius* or *túchē* was an integral part of the imperial cult, a display of both spiritual and political support for the Empire and its leader.

21. *Passion of Polycarp*, 5; Musurillo, *Acts of the Christian Martyrs*, 6. Polycarp receives a vision that the pillow on which he is sleeping bursts into flames; he understands that he is to be burnt alive.

22. On the persecution of Valerian, see Frend, *Martyrdom and Persecution*, 413–27.

23. *Passion of Marian and James*, 11.7–8. Musurillo, *Acts of the Christian Martyrs*, 208. See Sordi, *Christians*, 6, 108; Frend, *Martyrdom*, 391ff.

24. For the significance of *gloria* in martyrdom, see chapter 4.

25. On the Providential activity of God in martyrdom, see chapter 5.

26. This attitude toward divine support for the enemies of God as instruments in achieving a desired end has both Old and New Testament parallels. We have already noted Sisera's divine sanction as a punitive foreign conqueror of Israel; another important thread of this theme in separatist Christian literature is the claim of culpability of the Jews for Jesus's death; see *New Catholic Encyclopedia*, 17 vols. (New York: McGraw-Hill, 1967), 1:634, *sub verbo* "Anti-Semitism: Christian Antiquity" (henceforth *NCE*).

27. The context of apologetic literature, and its relation to martyrial texts, will be discussed in greater detail in chapter 7.

28. Justin Martyr, *First Apology for the Christians*, 11. See Grant, *Augustus to Constantine*, 51; Hugo Rahner, SJ, *Kirche und Staat im Frühen Christentum* (Munich, 1961), trans. L. D. Davis, SJ, *Church and State in Early Christianity* (San Francisco: Ignatius Press, 1992), 4–13; C. Munier, *L'Apologie de Saint Justin philosophe et martyr* (Fribourg: Editions Univérsitaires de Fribourg, 1994), 2–3.

29. There are two ways of reading this phrase: either the judges are sitting just below the peak of the *civitas*, i.e., just below the Augustus in rank, or the peak of the *civitas* on which they sit is no peak at all.

30. The participle *operata*, from *operor*, implies ritual service to the Roman gods in the carrying out of an action.

31. Tertullian, *Apologetic*, 1. See Salisbury, *Perpetua*, 71–72.

32. On the official duties of *judices* in the late second century, see P. Garnsey, *Social Status and Legal Privilege in the Roman Empire* (Oxford: Clarendon, 1970), 251ff; P. Garnsey and R. P. Saller, *The Roman Empire: Economy, Society, and Culture* (Berkeley: University of California Press, 1987), 20ff; Millar, *Emperor*, 228–51.

33. This will be more fully established in chapters 4 and 5.

34. The role of imperial authorities in Christian sources in carrying out the divine Providential plan has already been alluded to; see also chapter 3.

35. 1 Tm 4:10.

36. Clement of Alexandria, *Exhortation to the Nations*, 9. See Sordi, *Christians*, 90; Edwards, *Religion and Power*, 44–45; W. H. Wagner, *After the Apostles: Christianity in the Second Century* (Minneapolis: Fortress Press, 1994), 182–84.

37. Though Arnobius died about 327, Jerome implies that his *Disputation* was composed prior to 311: see *NCE* 1:843, and Michael Bland Simmons, *Arnobius of Sicca: Religious Conflict and Competition in the Age of Diocletian* (Oxford: Clarendon, 1995). Simmons (6ff) insists that Arnobius should not be considered an apologist, because his text was never intended to be used as part of an argument between Christians and non-Christians; I do include his *Disputation* as an apology, for precisely the same reason: it was a text intended for a Christian audience, to display the incompatibility of Christian and pagan beliefs. See chapter 7.

38. Arnobius, *Disputation against the Nations*, 2.76. See Frend, *Martyrdom*, 456.

39. Simmons, *Arnobius of Sicca*, 4–9.

40. Jerome, *Chronicon sub anno*, 326–27 (text cited in Simmons, p. 6, n. 31, without reference to edition); *PL* 27:675–76 (where *sub anno* 329–30).

41. That is, in addition to enjoyment in heaven.

42. That is, living in the world.

43. Tertullian, *On Spectacles*, 28.

44. Salisbury, *Perpetua*, 122–29.

45. Tertullian, *On Spectacles*, 29.

46. Clement of Alexandria, *Instructor*, 2.1.

47. On the indifference of the soul to states of the body, see also Clement's *Stromata*. "It is worthy to admire the Stoics, who said that the soul is in no way acted upon by the body, not for evil by disease, nor for good by health; but they said that these two things [i.e., body and soul] are [mutually] indifferent."

48. Clement of Alexandria, *Instructor*, 2.1.

49. On this expectation, see chapter 6.

50. Clement of Alexandria, *Instructor*, 2.2.

51. Ibid. and following.

52. Ibid., 2.3.

53. Danielou, *L'Eglise*, 185.

54. Cyprian, *On the Lapsed*, 12.

55. Ibid., 5.

56. Salisbury, *Perpetua*, 159–61; Wardman, *Religion and Statecraft*, 139.

57. *Zábulos* or *Zábolos*, for *Diábolos*, the devil.

58. Commodianus, *Instructions against the Nations*, 57, vs. 1–9, 12–13, 19–20; see Hippolyte Delehaye, *Sanctus: Essai sur le culte des saints dans l'Antiquité, Subsidia Hagiographica* (Brussels: Société des Bollandistes, 1927), 17:109–11.

59. Tertullian also describes the circus events in much the same "diabolical" terms in *On Spectacles*: "Therefore, if it is established that the complete preparation of the shows consists in idolatry, then without doubt it will be judged that the oath of our renunciation (*renuntiatio*) in the laver [i.e., of baptism] pertains even to the shows, which are given over to the devil and to his pomp and angels, precisely because of idolatry" (4).

60. See *NCE* 2:496–501, *sub verbo* "Bible VI: Exegesis"; *NCE* 5:707, *sub verbo* "Exegesis."

61. Rom 7:14.

62. Origen, *Homily on Numbers*, 1.1.3; *SC* 415:32–35. Origen's homiletic material survives only in Rufinus's Latin translation, made in the early fifth century: *NCE* 10:768.

63. Origen, *Homily on Leviticus*, 16.1; *SC* 287:262–65.

64. Origen, *Homily on Judges*, 7.1; *SC* 389:172–75. See R. A. Markus, *The End of Ancient Christianity* (Cambridge: Cambridge University Press, 1990), 101–2.

65. Tertullian, *On Prayer*, 2.

66. See Mt 13:3, 18:1–5, both quoted immediately preceding this passage.

67. Mt 18:3: "And he said, 'I tell you the truth, unless you change and become like little children, you will never enter the kingdom of heaven.' "

68. Clement of Alexandria, *Instructor,* 1.5; see Edwards, *Religion and Power,* 74–75, 86–87.

69. Origen, *Treatise on Prayer,* 17.

70. 2 Cor 6:14–15.

71. Rom 6:12.

72. Col 3:5.

73. See Gal 5:22; Jn 15:8,16.

74. See Jn 3:8; 2 Cor 6:16.

75. Origen, *Treatise on Prayer,* 25.

76. On the social-prestige value of exclusivity and of very difficult ideals in attracting adherents to Christianity, see R. Stark, *The Rise of Christianity: A Sociologist Reconsiders History* (Princeton: Princeton University Press, 1996), 163ff, 179ff.

77. 1 Cor 2:15.

78. Nm 2:2.

79. 1 Cor 14:40.

80. Mt 6:33.

81. Mt 6:33.

82. Origen, *Homily on Numbers,* 2.1.3; *SC* 415:56–59: see G. E. Caspary, *Politics and Exegesis: Origen and the Two Swords* (Berkeley: University of California Press, 1979).

83. Methodius, *Banquet of the Ten Virgins,* 3.8.

84. Ibid., 1.1.

85. Ibid., 1.5: "And so what did the Lord, the truth and the light, undertake when he descended [i.e., from Heaven]? When he had adorned himself [i.e., with a human body], he guarded his flesh uncorrupt in virginity, so that we also, if we would be according to the likeness of God and of Christ, could aspire to honor virginity. For the likeness of God flees corruption [i.e., sin]."

86. Ibid., 8.4; see Peter Brown, *The Body and Society: Men, Women, and Sexual Renunciation in Early Christianity* (New York: Columbia University Press, 1988), 181–86. Brown's insightful connections among virginity, marriage, and developing monastic traditions are correct, but Methodius also uses the concept of virginity in a broader sense (that of renunciation).

87. Irenaeus, *Against Heresies,* 3.25.1. The "certain Gentiles" mentioned here include pagan philosophers like Plato and his followers, who, Irenaeus implies just below the passage cited here, understood the nature of God and his relationship to man and the world better than the Gnostics, even though lacking the advantage of revelatory knowledge; but Irenaeus refers especially to converts to Christianity from philosophical disciplines, such as (most famously) Justin Martyr, whose conversion he himself described in his *First Apology;* see chapter 7.

88. Athenagoras, *Embassy for Christians*, 24. For more on this demonization of matter, see chapter 7; for the salvation of matter after Christ's return, see chapter 6.

89. Living in the world is part of the "testing" which all Christians must undergo; see chapter 4.

90. Tertullian, *Against Marcion*, 1.24.

91. Elaine Pagels, *The Gnostic Gospels* (New York: Random House, 1979); Pheme Perkins, *The Gnostic Dialogue: The Early Church and the Crisis of Gnosticism* (New York: Paulist Press, 1980), 145–94.

92. Hippolytus of Rome, *Refutation of All Heresies*, 10.29. On the significance of suffering as an imitation of Christ, see chapter 4.

93. For more on the salvation of matter with the Parousia, see chapter 6.

THREE: Separatist Christianity and the Roman Empire

1. It does, however, show some early changes visible in attitudes toward Jews; see M. Simon, "The Bible in the Earliest Controversies between Jews and Christians," in *The Bible in Greek Christian Antiquity*, ed. P. M. Blowers (Notre Dame: University of Notre Dame Press, 1997), 49–68.

2. Mt 22:15–21, and parallel passages at Mk 12:17, Lk 20:25. I have used the Greek text established by E. Nestle, and the English translation of the New International Version (NIV). Quoted here from Alfred Marshall, ed., *The Interlinear KJV-NIV Parallel New Testament in Greek and English.* (Grand Rapids, Mich.: Zondervan Publishing, 1975), 72–73.

3. On the Pharisees, see *NCE* 11:252, *sub verbo* "Pharisees"; G. Stemberger, *Jewish Contemporaries of Jesus: Pharisees, Sadducees, Essenes* (Minneapolis, Minn.: Fortress Press, 1995); M. Pelletier, *Les Pharisiens: Histoire d'un parti méconnu* (Paris: Edition du Cerf, 1990); J. Neuser, ed., *The Pharisees and Other Sects,* trans. A. W. Mahnke, vol. 2 of *Origins of Judaism* (New York: Garland, 1990).

4. On the Zealots, see *NCE* 14:1114, *sub verbo* "Zealots"; Neuser, *Pharisees and Other Sects;* Brandon, *Jesus and the Zealots;* M. Hengel, *Die Zeloten: Untersuchungen zur jüdischen Freiheitsbewegung in der Zeit von Herodes I bis 70 n. Chr.* (Leiden: E. J. Brill, 1961), trans. D. Smith, *The Zealots: Investigations into the Jewish Freedom Movement in the Period from Herod I until 70 A.D.* (Edinburgh: T. & T. Clark, 1989).

5. Augustine discusses this passage in several places: *Sermon*, 40.10 (P. Schaff, ed., *A Select Library of Nicene and Post-Nicene Fathers of the Christian Church*, 28 vols. [1886; Grand Rapids, Mich.: Eerdmans, 1978], vol. 6; henceforth *NPNF*); *Tractates on John*, 40.9, 41.2 (*NPNF 7*); *Commentary on the Psalms*, 4.8, 58.8 (*NPNF 8*). In each case, Augustine stresses the parallel between the image of Caesar on the coin and the image of God in humans; no literal meaning about taxation is considered. See Marc Meslin, *Le Christianisme dans l'Empire romaine* (Paris: Presses Univérsitaires de France, 1970), 101–2; Rahner, *Church and State*, 3–4.

6. Mt 6:24.

7. Mt 6:24.

8. Jn 8:34.

9. Irenaeus, *Against Heresies*, 3.8.1.

10. Tertullian, *On the Crown*, 12.

11. Lk 12:48.

12. Justin Martyr, *First Apology*, 17.

13. The significance of this claim will be developed in chapter 7.

14. Justin Martyr, *First Apology*, 5.

15. *doûloi*, literally "slaves."

16. 1 P 2:13–21: Marshall, *Interlinear New Testament*, 688–89.

17. A. J. Malherbe, *Social Aspects of Early Christianity* (Baton Rouge: Louisiana State University Press, 1977), 52–53, 67; Danielou, *L'Eglise*, 43, 92; Grant, *Augustus to Constantine* 48.

18. Tobit 4:10.

19. Polycarp of Smyrna, *Epistle to the Philippians*, 10.

20. As noted by Irenaeus, *Against Heresies* 3.25.1.

21. Tatian, *Address against the Greeks*, 4.

22. Oscar Cullmann, *State in the New Testament*, 55–63, warned against taking the first verses (vs.1–7) of this passage out of the context of the following verses.

23. Marshall, *Interlinear New Testament*, 474–77.

24. For more on this, see chapter 6.

25. Origen, *Against Celsus*, 7.65.

26. Irenaeus, *Against Heresies*, 5.24.1–3.

27. Tertullian, *On Spectacles*, 5.

28. Origen, *Against Celsus*, 1.1.

29. *Passion of the Scillitan Martyrs*, 6.

30. This claim is relevant because of the demands for obedience to the state in matters that do not involve transgressing divine commandments, as described in the first three sections of this chapter.

31. See Musurillo, *Acts of the Christian Martyrs*, 87; Barnes, "Pre-Decian *Acta Martyrum*," 519; Delehaye, *Passions*, 47–49.

32. On the use of imperial titulature to refer to God in separatist Christianity, see Delehaye, *Sanctus*, 4ff, 33ff, 60ff.

33. *Passion of the Thessalonican Saints*, 3.4, 4.1. Musurillo entitles this text "The Martyrdom of Saints Agapê, Irenê, and Chionê at Saloniki."

FOUR: Martyrdom and Salvation

1. In addition to the citations noted within the following passages, see the books of Daniel and Maccabees, esp. Dn 3:1–30, 6:1–28; 1 Mc 1:41–64, 2:29–38; and 2 Mc 6:1–7:42.

2. Frend, *Martyrdom*, 44, 90–91; Rahner, *Church and State*, 5.

3. While these ideas are not restricted to martyrial literature, this is naturally enough their main genre for expression; martyrial texts therefore make up the bulk of primary evidence for this chapter.

4. Origen, *Homily on Judges*, 7.2. Other instances in these homilies of this theme are Homily 2.3–5; 3.1–2, 5; 4.3–4; 7.1.

5. Jgs 6:1. This is also related to the idea of martyrdom as punishment for sin.

6. Jgs 7:4. Literally, "I [i.e., God] will purify." The three hundred are chosen by how they drink water at a river, which Origen interprets as a symbol for baptism. The "choice" by which the three hundred are separated from the rest of Gideon's followers is both a test—did they drink this way or that?—and a purification. The two ideas are often inextricable one from the other; on martyrdom as purifying punishment, see below.

7. *Homily on Judges*, 9.2.

8. Dt 13:3; compare Mt 22:37, Dt 6:5.

9. Origen, *Exhortation to Martyrdom*, 6.

10. Tertullian, *On Flight*, 2.

11. Tertullian, *Antivenom against the Gnostics*, 6.

12. On the common image of Christian martyrs as "athletes," see for example *Martyrdom of Carpus, Papylus, and Agathonice*, 35; *Martyrs of Lyons*, 17, 36.

13. Dt 13:3.

14. Ecclesiasticus 27:6.

15. Rom 5:2–5.

16. Cyprian, *To Fortunata*, 9.

17. Apollonius, third fragment, "Concerning Montanism," quoted from A. Roberts and J. Donaldson, eds., *The Ante-Nicene Fathers: Translations of the Writings of the Fathers Down to AD 325*, 10 vols. (New York: Scribner, 1926, 1885), vol. 8.; henceforth *ANF*. See Eusebius, *Ecclesiastical History*, 5.18.

18. Tertullian, *On Flight*, 4.

19. See for example Epistle 10.

20. Eps. 5 through 43 (*Corpus Scriptorum Ecclesiasticorum Latinorum*, 91 vols. [Vienna: Austrian Academy of Learning, 1866–1998], 3.2.478–597; henceforth *CSEL*) all date from the period during which Cyprian remained in hiding because of the Decianic persecution; see L. Duquenne SJ, *Chronologie des lettres de S. Cyprien: le dossier de la persécution de Dèce*, vol.54 of *Subsidia Hagiographica* (Brussels: Société des Bollandistes, 1972).

21. Eps. 2.1, 3, 6. G. F. Diercks, ed., *Novatiani Opera*, vol. 4 of *Corpus Christianorum, series latina* (Turnholt: Brepols, 1972). Novatian's condemnation of Cyprian and others who hide rather than face martyrdom is not strong in this letter—he is trying to make common cause with Cyprian in favor of episcopal control over the potential readmission of the lapsed; the two have not yet begun to disagree over how that readmission should be handled by bishops—but Novatian nevertheless makes it clear that martyrdom is by far the most desirable state, and those who seek to avoid it at least risk, if not actually lose, their hope of salvation.

22. Cyprian, Eps. 5–7, 10–19 (*CSEL* 3.2:478–526) are particularly exhortative; the much smaller Dionysian epistolary corpus, being preserved only by fragmentary citations in Eusebius's *Ecclesiastical History*, does not in its present state include a similarly explicit exhortation to martyrdom.

23. The primary institutional means available was a period of penitential exclusion from communion, which in effect reduced the transgressor back to the level of the catechumens. This was intended to cope with minor individual transgressions; as a system, it was stretched to its limits in the 250s and 260s, following the persecutions of Decius and Valerian, with the large numbers of apostates who sought readmission. This means did not, strictly speaking, expunge sin as baptism had done for the convert; forgiveness remained the unique purview of God.

24. On the sacrament of baptism in the separatist period, see P. F. Bradshaw, *The Search for the Origins of Christian Worship: Sources and Methods for the Study of Early Liturgy* (London: Society for Promoting Christian Knowledge, 1992); E. C. Whitaker, *Documents of the Baptismal Liturgy* (London: SPCK, 1970); A. Benoît, *Le Baptême Chrétien au Second Siècle: la théologie des pères* (Paris: Presses Univérsitaires de France, 1953).

25. Origen, *Exhortation to Martyrdom*, 30.

26. Martyrdom was sometimes considered superior to baptism, for unbaptised martyrs were still considered saved. See, for example, the martyr Primolus: "His confession of faith but a few months before baptized him" (*Martyrdom of Montanus and Lucius* 2.2).

27. Tertullian, *On Flight*, 5.

28. Cyprian, *On the Lapsed*, 5.

29. Eps. 1.3, 3.2. Diercks, *Corpus Christianorum, series latina*, 4:201–2, 248–49. Note that in the view even of the extremely rigorist Novatian, apostates have not lost all hope of salvation, because God can still forgive the sin of idolatry for the truly repentant; but the Church, either through bishops or through confessors, cannot. For examples of martyrdom purging previous apostasy, see Tertullian, *On Flight* and *The Martyrs of Lyons and Vienne*.

30. *On the Lapsed*, 18, 33, 35; *Epistle 17*.

31. The topography of the afterlife was still extremely vague in the separatist period; ideas of "heaven" and "hell" generally meant only proximity to or exclusion from the divine. J. LeGoff, *La Naissance du Purgatoire* (Paris: Gallimard, 1981), trans. A. Goldhammer, *The Birth of Purgatory* (Chicago: University of Chicago Press, 1984), 52ff.

32. Ps 115:15.

33. Ps 50:19.

34. Wis 3:4–8.

35. Cyprian, *Epistle 6.2*.

36. Particularly exemplary are the visions of Perpetua while in prison and awaiting her martyrdom: *Martyrdom of Perpetua and Felicity*, 4, 7, 8, 10. As a general martyrial phenomenon, these visions are beyond the scope of the present work; they have recently been examined in detail by Salisbury, *Perpetua*, 92ff.

37. The Latin *adlocutionem* is here ambiguous. Its root meaning, from *adloquor,* is "a speaking to"; hence the two main extended meanings, "exhortation" and "consolation." Both are appropriate here. The martyrs are exhorted by the example of Christ's suffering, and consoled by the reward Christ's suffering has gained them, namely Heaven.

38. *Martyrdom of Montanus and Lucius,* 7.

39. Most clearly in Frend, *Martyrdom,* 14–15, 83–91, 196–98, 349; Delehaye, *Origines.*

40. Mt 10:22.

41. Mt 10:25.

42. Tertullian, *Antivenom against the Gnostics,* 9.

43. 1 P 4:12–14.

44. Cyprian, *To Fortunata,* 9.

45. Jn 12:25; Cyprian reads *animam* for the Greek *psychēn,* usually translated to English as "life." See Marshall, *Parallel New Testament,* 310–11.

46. Mt 10:28.

47. Rom 8:16–17.

48. Rom 8:18.

49. Cyprian, *Epistle 6.2.*

50. Although the antecedent for *autoû* is here grammatically ambiguous between Christ and Polycarp, contextually it can only be Christ, for two reasons; one, Polycarp cannot imitate himself in doing something for the first time, and therefore the audience cannot "also" become Polycarp's imitators; and second, the quotation from Philippians, here in apposition to "we," the audience, refers to Christ, not Polycarp.

51. Phil 2:4.

52. *Passion of Polycarp,* 1.2.

53. Heb 12:2.

54. Mt 10:34.

55. Origen, *Exhortation to Martyrdom,* 37.

56. A fourth possibility originally open, that of prophecy, visions, glossolalia, and other "spiritual gifts," was largely contained by developing episcopal authority in the early second century, a development against which some Christians reacted; see Robin Lane Fox, *Pagans and Christians* (New York: Knopf, 1989), 404–10.

57. On Eucharist in the separatist period, see R. C. D. Jasper and G. J. Cuming, *Prayers of the Eucharist: Early and Reformed* (Collegeville, Minn.: Liturgical Press, 1992); C. W. Dugmore, "The Study of the Origins of the Eucharist: Retrospect and Reevaluation," in *Studies in Church History II,* ed. G. J. Cuming (London: Nelson, 1985), 1–18; W. Rordorf, ed., *The Eucharist of the Early Christians,* trans. M. J. O'Connell (New York: Pueblo, 1978).

58. Lk 12:50.

59. Jn 5:6.

60. See Jn 19.

61. Tertullian, *On Baptism,* 16.

62. Lk 12:50.
63. Origen, *Homily on Judges*, 7.2.
64. Ps 115:15.
65. Cyprian, *Epistle 10.2–3*.
66. *Letter of the Churches of Lyons and Vienne*, 1.23.

FIVE: The Martyr and the Community

1. Arnobius, *Disputation against the Nations*, 2.76.
2. *Thessalonikan Martyrs*, 2.
3. Justin Martyr, *First Apology*, 8. See also Grant, *Augustus to Constantine*, 87–89; Meslin, *Christianisme*, 94.
4. Clement in the *Stromata* never uses this word to refer to the collection of quasi-Christian sects known to modern scholars under the rubric of Gnosticism, but rather to his ideal of the "true Christian" who knows rightly the wisdom of Christ as set forth in the Gospels.
5. Clement of Alexandria, *Stromata*, 4.21. This passage is specifically mentioned by Grant, *Augustus to Constantine*, 200–201, as one which proves that martyrdom is important to separatist Christianity *only* as a response to persecution; compare Delehaye, *Sanctus*, 109–10; R. A. Markus, *Christianity in the Roman World* (New York: Scribner, 1974), 46.
6. The dating of the extant text of the *Martyrdom of Apollonius* is uncertain; Musurillo, *Acts of the Christian Martyrs* (xiii–xv), thinks it likely that the redaction is fourth-century or later. Barnes, "Pre-Decian *Acta Martyrum*," 520–21, accepts the first ten sections of the extant text as authentic, and the remainder only as a later addition. Delehaye, *Passions*, 87, and *Origines* 263, considers the whole text to be of probable third-century origin. The text clearly is intended to serve an apologetic function within the Christian community, which lends weight to its earlier dating.
7. *Martyrdom of Apollonius*, 26–27.
8. *Martyrdom of Justin*, A5.
9. *Martyrdom of Montanus and Lucius*, 4.
10. See 2 Cor 3:18.
11. *Martyrdom of Marian and James*, 3.
12. For other examples of this common motif in martyrial literature, see *Martyrdom of Polycarp*, 1; *Martyrdom of Carpus, Papylus, and Agathonice*, 42–44; *Martyrdom of Apollonius*, 47; *Martyrdom of Perpetua and Felicity*, 1.
13. Tertullian demonstrates this injunction on the basis of Old Testament passages against idolatry, citing Ex 20:2, 22–23; Dt 6:4, 12; Dt 11:27; Dt 12:2–3, 30; Dt 13:1, 6, 16; Dt 27:15; Lv 25:55, 26:1; Ps 135:15; Ps 115:4.
14. Tertullian here advances several passages regarding the Israelites' sojourn in the desert after their flight from Egypt: Ex 32; Nm 25:1; Jgs 2:8–13, 20–21.
15. Tertullian, *Antivenom against the Gnostics*, 2–5.
16. Tertullian, *On Spectacles*, cited above, chapter 2.

17. These reasons were discussed in chapter 4: martyrdom is a test of faith, a punishment for sin, and a sure path to salvation, while simultaneously being an imitation of Christ's own violent death.

18. *Acts of Perpetua and Felicity*; see Salisbury, *Perpetua*, 70–71.

19. For other examples of this explicit demand, see *Martyrdom of Polycarp*, 1; *Martyrdom of Apollonius*, 47; *Martyrs of Lyons*, 2.2–4; *Martyrdom of Pionius*, 22; *Martyrdom of Cyprian*, 5; *Martyrdom of Montanus and Lucius*, 1, 14; *Martyrdom of Maximilian*, 3.2; *Thessalonikan Martyrs*, 1.

20. *Martyrdom of Marian and James*, 1.

21. The theme of apocalyptic expectations will be treated fully in chapter 6.

22. Tertullian, *Apologetic*, 1; see Salisbury, *Perpetua*, 71–72; Grant, *Augustus to Constantine*, 51, 88–89.

23. *Acts of the Scillitan Martyrs*, 14–15.

24. *Acts of Cyprian*, 4–5.

25. *Martyrdom of Montanus and Lucius*, 6.

26. Cyprian, *Epistle 12.1*; Hartel, *CSEL* 3.2:502–3.

27. While it is not possible to argue that all or even a majority of separatist Christians accepted in practice the exhortations to martyrdom being taught by Christian leaders, the fact that any Christians at all were willing to accept martyrdom demonstrates the successful perpetuation of the ideal. Moreover, those who did not accept martyrdom but still wished to be Christians universally accepted that some form of penitential action was required for their failure to live up to Christian norms, as the debate between Cyprian and Novatian in the aftermath of the Decianic persecution proves.

28. See below, chapter 7. The consistency of the Roman accusations against Christianity as countercultural or subversive of culture is striking.

29. *Acts of Perpetua and Felicity*, 15. One notes also the number of separatist *Acta* that commemorate groups of martyrs as opposed to a single martyr: of the twenty-eight texts accepted by Musurillo as authentic to the separatist period, fifteen commemorate groups of martyrs; of the remaining thirteen, four commemorate bishops (distinguished by their rank) and five commemorate military martyrs (incapable of being part of a group due to their unique circumstances). Thus only four of twenty-eight texts commemorate "ordinary" Christians who were martyred in isolation from a group.

30. On the social significance of Felicity's martyrdom, and of the role of her pregnancy in it, see Salisbury, *Perpetua*, 116. This excellent treatment does not, however, emphasize sufficiently the extent to which the communal nature of martyrial salvation was operating here. Salisbury emphasizes (rightly) the links among the group of martyrs and Felicity's disappointment at the prospect of dying apart from them, but does not develop how the martyrs fulfill expectations for the rest of the Carthaginian Christian community.

31. *Acts of Perpetua and Felicity*, 5.2.

32. Literally, "whose throats are cut in sacrifice."

33. Rv 6:9.

34. Origen, *Homily on Numbers*, 10.2.1–2.

35. On the dating of Origen's homilies, see R. Greer, *Origen* (New York: Paulist Press, 1979), 4.

36. Eusebius, *Ecclesiastical History*, 6.1–3, relates an account of Origen's life, including his early zeal for martyrdom (frustrated by his mother) and his ascetic practices. Greer, *Origen*, 4–5, emphasizes rather Origen's desire to support both conversions and the developing institutions of Christianity.

37. *Martyrdom of Montanus and Lucius*, 1.

38. Delehaye, *Sanctus*, 123.

39. Ibid., 123ff. On the Christian version of the traditional Roman *refrigerium*, which was an annual graveside meal celebrated by the family or community of a deceased to emphasize the continued presence of the deceased, see ibid., 135ff.

40. Salisbury, *Perpetua*, 156ff, esp. 165.

SIX: Apocalyptic Expectations

1. E.g., Grant, *Augustus to Constantine*, 48–52; Rahner, *Church and State*, 15–17.

2. Danielou, *L'Eglise*, 86–88, attributes apocalypticism to the mystical imagination of Gnostics from the late second century on; Sordi, *Christians*, 5–6, attributes it to the disciplinary fervor and martyrial commitment of the Montanists.

3. 1 Thes 4:15–17; see also Mt 24:34: "This generation [*genea*] will certainly not pass away until all these things have happened."

4. Rv 22:12,14–15.

5. Tt 3:5.

6. Tertullian, *On Modesty*, 1.

7. Sordi, *Christians*, 5–6. Barnes, *Tertullian*, Introduction, assigns this work to the first or second decade of the third century, by which time Tertullian was openly attached to the Montanist movement.

8. Irenaeus, *Against Heresies*, 5.1.3.

9. The whole first chapter of Book 5 concerns Adam's salvation as a prerequisite for any salvation. Although Adam transgressed the will of God in the garden, still the fact that he did not flee or lie about it (like Cain) indicates some level of repentance, which in turn implies his salvation once Christ had made that possible by dying on the cross.

10. Mt 24:42.

11. Clement seems here to read *kurion* for *kairon*; see *ANF* vol. 2.

12. Rom 13:11–12.

13. Clement of Alexandria, *Stromata*, 4.22.

14. This is much different from Eusebius's identification of the Parousia with Constantine's conversion; see chapter 8.

15. 1 Cor 15:20–26, 28.

16. This is the transformation of the corporeal nature of matter to a spiritual nature; see below.

17. On Paul's identification of "death" with "pride," see 1 Cor 5:2–5; Gal 5:19–25; Eph 2:1–7; Phil 3:18–21.

18. Rv 6:9–11.

19. See Rv 14:1–5.

20. Rv 7:9, 13–14.

21. See Rv 12:17–13, 17. As was noted in chapter 3, separatist Christians could characterize Roman authority as both demonic and illegitimate.

22. Hermas, *Pastor*, bk. 1, vis.3, ch. 1–2.

23. Danielou, *L'Eglise*, 86–87, considers the *Shepherd* to be "apocalyptic" only in a mystical, gnostic-influenced sense. In other respects, he argues, it reflects very early attenuation of apocalyptic expectations and increasing desire to win toleration from the Roman state.

24. The "gifts" are those of the Holy Spirit; the "promises," those of salvation.

25. Tertullian, *Apologetic*, 48.

26. Ibid., 50; see Wagner, *Apostles*, 170, 200–1; Edwards, *Religion and Power*, 42.

27. See above, where it is shown how in the same chapter Clement describes this "striving after perfection" as renunciation and preparation for martyrdom. Complete perfection is only reached through martyrdom, on the example of Christ, but willingness for martyrdom without opportunity for martyrdom also allows salvation.

28. 2 Cor 6:3–4.

29. Clement is not here supporting a pro-imperial Christianity, but rather defending martyrdom as a defense against idolatry; this is consistent with all that we have already seen.

30. 2 Cor 7:1.

31. 2 Cor 7:9.

32. Eph 4:11–13.

33. Clement of Alexandria, *Stromata*, 4.21; see Markus, *End of Ancient Christianity*, 71; Brown, *Body and Society*, 124–25.

34. Origen, *On Prayer*, 25.1.

35. Phil 3:13.

36. Especially 2 Cor 6:14–16, noted above by, for example, Clement, and again below by Origen.

37. 1 Cor 15:24.

38. Origen, *On Prayer*, 25.2.

39. Origen, *On Prayer*, 26.3.

40. 2 Thes 1–12.

41. Dn 7:23–26.

42. Origen, *Against Celsus*, 2.50; see also 6.45–46.

43. Ibid., 1.8.

44. See for example Irenaeus, *Against Heresies*, 3.23.7; Cyprian, *Exhortation to Martyrdom*, 8. Cyprian collects many of the same biblical passages in favor of martyrdom as part of the expected violence accompanying Christ's return as Origen (see above).

45. On the mid-third-century plagues and Christians' reactions to them, see Stark, *Rise of Christianity*, 73ff.

46. Cyprian, *On Mortality*, 2.

47. Ibid., 8, 9.

48. *Quaestio* is used here in its technical sense of judicial investigation under torture. The implication is that Christians who question the rightness of Christian dogma persecute God.

49. Arnobius, *Disputation against the Nations*, 2.78.

50. See above, Arnobius, *Disputation*, 2.76.

51. Mt 17:1–8; Mk 9:2–8; Lk 9:28–36.

52. *oikía toû skēnous*, literally "home of the tabernacle."

53. *oikía*, parallel with the previous clause.

54. 2 Cor 5:1–4.

55. Rv 22:1–4.

56. Rv 21:22–23.

57. This anti-Jewish theme is typical of the period between the two Jewish revolts, when Christianity began to define itself in opposition to Pharisaic Judaism; see chapter 1.

58. 2 Cor 12:9.

59. Lk 5:31.

60. 1 Cor 12:23.

61. Lk 19:10.

62. Ez 18:23.

63. Dt 32:39.

64. Tertullian, *On the Resurrection of the Flesh*, 9.

65. This same argument is employed by Origen, in *On First Principles*, to support the eventual repentance and salvation of Satan. For God to remove any part of his creation from himself permanently, without any hope of restoration, reduces God's perfect mercy and justice.

66. Methodius, *Banquet of the Ten Virgins*, 3.6.

67. Irenaeus, *Against Heresies*, 5.2.2.

68. Ibid., 5.2.3.

69. Jn 2:19.

70. 1 P 2:5; see also Hermas, *Shepherd*, where the vision of the Church as a tower of stones being built (and almost finished) recalls the same text.

71. 1 Cor 12:27.

72. Ez 37:11.

73. Origen, *Commentary on John*, 10.20.

SEVEN: Apologetic Evidence

1. On positive attitudes toward martyrdom in apologetic literature, see above, chapter 2.

2. Roman success was thus an effect of Roman piety. See Jones, *Later Roman Empire*, 940–41; Lane Fox, *Pagans and Christians*, 80, 98; MacMullen, *Paganism in the Roman Empire*, 7, 109, 141.

3. E.g., P. Keresztes, *Imperial Rome and the Christians, from Herod the Great to about 200 A.D.* (Lanham, Md.: University Press of America, 1989), 129; Rahner, *Church and State*, 9–10; Danielou, *L'Eglise*, 95–102; Edwards, *Religion and Power*, 44.

4. Grant, *Augustus to Constantine*, 89.

5. Athenagoras, *Embassy*, 24; see Cyril Richardson, ed. and trans., *Early Christian Fathers* (New York: Collier, 1970), 293–96; Brown, *Body and Society*, 66.

6. Theophilus, *To Autolycus*, 1.2; see Grant, *Augustus to Constantine*, 95.

7. Tatian, *Oration against the Greeks*, 13; see Richardson, *Fathers*, 24–25; Brown, *Body and Society*, 91–94.

8. 1 Cor 3:18–19.

9. Origen, *Against Celsus*, 1.13.

10. Melito of Sardis, *Apology*. Fragments only of this work from a Syriac version are extant; these are translated into Latin by J. P. Migne, ed., *Patrologia Cursus Completus, series Graeca*, 161 vols. (Paris: Garnier, 1857–66), 5:1229–30; henceforth *PG*.

11. Cyprian here means "accidents" in the philosophical sense of things that are not pertinent by nature of the subject.

12. Cyprian, *To Demetrian*, 18.

13. See above, chapter 4.

14. The best recent treatment of the various charges against Christians is S. Benko, *Pagan Rome and the Early Christians* (Bloomington: Indiana University Press, 1984).

15. Benko, *Pagan Rome*, 9ff, 156ff.

16. Theophilus, *To Autolycus*, 3.4; see Grant, *Augustus to Constantine*, 95.

17. Arnobius, *Disputation against the Nations*, 1.27; see especially Sordi, *Christians*, 123ff, where the anti-Roman evidence in Arnobius's apology is dismissed by a verdict of Montanist sympathies.

18. Justin Martyr, *Second Apology*, 4, 7. This sort of "address" to pagan audiences in the apologetic literature is always addressed to emperors and other high Roman officials by name; I believe that this is merely a rhetorical stance, and one that in fact heightens the illegitimacy of Roman use of authority, because, if the Roman officials were indeed just, they would clearly listen and cease unjust persecutions.

19. On the culpability of Christians "by the name" and the rescripts of Hadrian and Trajan on this topic, see Benko, *Pagan Rome*, 4ff; Sordi, *Christians*, 59ff; Keresztes, *Imperial Rome*, 103ff.

20. Athenagoras, *Embassy*, 2; see Meslin, *Christianisme*, 72; Keresztes, *Imperial Rome*, 141–42.

21. It is possible that the Christians denounced to Pliny the Younger in Bithynia about 112 were accused under such a law; see Benko, *Pagan Rome*, 10–11. Pliny's subsequent investigations certainly included judicial examination by torture of two Christian slaves, to discover the content of the Christians' nocturnal meetings, which indicates Pliny's concern that Christians, like some other groups with secret or nocturnal meetings, might be politically subversive.

22. Origen, *Against Celsus*, 1.1. A. Momigliano, *On Pagans, Christians, and Jews* (Middletown, Conn.: Wesleyan University Press, 1987), 151ff, argues that Origen is deriding only anti-Christian activity by the otherwise providential Roman government as comparable to Scythian barbarity.

23. On the Scythians, see H. Wolfram, *Geschichte der Goten* (Munich: C. H. Beck'sche Verlagsbuchhandlung, 1979), trans. T. J. Dunlap, *History of the Goths* (Berkeley: University of California Press, 1988).

24. Minucius Felix, *Octavius*, 25.

25. Jones, *Later Roman Empire*, 32–35, 71–76; Benko, *Pagan Rome*, 4; R. MacMullen, *Christianizing the Roman Empire, A.D. 100–400* (New Haven: Yale University Press, 1984), 16.

26. Tertullian, *Apologetic*, 25.

27. Ibid., 10.

28. Melito of Sardis, *Apologia*. On this and the previous passage, see Grant, *Augustus to Constantine*, 91–92; Sordi, *Christians*, 168–72; Keresztes, *Imperial Rome*, 134ff, 154ff.

29. Melito's *Apology* was written about 175; within the previous generation, well-remembered persecutions had taken place in Rome (Justin), Lyons, and Smyrna (Polycarp).

30. See above, chapter 3.

31. Cyprian, *To Demetrian*, 5.

32. Cyprian makes this claim explicitly in his *On Mortality*.

33. On the irremissibility of idolatry, see, for example, Tertullian, *On Idolatry*, 6–7.

34. Tertullian, *Apologetic*, 30, 32.

35. Theophilus, *To Autolycus*, 11.

36. Athenagoras, *Embassy*, 37.

37. E.g., Meslin, *Christianisme*, 94; Grant, *Augustus to Constantine*, 95–96; Edwards, *Religion and Power*, 42–44; Markus, *Christianity in the Roman World*, 91–98; Richardson, *Early Christian Fathers*, 293–96; Jaroslav Pelikan, *The Christian Tradition*, 5 vols. (Chicago: University of Chicago Press, 1971–84), 1:129–30.

38. The expectation of the Parousia became embedded in baptismal creeds as an article of faith during the separatist period; see Philip Schaff, *The Creeds of Christendom*, 6th ed. (New York: Harper, 1919).

39. This idea has not been fully expounded in this work, but see above, the

discussion of Cyprian's *On Mortality* in chapter 6. See also the treatises on prayer by Tertullian (*PL* 1:1249–1304), Cyprian (*PL* 4:519–44), and Origen (*PG* 11:415–562), where this idea is more clearly expressed; Commodianus, *Instructions*, 79: *Tu sane si nudus benefactis Deum adores* (You adore God rightly if devoid of benefits); and D. A. Lopez, "Holy Man and Holy Relic in the Fourth Century: Healer or Exorcist?" *Publications of the Medieval Association of the Midwest* 5 (1998): 85–95.

40. E.g., Mt 5:44; Rom 12:20. It is beyond the scope of this study to examine the objects of Christian prayer in this and other contexts; I hope to devote another study to that topic in the near future.

41. Nor do I think it tenable to argue that these apologetic sources were *also* or perhaps *sometimes* intended to be read by pagan audiences. In the first place, the anti-Roman sentiments are too strongly expressed, even in apologetic, for that literature to be intentionally aimed at Romans—unless apologetic is intended to *provoke* persecution by insulting and angering Romans, which seems unlikely. In the second place, as the quotation from Origen in chapter 5 (note 34) shows, separatist Christian leaders did not generally desire a reduction in persecution: persecution was good, because it created martyrs. The one problem with persecution was that it also created apostates; but this, I believe, only corroborates my thesis about the marginal Christian audience of apologetic literature. In the third place, there is absolutely no evidence that any pagan Roman official ever read an apologetic text, was ever swayed to avoid or halt a persecution because of them, or ever converted to Christianity because of apologetic arguments.

42. Lit., "those entirely untasting the faith of Christ"; I read this as hyperbolic reference to the catechumenate, parallel to the following clause. On hyperbole and other rhetorical devices in Origen, see C. Blönnigen, *Der griechische Ursprung der jüdisch-hellenistischen Allegorese und ihre Rezeption in der alexandrinischen Patristik*, vol. 59 of *Europäische Hochschulschriften, Reihe XV, Klassische Sprachen und Literatur* (Frankfurt am Main: P. Lang, 1992); A. Quacquarelli, *Retorica patristica e sue istituzioni interdisciplinari* (Rome: Città nuova, 1995).

43. Rom 14:1.

44. Origen, *Against Celsus: Preface*, 6.

45. Justin Martyr, *Second Apology*, 12.

46. Justin's *Second Apology* opens with an account of three recent Roman martyrs; see Musurillo, *Acts of the Christian Martyrs*, 38–41.

47. Heb 12:22–23.

48. Mt 25:41, 46.

49. Clement of Alexandria, *Exhortation against the Nations*, 9.

50. Aristides, *Apology*, 15. Quoted from the Greek fragments, edited by Carlotta Alpigiano, *Aristide di Atene: Apologia* (Florence: Nardini, 1988), 114.

51. Tertullian, *To Scapula*, 2.

52. Minucius Felix, *Octavius*, 14.

EIGHT: Constantine, Eusebius, and the Triumph of Christianity

1. Jones, *Later Roman Empire*, 71–76; Lane Fox, *Pagans and Christians*, 592–608.

2. On Donatism, the best work remains W. H. C. Frend, *The Donatist Church* (1952; Oxford: Clarendon, 1985). On Montanism, Christine Trevett, *Montanism: Gender, Authority, and the New Prophecy* (Cambridge: Cambridge University Press, 1996), provides excellent, subtle analysis. On asceticism, see Marilyn Dunn, *The Emergence of Monasticism: From the Desert Fathers to the Early Middle Ages* (Oxford: Blackwell, 2000); David Brakke, *Athanasius and the Politics of Asceticism* (Oxford: Clarendon, 1995); Susanna Elm, *Virgins of God: The Making of Asceticism in Late Antiquity* (Oxford: Oxford University Press, 1994); Philip Rousseau, *Ascetics, Authority, and the Church in the Age of Jerome and Cassian* (Oxford: Oxford University Press, 1978).

3. Brox, *Concise History*, 40–41.

4. Ibid., 41; Benko, *Pagan Rome*, 4; Jones, *Later Roman Empire*, 35.

5. On Decius's death on campaign against the Goths, and Valerian's capture by Persians, see Jones, *Later Roman Empire*, 34.

6. On Valerian's son Gallienus's disinterest in persecution and repression of revolts after Valerian's end in 260, see Lane Fox, *Pagans and Christians*, 553. On the emperors of the 270s, see Jones, *Later Roman Empire*, 35–36.

7. Lane Fox, *Pagans and Christians*, 556; Sordi, *Christians*, 116, 123; Grant, *Augustus to Constantine*, 172.

8. Stark, *Rise of Christianity*, 73–75.

9. Sordi, *Christians*, 85–90, and Grant, *Augustus to Constantine*, 90–95, both argue strongly for the presence of Christians in the army and bureaucracy as early as about 180.

10. See above, esp. chapter 2.

11. See, for example, Dionysius of Alexandria's letters throughout books 6 and 7 of Eusebius's *Ecclesiastical History;* Peter of Alexandria's *Canonical Epistle* (*ANF* 6); or Gregory of Pontus's *Canonical Letter* (*PG* 10:1020A ff; see also Lane Fox, *Pagans and Christians*, 528–42).

12. Lane Fox, *Pagans and Christians*, 597.

13. Paolo Mastandrea, "Passioni di martiri donatisti (BHL 4473 e 5271)," *Analecta Bollandiana* 113 (1995): 39–88.

14. Jones, *Later Roman Empire*, 76.

15. Lane Fox, *Pagans and Christians*, 597–98.

16. Jones, *Later Roman Empire*, 76–77.

17. What follows is only a rapid sketch of Constantine's rise. For a thorough treatment of this subject, see Michael Grant, *Constantine the Great: The Man and His Times* (New York: Scribner, 1993); A. H. M. Jones, *Constantine and the Conversion of Europe* (New York: Collier, 1962), and *Later Roman Empire*, 77–111.

18. On Constantius and his role in Diocletian's Tetrarchy, see Jones, *Later Roman Empire*, 38–42.

19. Ibid., 74.

20. Grant, *Constantine the Great*, 16–17, 134.

21. Bede, *Ecclesiastical History of the English People*, 1:7; Gildas, *On the Ruin of Britain*.

22. On Albanus's martyrdom and *cultus*, see Philip Thornhill, "St. Albanus and the End of Roman Britain," *Mankind Quarterly* 41, no. 1 (Fall 2000): 3–43; "The British Martyrs, Aaron and Julius," *Mankind Quarterly* 39, no. 4 (Summer 1999): 467–508.

23. For Constantine's campaign and propaganda against Maxentius, see Grant, *Constantine the Great*, 31–40.

24. On Licinius's career, see Jones, *Constantine and the Conversion of Europe*, 76–80; *Later Roman Empire*, 79–80.

25. On the wars between Constantine and Licinius, see Grant, *Constantine the Great*, 40–48.

26. Eusebius, *Ecclesiastical History*, 10.5.1–12; Lactantius, *On the Deaths of the Persecutors*, 48.

27. Quoted from translation by Grant, *Constantine the Great*, 157.

28. Ibid., 39–41.

29. In addition to note 17 above, see Lane Fox, *Pagans and Christians*, 609ff; Markus, *Christianity in the Roman World*, 87ff; R. MacMullen, *Constantine* (New York: Dial Press, 1969); A. Momigliano, ed., *The Conflict of Paganism and Christianity in the Fourth Century* (Oxford: Clarendon, 1963); S. L. Greenslade, *Church and State from Constantine to Theodosius* (London: SCMP, 1954); T. D. Barnes, *Constantine and Eusebius* (Cambridge, Mass.: Harvard University Press, 1981).

30. Jones, *Later Roman Empire*, 93; *Constantine and the Conversion of Europe*, 89.

31. John Meyendorff, *Imperial Unity and Christian Divisions* (Crestwood, N.Y.: St. Vladimir's Seminary Press, 1989), 16, 32–33; Grant, *Constantine the Great*, 81–85, 162.

32. Jones, *Later Roman Empire*, 80–81.

33. Ibid., 81–82; Grant, *Constantine the Great*, 164–67.

34. *Ecclesiastical History*, 10.7.

35. Grant, *Constantine the Great*, 167. Much of Constantine's anti-Donatist legislation survived to be included in the Theodosian Code, especially in book 16; see Clyde Pharr, *The Theodosian Code and Novels, and the Sirmondian Constitutions: A Translation with Commentary, Glossary, and Bibliography* (1952; New York: Greenwood Press, 1969).

36. T. D. Barnes, "The Editions of Eusebius's *Ecclesiastical History*," reprinted in *Early Christian and the Roman Empire* (London: Variorum, 1984); but see Lane Fox, *Pagans and Christians*, 607–8, for the view that the work does not predate 312/13.

37. *Ecclesiastical History*, 4.12–14.

38. Ibid., 4.15.1.

39. Ibid., 4.15.18.

40. Ibid., 8.2.4–5.
41. Ibid., 8.3.2–4.
42. Ibid., 6.3.8–11.
43. Ibid., 6.3.13
44. Ibid., 6.5.5.
45. For example, Cyprian, *On Mortality,* and Arnobius, *Disputation,* both assert that natural disasters like these should be taken as evidence of the imminent Parousia.
46. This idea reflects Paul's positive attitudes toward the Empire as divine institution, and surfaces primarily in the apologetic literature during the separatist period.
47. Eusebius, *Oration in Praise of Constantine,* 2.1–4; cited from *NPNF,* series 2, vol. 1.
48. Eusebius, *Life of Constantine,* Preface, 1.2.
49. Ibid., 1.3.
50. Ibid., 4.24.

Select Bibliography

I. REFERENCE WORKS

Alpigiano, C. *Aristide di Atene: Apologia.* Florence: Nardini, 1988.
Brenton, L. C. L. *The Septuagint with Apocrypha: Greek and English.* 1851. London: Hendrickson Publishing, 1995.
Corpus Christianorum, series latina. 176 vols. Turnholt: Brepols, 1954–65.
Corpus Scriptorum Ecclesiasticorum Latinorum. 91 vols. Vienna: Austrian Academy of Learning, 1866–1998.
Lampe, G. W. H., ed. *Patristic Greek Lexicon.* Oxford: Clarendon, 1961.
Lewis, C. T., and C. Short, eds. *A Latin Dictionary.* 1879. Oxford: Clarendon, 1989.
Liddell, H. G., and R. Scott, eds. *Greek-English Lexicon.* 9th ed. Oxford: Clarendon, 1940.
Marshall, A., ed. *The Interlinear KJV-NIV Parallel New Testament in Greek and English.* Grand Rapids, Mich.: Zondervan Publishing, 1975.
Migne, J. P., ed. *Patrologia Cursus Completus, series Graeca,* 161 vols. Paris: Garnier, 1857–66.
———, ed. *Patrologiae Cursus Completus, series Latina,* 217 vols. Paris: Garnier, 1844–64.
Mondésert, C., ed. *Sources Chrétiennes.* 430 vols. Paris: Edition du Cerf, 1968–98.
Musurillo, H. *The Acts of the Christian Martyrs: Introduction, Texts, and Translations.* Oxford: Clarendon Press, 1972.
Pharr, Clyde. *The Theodosian Code and Novels, and the Sirmondian Constitutions: A Translation with Commentary, Glossary, and Bibliography.* 1952. New York: Greenwood Press, 1969.
Roberts, A., and J. Donaldson, eds. *The Ante-Nicene Fathers: Translations of the Writings of the Fathers Down to A.D. 325.* 10 vols. 1885. New York: Scribner, 1926.
Schaff, P. *Creeds of Christendom.* 6th ed. New York, 1919.
Schaff, P., ed. *A Select Library of the Nicene and Post-Nicene Fathers of the Christian Church.* 28 vols. 1886. Grand Rapids, Mich.: Eerdmans, 1978.
New Catholic Encyclopedia. 17 vols. New York: McGraw-Hill, 1967.

II. PRIMARY SOURCES

Acta Apollonii.

Acta Cypriani.

Acta Justini.

Acta Maximiliani.

Acta Perpetuae et Felicitatis.

Aristides. *Apologia.*

Arnobius of Sicca. *Disputatio adversus gentes.*

Athenagoras. *Presbeia* (*Legatio pro Christianis*).

Augustine, Saint, Bishop of Hippo. *Commentaria in Psalmos.*

————. *De civitate dei.*

————. *De doctrina christiana.*

————. *Sermones.*

————. *Tractates in Johannem.*

Clement of Alexandria. *Cohortatio ad gentes.*

————. *Paedagogus.*

————. *Stromata.*

Commodianus. *Instructiones.*

Cyprian, Saint, Bishop of Carthage. *Ad Demetrianum.*

————. *Ad Fortunatam de exhortatione martyrii.*

————. *De dominica oratione.*

————. *De mortalitate.*

————. *Epistolae.*

————. *Liber de lapsis.*

Epistola de martyribus Lugdunensis.

Eusebius of Caesarea. *Historia Ecclesiastica.*

Hermas. *Pastor.*

Irenaeus of Lyons. *Contra Haeresias.*

Jerome. *Chronicon.*

Justin Martyr. *Apologia Prima pro Christianis.*

————. *Apologia Secunda pro Christianis.*

Lactantius. *De mortuibus persecutorum.*

Melito of Sardis. *Apologia.*

Methodius. *Convivium decem virginum.*

Minucius Felix. *Octavius.*

Novatian. *Epistolae.*

Origen. *Contra Celsum.*

————. *Exhortatio ad martyrium.*

————. *Homiliae in Judicos.*

————. *Homiliae in Leviticum.*

————. *Homiliae in Numeros.*

————. *Libellus de Oratione.*

Passio Carpi, Papyli, et Agathonice.

Passio Mariani et Jacobi.
Passio Montani et Lucii.
Passio Pionii.
Passio Polycarpi.
Passio sanctorum Scillitanorum.
Passio sanctorum Thessalonikorum.
Tatian. *Oratio adversus Graecos.*
Tertullian. *Ad martyres.*
――――. *Ad Scapulam.*
――――. *Adversus Gnosticos Scorpiace.*
――――. *Apologeticus.*
――――. *De Baptismo.*
――――. *De Corona.*
――――. *De Fuga.*
――――. *De Idololatria.*
――――. *De Oratione.*
――――. *De Spectabulis.*
Theophilus. *Ad Autolycum.*

III. SECONDARY SOURCES

This section comprises the works directly referred to in this study. For a more complete bibliography of the period, see T. A. Robinson, *The Early Church: An Annotated Bibliography of Literature in English* (Metuchen, N.J.: Scarecrow Press, 1993).

Barnes, T. D. *Constantine and Eusebius.* Cambridge, Mass.: Harvard University Press, 1981.

――――. "Pre-Decian *Acta Martyrum.*" *Journal of Theological Studies* n.s. 19 (1968). Reprinted in *Early Christianity and the Roman Empire.* London: Variorum Reprints, 1984.

――――. *Tertullian: A Historical and Literary Study.* Oxford: Clarendon, 1971.

Bayet, J. *Histoire politique et psychologique de la religion romaine.* Paris: Payot, 1957.

Beaujeu, J. *La Religion romaine à l'apogée de l'Empire.* Paris: Société d'Edition "Les Belles Lettres", 1955.

Benko, S. *Pagan Rome and the Early Christians.* Bloomington: Indiana University Press, 1984.

Benoît, A. *Le Baptême Chrétien au Second Siècle: la théologie des pères.* Paris: Presses Univérsitaires de France, 1953.

Blowers, P. M., ed. *The Bible in Greek Christian Antiquity.* Notre Dame, Ind.: University of Notre Dame Press, 1997.

Bowersock, G. *Augustus and the Greek World.* Oxford: Clarendon, 1965.

Bradshaw, P. F. *The Search for the Origins of Christian Worship: Sources and Methods for the Study of Early Liturgy.* London: SPCK, 1992.

Brakke, D. *Athanasius and the Politics of Asceticism.* Oxford: Clarendon, 1995.

Brandon, S. G. F. *Jesus and the Zealots: A Study of the Political Factor in Primitive Christianity.* Manchester: Manchester University Press, 1967.

Braun, R. "Christianisme et pouvoir impérial." In *Approches de Tertullien: vingt-six études sur l'auteur et l'oeuvre,* ed. R. Braun. Paris: Institut d'Etudes Augustiniennes, 1992.

Brown, P. *The Body and Society: Men, Women, and Sexual Renunciation in Early Christianity.* New York: Columbia University Press, 1988.

———. *The Making of Late Antiquity.* Cambridge, Mass.: Harvard University Press, 1978.

———. *Power and Persuasion in Late Antiquity: Towards a Christian Empire.* Madison: University of Wisconsin Press, 1992.

———. *The Rise of Western Christendom: Triumph and Diversity, A.D. 200–1000.* Cambridge, Mass.: Blackwell, 1994.

Caspary, G. E. *Politics and Exegesis: Origen and the Two Swords.* Berkeley: University of California Press, 1979.

Cullmann, O. *The State in the New Testament.* New York: Scribner, 1956.

Danielou, J. *L'Eglise des premiers temps: des origines à la fin du troisième siècle.* 1963. Paris: Editions du Seuil, 1985.

Delehaye, H. *Les Origines du culte des martyrs.* 2d ed. Volume 20 of *Subsidia Hagiographica.* Brussels: Société des Bollandistes, 1933.

———. *Les Passions des martyrs et genres littéraires.* 2d ed. Volume 13B of *Subsidia Hagiographica.* Brussels: Société des Bollandistes, 1966.

———. *Sanctus: Essai sur le culte des saints dans l'Antiquité.* Volume 17 of *Subsidia Hagiographica.* Brussels: Société des Bollandistes, 1927.

Dugmore, C. W. "The Study of the Origins of the Eucharist: Retrospect and Reevaluation." In *Studies in Church History II.* Edited by G. J. Cuming. London: Nelson, 1985.

Dunn, M. *The Emergence of Monasticism: From the Desert Fathers to the Early Middle Ages.* Oxford: Blackwell, 2000.

Duquenne, L., SJ. *Chronologie des lettres de S. Cyprien: le dossier de la persécution de Dèce.* Volume 54 of *Subsidia Hagiographica.* Brussels: Société des Bollandistes, 1972.

Edwards, D. R. *Religion and Power: Pagans, Jews, and Christians in the Greek East.* New York: Oxford University Press, 1996.

Elm, S. *Virgins of God: The Making of Asceticism in Late Antiquity.* Oxford: Clarendon, 1994.

Festugière, A.-J. *La Sainteté.* Paris: Presses Univérsitaires de France, 1949.

Frend, W. H. C. *The Donatist Church.* 1952. Oxford: Clarendon, 1985.

———. *Martyrdom and Persecution in the Early Church: A Study of Conflict from the Maccabees to Donatus.* Oxford: Blackwell, 1965.

Garnsey, P. *Social Status and Legal Privilege in the Roman Empire.* Oxford: Clarendon, 1970.

Garnsey, P., and R. P. Saller. *The Roman Empire: Economy, Society, and Culture.* Berkeley: University of California Press, 1987.

Grant, M. *Constantine the Great: The Man and His Times.* New York: Scribner, 1993.

Grant, R. M. *Augustus to Constantine: The Thrust of the Christian Movement into the Roman World.* New York: Harper and Row, 1970.

Greenslade, S. L. *Church and State from Constantine to Theodosius.* London: SCM Press, 1954.

Greer, R. *Origen.* New York: Paulist Press, 1979.

Hazlett, I., ed. *Early Christianity: Origins and Evolution to A.D. 600.* London: Abingdon, 1991.

Hengel, M. *Die Zeloten: Untersuchungen zur jüdischen Freiheitsbewegung in der Zeit von Herodes I bis 70 n. Chr.* Leiden, 1961. Translated by D. Smith, *The Zealots: Investigations into the Jewish Freedom Movement in the Period from Herod I until 70 A.D.* Edinburgh: T. & T. Clark, 1989.

Jasper, R. C. D., and G. J. Cuming. *Prayers of the Eucharist: Early and Reformed.* Collegeville, Minn.: Liturgical Press, 1992.

Jones, A. H. M. *Constantine and the Conversion of Europe.* 1948. New York: Collier Books, 1962.

———. *The Later Roman Empire.* 2 vols. Oxford: Blackwell, 1964.

Keresztes, P. *Imperial Rome and the Christians, from Herod the Great to about 200 A.D.* Lanham, Md.: University Press of America, 1989.

Lane Fox, R. *Pagans and Christians.* New York: Knopf, 1989.

LeGoff, J. *La Naissance du Purgatoire.* Paris: Gallimard, 1981. Translated by A. Goldhammer, *The Birth of Purgatory.* Chicago: University of Chicago Press, 1984.

Liebeschuetz, J. H. W. G. *Continuity and Change in Roman Religion.* Oxford: Clarendon, 1979.

Lopez, D. A. "Holy Man and Holy Relic in the Fourth Century: Healer or Exorcist?" *Publications of the Medieval Association of the Midwest* 5 (1998): 85–95.

MacMullen, R. *Christianity and Paganism from the Fourth to the Eighth Centuries.* New Haven: Yale University Press, 1997.

———. *Christianizing the Roman Empire, A.D. 100–400.* New Haven: Yale University Press, 1984.

———. *Constantine.* New York: Dial Press, 1969.

———. *Paganism in the Roman Empire.* New Haven: Yale University Press, 1981.

Malherbe, A. J. *Social Aspects of Early Christianity.* Baton Rouge: Louisiana State University Press, 1977.

Markus, R. A. *Christianity in the Roman World.* New York: Scribner, 1974.

———. *The End of Ancient Christianity.* Cambridge: Cambridge University Press, 1990.

Mastandrea, P. "Passioni di martiri donatisti (BHL 4473 e 5271)." *Analecta Bollandiana* 113 (1995): 39–88.

Meeks, W. A. *The First Urban Christians: The Social World of the Apostle Paul.* New Haven: Yale University Press, 1983.

Meslin, M. *Le Christianisme dans l'Empire romaine.* Paris: Presses Univérsitaires de France, 1970.

Meyendorff, J. *Imperial Unity and Christian Divisions: The Church 450–680 A.D.* Crestwood, N.Y.: St. Vladimir's Seminary Press, 1989.

Millar, F. *The Emperor in the Roman World.* Ithaca, N.Y.: Cornell University Press, 1977.

Mirgeler, A. *Rückblick auf das abendländische Christentum.* Mainz, 1961. Translated by E. Quinn, *Mutations of Western Christianity.* New York: Herder and Herder, 1964.

Momigliano, A., ed. *The Conflict of Paganism and Christianity in the Fourth Century* Oxford: Clarendon, 1963.

———. *On Pagans, Christians, and Jews.* Middletown, Conn.: Wesleyan University Press, 1987.

Munier, C. *L'Apologie de Saint Justin philosophe et martyr.* Fribourg: Editions Univérsitaires de Fribourg, 1994.

Neuser, J., ed. *The Pharisees and Other Sects.* Translated by A.W. Mahnke. Volume 2 of *Origins of Judaism.* New York: Garland, 1990.

Osborn, E. F. *Tertullian, First Theologian of the West.* Cambridge: Cambridge University Press, 1997.

Pagels, E. *The Gnostic Gospels.* New York: Random House, 1979.

Pelikan, J. *The Christian Tradition.* 5 vols. Chicago: University of Chicago Press, 1971–84.

Pelletier, M. *Les Pharisiens: Histoire d'un parti méconnu.* Paris: Edition du Cerf, 1990.

Perkins, P. *The Gnostic Dialogue: The Early Church and the Crisis of Gnosticism.* New York: Paulist Press, 1980.

Price, S. R. F. *Rituals and Power: The Roman Imperial Cult in Asia Minor.* Cambridge: Cambridge University Press, 1984.

Rahner, H., SJ. *Kirche und Staat im Frühen Christentum.* Munich, 1961. Translated by L. D. Davis, SJ., *Church and State in Early Christianity.* San Fransisco: Ignatius Press, 1992.

Rankin, D. *Tertullian and the Church.* Cambridge: Cambridge University Press, 1995.

Richardson, Cyril C., ed. and trans. *Early Christian Fathers.* New York: Collier Books, 1970.

Rordorf, W., ed. *The Eucharist of the Early Christians.* Translated by M. J. O'Connell. New York: Pueblo, 1978.

Rousseau, P. *Ascetics, Authority, and the Church in the Age of Jerome and Cassian.* Oxford: Oxford University Press, 1978.

Salisbury, J. E. *Perpetua's Passion: The Death and Memory of a Young Roman Woman.* New York: Routledge, 1997.

Simmons, M. B. *Arnobius of Sicca: Religious Conflict and Competition in the Age of Diocletian.* Oxford: Clarendon Press, 1995.

Sordi, M. *I cristiani e l'impero romano.* Translated by A. Bedini, *The Christians and the Roman Empire.* Norman: University of Oklahoma Press, 1986.

Stark, R. *The Rise of Christianity: A Sociologist Reconsiders History.* Princeton: Princeton University Press, 1996.

Stemberger, G. *Jewish Contemporaries of Jesus: Pharisees, Sadducees, Essenes.* Minneapolis: Fortress Press, 1995.

Thornhill, P. "The British Martyrs, Aaron and Julius." *Mankind Quarterly* 39, no. 4 (Summer 1999): 467–508.

———."St. Albanus and the End of Roman Britain." *Mankind Quarterly* 41, no. 1 (Fall 2000): 3–43.

Trevett, C. *Montanism: Gender, Authority, and the New Prophecy.* Cambridge: Cambridge University Press, 1996.

Wagner, W. H. *After the Apostles: Christianity in the Second Century.* Minneapolis, Minn.: Fortress Press, 1994.

Wardman, A. *Religion and Statecraft among the Romans.* Baltimore, Md.: Johns Hopkins University Press, 1982.

Whitaker, E. C. *Documents of the Baptismal Liturgy.* London: SPCK, 1970.

Wolfram, H. *Geschichte der Goten.* Munich, 1979. Translated by J. D. Dunlap. *History of the Goths.* Berkeley: University of California Press, 1988.

Index

acta of martyrs: defined, 13; on desire for martyrdom, 83; significance 57; visions, 66

Agapê, martyr, 54–5, 73–4

Agapius, bishop and martyr, 77–8

Albanus, martyr, 138

anticonspiracy laws, 118–9

apocalypticism: and apologetic, 126–8; in both rigorist and nonrigorist traditions, 91–3; in Jewish revolts, 8; not attenuated in separatist period, 89–90, 97, 99, 124; significance beyond persecution, 101–2. *See also* nonrigorist tradition; Parousia; rigorist tradition

Apollonius, martyr, 75–6; anti-Montanist fragments, 62

apologia: anti-Roman attitudes in, 116–20; apocalypticism in, 124; audience of, 110, 116, 120–1, 129–33; defined, 11; lacking Augustinian-like distinctions, 110–5; purpose, 109–10, 116

apostasy: problem of apostates, 65–6, 135; targeted by apologetic, 109–10

Aristides: about, 11; apologetic audience, 131; Christian truth superior, 131

Arnobius: about, 13, 22; irrelevance of corporeal to salvation, 21, 73; on pagan ignorance, 21, 117; on Parousia, 102

asceticism: lifestyle required by renunciation, 24–6; "modesty" and Parousia, 91–2; preparation for martyrdom, 74–8; significance in Eusebius, 143–5

Athenagoras: about, 11–12; demonization of matter, 34, 111; injustice of Roman authority, 118; lacking Augustinian-like distinctions, 127; on prayer for emperors, 126

Augustine, bishop: about, 3; anachronistically understood, 150; state/religion distinction, 4; use/enjoyment distinction, 4

baptism, 58; martyrdom as second baptism, 69–70; and Parousia, 95–6; sin after, 63–5, 86

Basilides, martyr, 144–5

Caecilian, bishop, 140

Chionê, martyr, 55, 73–4

Christology: and Gnosticism, 35–6; and martyrdom, 67–72; and Parousia, 92, 94–5, 103–4; renunciation as perfection of holiness, 98; resurrection of the body, 35–6, 104–6

Clement (of Alexandria): about, 12; apologetic audience, 130–1; on living renunciation, 24–6, 75, 92–3, 98; on Christian childlikeness, 29; on choosing salvation, 20–1; lacking Augustinian-like distinctions, 25; on Parousia, 92–3, 98

Commodianus, bishop, 12, 27

Constantine, emperor: "Bishop for external affairs," 147; career, 137–8; conversion, 139; Edict of Milan, 138–9; and Logos, 146; as martyr, 146–7; as Pontifex Maximus, 139–40

Constantius, emperor, 137–8

Consualia, 51

corporeal (*saecularis, kosmikós*): defined, 3;
    demonized, 33–4, 51, 53–5, 127; in
    Eusebius, 134–5; ideas conflated in, 18,
    22, 27, 32, 48, 109; incorruptible after
    Parousia, 103–5; same definition in
    apologetic, 109

cult of martyrs, 87–8

cult of saints, 152

Cyprian, bishop: about, 13; apocalypticism,
    101, 124; avoided persecution, 62; on
    causes of persecution, 64; on Christ pres-
    ent in martyrs, 71; lacking Augustinian-
    like distinctions, 26–7; martyrdom
    fulfills expectations, 83–4; on material
    possessions, 26; on salvation of martyrs,
    65–6, 71; on suffering, 114–5; on test of
    faith, 61–2, 64, 71, 114–5

demons. *See* corporeal, demonized

devotion, tested by God, 59

Diocletian, emperor, 135, 137

Dionysius, bishop, 62

Domitian, emperor, 10

Donatus, bishop, 140

Edict of Milan, 138–9

Eucharist, 69, 152–3, 166n57

Eusebius, bishop: on Origen, 144; on
    Polycarp, 141; redefines corporeal and
    spiritual concepts, 134–5; redefines sig-
    nificance of asceticism, 143; redefines
    significance of martyrdom, 141; re-
    defines significance of Parousia, 145–6

exegesis, 27–8

Felicity, martyr, 80–1, 85–6

fortuna: accusation of injury rebutted,
    120–4, 124–9; Christians accused of
    injury, 109–11; defined, 110; not sup-
    ported by Christians, 128–9

Galerius, emperor, 137

glory (*gloria, doxá, chárisma*): in martyrs,
    68, 71; and Parousia, 103–4

Gnosticism. *See* heresy, Gnosticism

grace, after separatist period, 152–3

Great Persecution (of Diocletian), 135,
    136

Hadrian, emperor, anti-Christian legisla-
    tion, 118

heresy: Donatism, 140; dualism, 34–5;
    Gnosticism, 35–6, 103; Montanism, 62

Hermas: about, 11; on Parousia, 95–6

Hippolytus (of Rome), Christ's full
    humanity, 35–6

idolatry. *See* renunciation, failure of, as
    idolatry

imperial cult, Christian rejection, 17

Irenaeus: on "giving to Caesar," 40–1; on
    moral discipline, 33; on conversion, 33;
    on New Adam, 92; on Parousia, 92,
    106; on providence, 33, 50–1; on resur-
    rection of the body, 106

Irenê, martyr, 54–5, 73–4

James, apostle, early followers, 9

Judaism: and Christianity 1–2; First and
    Second Revolts failed, 7–8, 10, 39, 94;
    Pharisees, 9, 39–40; Zealots, 9–10, 40

Justin Martyr: about, 11; apologetic
    audience, 130; on assurance of salva-
    tion, 76; on expected Kingdom, 18; on
    "giving to Caesar," 42–3; on injustice
    of Roman rule, 44, 117–8; lacking
    Augustinian-like distinctions, 43; on
    prayer for emperors, 44; on renuncia-
    tion and martyrdom, 74

libellus, 110

Licinius, emperor, 138–9

Logos. *See* renunciation, and Logos

Majorinus, bishop, 140

mammon, equated with Roman Empire,
    40–2

Marcion, dualist heretic, 34–5

martyrdom (*martyría*): and Christology,

67–72, 81, 103–4; commanded by God, 78–81; and communal salvation, 85–8; as consolation, 77, 84; cult of martyrs, 87–8; desire for qualities as, 84–5; martyr as athlete, 60–1; martyr as intercessor, 86; martyr as proven leader, 62; as punishment, 63–5; quotidian significance, 73, 81, 82–5, 86; renunciation as preparation for, 74–8, 81; as reward, 65–7, 81, 103–4; as second baptism, 63–4, 70; significance in Eusebius, 141–3; as test of faith, 58–63, 81; visions, 66

Masada, 8

Maxentius, emperor, 138

Maximilian, martyr, 16

Melito, bishop: about, 12; corporeal concept in apologetic, 113–4; expectation of Kingdom, 123; on injustice of Roman rule, 123; on resurrection of the body, 114

messianism, 8

Methodius: about, 13; on resurrection of the body, 105–6; on social standing, 31–2; on virginity, 32

Milvian Bridge, battle of, 138

Minucius Felix: about, 12; anti-Roman attitude, 120; apologetic audience, 132

miracle, 72, 86

Mithraism, 137

mob violence, 17, 20

Montanism. *See* heresy, Montanism

Nero, emperor, 10

Nicea, first ecumenical council, 147

nonrigorist tradition: apocalypticism in, 99; defined, 57; necessity of martyrdom, 62, 80–1, 97–100; polarized by Constantine's conversion, 139–40. *See also* Cyprian; Origen

Novatian, bishop, 65

oaths: by imperial *genius*, 10; refused by Christians, 54

Origen: about, 12; allegorical interpretation, 2, 58; apologetic audience, 129; on imitating Christ, 69; on intercession of martyrs, 86; on Judges, 2, 58; lacking Augustinian-like distinctions, 6, 113; on martyrdom as baptism, 63, 70–1; on Parousia, 99, 106–7; on perfection of virtue, 98–9; on prayer, 29–30, 98–9; rejecting Roman authority, 49–50, 52–3, 119; renunciation and social order, 31; "spiritual" exegesis, 28; on test of faith, 58–9; two incompatible kingdoms, 30, 113; using rigorist tradition, 100

Parousia: and Christology, 92, 94–5; imminence of, 49, 90–3, 101; redefined by Eusebius, 145–7; transformation of matter with, 102–7; violence of, 93–102

Paul, apostle: ambiguous about corporeal, 3, 104; early followers, 9; on New Adam, 94; on Parousia, 90, 94, 102–3; on Roman legitimacy, 48–9

penitential traditions limited, 63

Perpetua, martyr, 80–1, 87

persecution: caused by laxity, 64; difficult to justify avoiding, 62–4; distinctive of separatist period, 10–1; failed as imperial policy, 139; natural disasters as, 101; necessary for Christians, 60–2

Polycarp, bishop: imitated Christ, 69; not subject to Roman rule, 46; rejecting imperial cult, 17

Pontifex Maximus, 128

Potamiaena, martyr, 144–5

prayer, for emperors, limited, 127–9

Providence: instrumentality of persecuting officials, 18, 20, 59, 122–3; instrumentality of Satan, 34; and Roman Empire, 49–53; testing faith, 59

refrigerium, 87

renunciation (*renunciatio, apotassô*): and civic spectacles, 22–3, 27; correlation with social and moral standing, 31–2;

renunciation (*continued*)
  defined, 14–5; demanding ideal, 30–1;
    eroding in late third century, 136; and
    expectation of Kingdom, 19, 90–3;
    failure of, as idolatry, 47, 60, 64; and
    imperial cult, 17, 44; incompatible with
    corporeal and sin, 30; incomprehensi-
    ble to pagans, 21; and Logos, 32–6, 92,
    112; and material existence, 247; and
    military service, 16; preparation for
    martyrdom, 74–8
resurrection of the body, 34–6, 104–6,
  114
rigorist tradition: apocalypticism not
    attributable to, 92; defined, 57; neces-
    sity of martyrdom, 60–1, 78–80, 94–7;
    polarized by Constantine's conversion,
    139–40. *See also* Tertullian
Romanitas: contrasted with Christianity,
    1–2, 48, 77–8; inherently unjust, 19–
    20, 44–5, 49–53, 117–20; negative
    view in apologetic, 109–10, 116, 117–
    8, 121; not supported by Christians,
    128–9; renounced on conversion, 14,
    44; tolerating Christianity, 135–6; vio-
    lent confrontations, 57
Rutilius, martyr, 64

salvation: as choice, 21; communal signifi-
    cance, 85–8; immediate of martyrs, 65;
    problem of assurance of, 7, 76
Sanctus, martyr, 72
Scythians, 52, 119
Secundinus, bishop and martyr, 77–8
Severus, emperor, 137
Speratus, martyr, 54, 83
spiritual (*spiritualis, pneumatikós*): defined,

3; not different in apologetic genre,
    109; redefined by Eusebius, 134–5
superstitio, 116
syncretism, 139

Tatian: about, 11; corporeal concept in
    apologetic, 112; Roman rule illegiti-
    mate, 47
Tetrarchy, 137
Tertullian: about, 12; apologetic audience,
    132; on Christian truth, 19–20; on civic
    spectacles, 223; on dualism, 34–5; on
    expectation of martyrdom, 82; on imi-
    tating Christ, 67; on injustice of Roman
    rule, 19–20, 51–2, 121–2; lacking
    Augustinian-like distinctions, 23–4,
    127; on martyrdom as baptism, 70; on
    military service, 15–6, 41–2; on "mod-
    esty," 91–2; on not avoiding martyr-
    dom, 59–60, 64, 78–80; on pagan false-
    hood, 122, 132; on Parousia, 91–2, 96–
    7, 127; on prayer, 28, 125; on prison of
    the world, 15; on resurrection of the
    body, 104–5; on test of faith, 59–61
Theophilus, bishop: about, 12; apologetic,
    117; corporeal concept in apologetic,
    112; lacking Augustinian-like distinc-
    tions, 127; on prayer for emperors, 125
traditor, 140
Trajan, emperor, letter to Pliny, 10

Valentinus, Gnostic heretic, 36
virginity, 32. *See also* asceticism

will: free, 105, 114; knowable only in per-
    secution, 6; subordinate to divine, 5,
    29, 99